"This potential game-changer will help readers identify where opportunities lie and how to seize them." —*Publishers Weekly*

"Demonstrates just how far an inquisitive mind can take you." —*Bloomberg Businessweek*

The Book of Beautiful Questions

A More Beautiful Question:
The Power of Inquiry to Spark Breakthrough Ideas

CAD Monkeys, Dinosaur Babies and T-Shaped People:
Inside the World of Design Thinking

The Book of Beautiful Questions

THE POWERFUL QUESTIONS
THAT WILL HELP YOU DECIDE, CREATE,
CONNECT, AND LEAD

WARREN BERGER

BLOOMSBURY PUBLISHING
NEW YORK · LONDON · OXFORD · NEW DELHI · SYDNEY

BLOOMSBURY PUBLISHING
Bloomsbury Publishing Inc.
1385 Broadway, New York, NY 10018, USA

BLOOMSBURY, BLOOMSBURY PUBLISHING, and the
Diana logo are trademarks of Bloomsbury Publishing Plc

First published in the United States 2018

ISBN: HB: 978-1-63286-956-2; eBook: 978-1-63286-958-6

LIBRARY OF CONGRESS CATALOGING-IN-PUBLICATION DATA

Names: Berger, Warren, author.
Title: The book of beautiful questions : the powerful questions that will help
you decide, create, connect, and lead / Warren Berger.
Description: New York : Bloomsbury Publishing, [2018] | Includes
bibliographical references and index.
Identifiers: LCCN 2018014150 | ISBN 9781632869562 (hardback) |
ISBN 9781632869586 (e-book)
Subjects: LCSH: Creative ability in business. | Business communication. |
Inquiry-based learning.
Classification: LCC HD53 .B447 2018 | DDC 650.1—dc23
LC record available at https://lccn.loc.gov/2018014150

2 4 6 8 10 9 7 5 3 1

Typeset by Westchester Publishing Services
Printed and bound in the U.S.A. by Berryville Graphics Inc.,
Berryville, Virginia

To find out more about our authors and books visit
www.bloomsbury.com and sign up for our newsletters.

Bloomsbury books may be purchased for business or promotional use.
For information on bulk purchases please contact Macmillan Corporate
and Premium Sales Department at specialmarkets@macmillan.com.

Contents

The Book of Beautiful Questions

Why Question?

I am a questionologist.

You may be asking yourself: *Is that really a thing?* I asked myself that very question a few years ago. Then I did some research, which turned up hundreds of different types of "ologists," ranging from the acarologist (who studies ticks and mites) to the zoologist. But searching among the Qs, I found no entry for "questionologist." And this led me to inquire, *Why not? Isn't the study of questions as worthy of classification as the study of ticks and mites?*

My questioning then advanced from the "Why not?" to the "What if?" stage—as in, *What if I just declared myself a questionologist?* I did so in, among other places, the pages of the *New York Times*. And to my surprise, no one questioned it.

I have been using the term ever since, as I visit companies (including many Fortune 500 businesses), government agencies, such as NASA, and schools from grade-school level through university. I have been invited to various gatherings of farmers, accountants, artists, scientists, soldiers, political operatives, Hollywood agents, Danish pharmaceutical executives, and Australian school teachers. The interest in questioning crosses all lines, it seems.

And it should. When we are confronted with almost any demanding situation, in work or in life, simply taking the time and effort to ask questions can help guide us to better decisions and a more productive course of action. But the questions must be the *right* ones—the ones that cut to the heart of a complex challenge or that enable us to see an old problem in a new light.

The Book of Beautiful Questions contains many such questions—more than two hundred of them, covering everyday situations that range from getting out of a career rut to strengthening personal relationships. This book is about asking thoughtful questions at the right time in order to make the best choices when it matters most. It is aimed at thinkers, creators, problem solvers, and decision makers.

While there are many "answer" books available—the ones declaring, "Here is a four-step solution to your problem, and you can remember it via this four-letter acronym"—the philosophy behind this book is different. I am suggesting that we must figure out our own solutions and answers to the complex, individualized challenges we face, in work and in our personal lives. And that we have at our disposal a natural tool to help us think and "hack" our way to more successful outcomes. That tool is the humble question.

I FIRST BEGAN to appreciate the value of questions years ago, when I worked as a newspaper reporter. For me (and for journalists in general), a good, pointed question can serve as a spade for digging and unearthing bits of the truth of a story. Through the years, I tended to think of a question primarily as something you ask others in order to extract information from them. I'm sure that attorneys, pollsters, psychiatrists, and other "professional questioners" think of questioning the same way.

But my work as a journalist also brought me into contact with inventors, entrepreneurs, business leaders, artists, and scientists, who often were the subjects of my writing. I found that many of these people tended to use the questioning tool in a different way—their questions were often directed inward. They might be trying to solve a problem or create something original, and in doing so, were likely to begin with questions that they asked themselves: *Why does this problem or situation exist? What are the underlying forces, the larger issues at play? What might be an interesting new way to come at this challenge?*

This type of questioning helped lead these creative thinkers to original ideas and effective solutions. And this observation formed the basis of my previous book *A More Beautiful Question*, which made the case that questioning is a starting point of innovation. In that book, I showed that inventions from the instant camera to the cell phone, and startup businesses such as Netflix and Airbnb, could be traced to a "beautiful question"—one that shifted the current thinking, opened up a new possibility, and ultimately led to a breakthrough.

After the book came out, as I conducted press interviews, gave speeches, and engaged with audiences of readers, I found that while many agreed with the premise of the book and its "Ask more questions" message, there also seemed to be a hunger for something more targeted and specific. People wanted to know *which* questions they should be asking with regard to a particular problem they might be facing or a goal they were pursuing.

When I spoke to business leaders, for example, they tended to be most interested in questions that could help in running a company, whereas those at creative gatherings wanted to know how to ask questions that could spark ideas. Likewise with people seeking to improve personal relationships or with those grappling with difficult decisions about whether to accept a job or pursue a new passion—all were seeking the questions that might help them make better choices or achieve the best results in a specific situation.

So with this book I focus on sharing productive questions and questioning strategies that can be applied to everyday situations. The questions featured come from a variety of sources. They derive from ideas and insights shared by entrepreneurs, life coaches, kindergarten teachers, cognitive behavioral therapists, chief executives, psychology professors, and neuroscientists, as well as an FBI counterintelligence agent, an acclaimed novelist, a venture capitalist, an improv performer, a Pulitzer Prize–winning playwright, a Nobel Prize–winning physicist, a U. S. Marine officer, a hostage negotiator, a risk-management specialist, and others. I tried to include a range of perspectives on how questioning can be used in various situations. Some of the questions in the book were originally asked years ago by people who are no longer alive—though the question lives on. A handful of these questions were first mentioned in *A More Beautiful Question*, but I took the opportunity with this book to expand upon them and place them in a more specific context.

Quite a few of the questions I formulated myself, with collaborative input from others. I used reverse engineering in many cases. For example, as I identified a common problem or pitfall in, say, decision-making, my challenge was to then construct a question or series of questions that might help someone avoid that particular pitfall when making decisions in the future.

The result is a checklist manifesto, wherein the checklists are made up entirely of beautiful questions. What makes them beautiful? To me, any question that causes people to shift their thinking is a beautiful one. These questions are intended to do that—to remind you to slow down and think more, to broaden your perspective, to see past biases, creative blocks, and emotional reactions. In so doing they can help steer you in the right direction at critical moments when you're trying to 1) decide on something, 2) create something, 3) connect with other people, and 4) be a good and effective leader. These are the four broad themes of the book. In my conversations with readers and with audiences at my speeches, these four areas seemed to come up most—they are very much on people's minds.

How can questioning help us decide, create, connect, and lead?

In each of the four featured areas, questioning plays a central role. ***Decision-making*** (at least *good* decision-making) demands critical thinking—which is rooted in questioning. It has been suggested that critical thinking is in crisis today, as evidenced by a growing collective inability to distinguish fake news from the real thing (or real leaders from fake ones). We can blame the media or Facebook or the politicians themselves—but ultimately, it's up to each of us to work through the hard questions that enable us to make more enlightened judgments and choices. Asking oneself a few well-considered questions before deciding on something—a candidate, a possible career or life change, an opportunity that you or your business may be thinking about pursuing—can be surprisingly effective in helping to avoid the common traps of decision-making.

As for *creativity*, it often depends on our ability, and willingness, to grapple with challenging questions that can fire the imagination. For people within an organization trying to innovate by coming up with fresh ideas for a new offering or for an individual attempting to express a vision in an original and compelling way, the creative path is a journey of inquiry. It often starts with identifying a singularly powerful "Why?" or "What if?" question (so many well-known creative breakthroughs, in business and the arts, can be traced back to a question of this type). But it doesn't end there. Knowing the right questions to ask at each stage of the creative process can guide the creator forward—steadily advancing from early stages of finding an idea to the final challenges of getting that idea "out the door" and into the world.

Our success in *connecting* with others can be improved dramatically by asking more questions—of ourselves and of the people with whom we're trying to relate. Surprising new research suggests we become more likable to others by asking questions—as long as they're the right type of questions, asked in the right way. (When asked the wrong way, questions can be confrontational and downright annoying.) While many of us tend to rely on generic "How are you?" questions, more thoughtful and purposeful questions can do a better job of breaking the ice with strangers or bonding with clients and colleagues. They also enable us to forge an even stronger, deeper relationship with the people closest to us. And—worth noting in these polarizing times—questions can help us understand and begin to relate to those who see the world very differently.

Lastly, *leadership* is not usually associated with questioning—leaders are supposed to have all the answers—but it is becoming increasingly clear that the best leaders are those with the confidence and humility to ask the ambitious, unexpected questions that no one else is asking. Today's leaders—and I'm referring to not just top corporate executives but team leaders of any type, as well as civic leaders, social advocates, "thought leaders," family leaders, and educators—are facing unprecedented challenges in a world of exponential change. They must ask the questions that anticipate and address the needs of an organization and its people, questions that set the tone for curious exploration and innovation, and questions that frame a larger challenge others can rally around. Mission statements are no longer sufficient; the new leader must pose "mission questions."

WITHIN EACH OF the four distinct themes, there are different types of questions that tend to be most effective. Many of the decision-making questions are designed to help you work through your own biases. Creativity questions are more exploratory and inspirational. Relationship questions tend to be empathetic. Leadership questions are more visionary.

But what ties them all together is this: The simplest and most powerful thing that happens when we ask ourselves questions is that it forces us to think. More specifically, when we're working on questions in our minds we're engaged in "slow thinking," the term used by Nobel Prize–winning psychologist Daniel Kahneman to describe the kind of deliberate, effortful cognition that tends to lead to better decisions, choices, and actions.

This might involve something as simple as pausing before making a decision or pursuing a course of action to ask, *What am I really trying to achieve here?* That very basic question, in and of itself, encourages you to think more—and that's a good start. But there's much more you can do if you're armed with more sophisticated, situational questions. You can use them to prompt or remind yourself to look at that situation from multiple perspectives or to challenge your own assumptions about it. When we do this, we tend to open up more possibilities and options—which means we're not only thinking *more* about a particular challenge, we're also thinking about it in a more comprehensive and balanced way.

While one function of this book is to share predetermined questions that can be used in given situations, the larger goal is to encourage a questioning habit—so that you'll not only use the questions contained in the book but also develop your own customized questions, gradually coming up with new ones based on seeing what works for you.

Our ability to question well is like a muscle. You must continually work it in order to strengthen it. Even if you feel that you already have a knack for questioning, there are many ways to improve. There are approaches to learn, from "speculative inquiry" to "appreciative inquiry," which I'll cover throughout the book. There are techniques for building a better question and for sharing it with others—including nuances involving tone and phrasing. And there are also ways to encourage others around you to question more (particularly important if you are, or aspire to be, a leader).

But in order to do any of this, we must overcome what seems to be a general reluctance to ask thoughtful questions—of others and of ourselves. While the rest of the book will provide specific tips and tools for better questioning, I want to start by discussing, more generally, some of the obstacles that get in the way of good questioning—and why it's so important, particularly in today's world, to make the effort to surmount them.

What can we learn from a four-year-old girl?

When people ask, *How does one become a better questioner?*, I advise them to take a few lessons from a true "master questioner"—not Einstein or Socrates, but rather the typical four-year-old child. Studies have shown that children at that age may ask anywhere from one hundred to three hundred questions a day (interestingly, some research shows the four-year-old girl asks even more questions than a boy of that age. She is the ultimate questioning machine.)

Questioning at these early ages may seem like child's play, but it's a complex, high-order level of thinking. It requires enough awareness to *know that one does not know*—and the ingenuity to begin to do something to remedy that. As the Harvard University-based child psychologist Paul Harris points out, young children discover early on that the information they seek can be easily extracted from other human beings, merely by using that certain combination of words and vocal inflection that forms a question.

If you could peer inside the mind of a questioning child, you'd get a hint as to why kids seem to enjoy asking "Why?". Neurological research shows that merely wondering about an interesting question activates regions of the brain linked to reward-processing. Curiosity—the act of wondering—feels good in and of itself, and thus, questions beget more questions. Think of curiosity as a condition—"like an itch," says the neuroscientist Charan Ranganath. And that condition often leads to the action known as questioning, which is how we scratch the itch.

The four-year-old child scratches away—until, at some point, she is told to stop. But for a time, during her peak questioning years, she has no reluctance to ask about anything and everything—including the most fundamental questions, those basic "Why?" queries that many of us are loathe to ask for fear of looking stupid. The questioning child isn't weighed down by accumulated knowledge, biases, or assumptions about how the world works and why things are the way they are. Her mind is both open and expansive—an ideal condition for wondering, inquiring, and growing.

This seems to begin changing somewhere around age five or six. The asking of questions (at least the ones that are verbalized by young students in school) tends to subside steadily, year by year, according to research from the nonprofit Right Question Institute, which studies questioning and devises question-formulation exercises for schools. What was once a hundred-per-day questioning habit among four-year-olds dwindles down to a few questions—or none—among teenagers.

What are the five enemies of questioning?

It is convenient to blame this on our education system, which, for the most part, is test-driven and answers-based. And our schools could be doing much more to encourage questioning by students.

But clearly, a number of additional forces and pressures work against questioning.

Foremost among what I think of as the "five enemies of questioning" is *fear*. Though many young children start out as fearless questioners, they gradually get the message—from teachers, parents, other kids—that asking a question carries risks, including the risk of revealing what they don't know and perhaps ought to know. It is a near-paralyzing problem for young students and seems to get worse as they move into the peer-pressure-cooker environments of junior high and high school. Students fear they'll ask the "wrong" question—one that could be seen as off-topic or obvious—or that by asking *any* question, they'll potentially be seen as uncool. As children become teenagers, coolness is generally associated with being in-the-know already—or acting as if you don't care. To ask a question is an admission that 1) you don't know, and 2) you do care—doubly uncool.

As we move into adulthood, the fear of revealing that we "don't know" is still there and in some ways may be even stronger. Kids at least have the excuse of being young, but adults have no excuse for not knowing something important. Fear of asking questions can be particularly strong in the workplace, as employees worry: *Will asking questions make it seem as if I don't know how to do my job? Will it annoy my colleagues and supervisors? Or worse, will it threaten them in some way?* These concerns are legitimate—questions can, indeed, sometimes be irritating or confrontational. There are ways to address those problems, as we'll see later, but most people don't know them—because we don't teach "questioning" in school (or in college or in most employee training programs.)

The reluctance to question extends beyond the classroom or workplace to the privacy of our homes. Many of our closest personal relationships could benefit from more questions, particularly the kinds of queries that show genuine interest and a desire to understand. Yet we are far more inclined to offer opinions and dispense advice—to do more telling than asking.

Even in the privacy of our own minds—when we're mentally grappling with problems or trying to work through difficult decisions—we're apt to worry, stew, or gripe about something (or avoid thinking about it altogether). What we should be doing is asking ourselves questions that can help break down the problem or get to the crux of it. But we may be unsure of how to formulate those questions. And we may fear not having the answers to them.

If fear is the first enemy of questioning, running a close second is **knowledge**. The more you know, the less you feel the need to ask. But the problem here is twofold. First, we can easily fall into the "trap of expertise," wherein knowledgeable people begin to rely too much on what they already know and fail to keep expanding upon and updating that knowledge. This is particularly perilous in times of rapid change. And there's another problem with depending too much on our existing knowledge: To put it bluntly, we don't know as much as we think we do.

This brings up the third and fourth enemies of questioning, which are related to each other: **bias** and **hubris**. In terms of biases, some of them are hardwired in us; others may be based on our own limited experiences. But in either case, if we are predisposed to think something, we may be less open to considering questions that challenge that view. The book's second section, on decision-making, looks at some of the ways we can use self-questioning to better understand and challenge our own biases and assumptions.

But to do that, we also must contend with hubris—which can lead us to believe our biases are correct or are not biases at all. ("*Everyone else* is biased!") The relationship between humility and questioning is interesting—if you lack the former, you'll probably do less of the latter. You may be more inclined to think and say things like: "If I don't know it already, it can't be that important," or "I just go with my gut instincts—they're usually right," or "I don't have to sit through intelligence briefings because I'm a really smart guy."

The last enemy of questioning is **time** (or the supposed lack of it). We just don't seem to make time for questioning—starting in school. Ask any teacher about this; there is so much material to "download" that little time remains for student questions. And time is an even bigger source of pressure on adult questioning. To make this point at companies I visit, I often share a quote attributed to the late comedian George Carlin: "Some people see things that are and ask, 'Why?' Some people dream of things that never were and ask, 'Why not?' Some people have to go to work and don't have time for all that shit."

Carlin's joke did not reflect his own view (he was a passionate believer in the importance of questioning *everything*), but it does capture an attitude that is quite common in business and in everyday life—perhaps more today than ever before. As our lives move faster and have become more complicated little time is allotted for inquiry, contemplation, or critical thinking. We're under pressure to make quick decisions and render snap judgments, and to *do, do, do*—without necessarily asking *why* we're doing what we're doing or whether we should be doing it at all.

The paradox is that in the rush to do more with our limited time, we may end up using that time *less* efficiently—because rushed decisions and actions can send us down the wrong path. This was understood by some of the most successful—and busiest—people today and in recent times.

Case in point: The late founder of Apple, Steve Jobs, was one of the busiest people on the planet, yet he made a conscious effort to regularly ask fundamental "Why?" questions while making the rounds of his company's various departments. At each stop, whether in the marketing area or accounting, "I always asked why we're doing things the way we're doing them," Jobs said. As Jobs took on the role of the inquisitive four-year-old wandering the company, it had a powerful effect on him and those around him—forcing everyone to reexamine assumptions.

In my research, I found a similar questioning habit among many of the highly productive business leaders or creative professionals I studied. In the midst of hectic schedules, they seem to be able to find the time to ask thoughtful questions of themselves and others, particularly when confronting a new challenge, starting out on an endeavor, or forming a new relationship. The ability and inclination to maintain that fearless, open-minded approach of a young questioner is part of what makes them successful.

We can all do likewise; we can release that four-year-old questioner within. In question-storming sessions I've conducted at universities, businesses, and government agencies, I've found that under the right conditions, people very quickly become comfortable with asking *a lot* of questions as well as with asking *basic* questions. It doesn't take long for them to begin questioning like a curious child when encouraged and prompted to do so. And that prompting can come from oneself—which is one of the main points of this book. If you want to see things as a four-year-old might, you can start by asking yourself: *How might a four-year-old see this situation?*

How might we foster a questioning habit?

The hardest part may be getting yourself to do this habitually. It's easy to become a better questioner during a structured questioning exercise, but to really have an impact, the behavior has to become routine: It should be part of the way we do our jobs, something we do on the way to work in the morning or that we incorporate into our everyday interactions with others. And for that to happen, we must come to terms with those five forces that get in the way of questioning.

The fear of asking questions in front of others can only be overcome by doing it, one question at a time. There are group exercises that can help, and we'll look at some of them in this book. One of the biggest concerns for some is the risk of being seen as naïve by others (particularly when asking fundamental "Why?" questions or imaginative "What if?" questions). It's a risk worth taking, however; those so-called naïve questions can be the most powerful ones in terms of producing insights and bringing about change. So be bold enough to ask, and let the non-questioners think what they will.

ARE YOU A BEAUTIFUL QUESTIONER? ASK YOURSELF THE FOLLOWING

- *Am I willing to be seen as naïve?*
- *Am I comfortable raising questions with no immediate answers?*
- *Am I willing to move away from what I know?*
- *Am I open to admitting I might be wrong?*
- *Am I willing to slow down and consider?*

As I mentioned earlier, fear of questioning extends even to self-questioning. Though no one is judging, the worry is, *What if I find that I have no ready answer for the serious questions I ask myself?* The expectation that every question can and should be quickly answered is nurtured in school and reinforced, unfortunately, by Google, but it simply doesn't apply to many of the most challenging and important questions.

There is value in asking yourself challenging questions even when—perhaps *especially* when—you don't have a ready answer. Just thinking about a difficult question—a tough decision, a creative problem that needs solving, a change you may want to make in your life—begins to put your mind to work on that issue and can soon start to yield insights and greater clarity. So the trick is to become more comfortable living with a question, working on it, learning from it—and knowing that you don't need to have an answer right away.

With regard to combating "question enemies" two through four—knowledge, bias, and hubris—the main requirement is a willingness to step back from what we know (or think we know) and be open to new perspectives, ideas, and possibilities. *How do we train ourselves to do this?* That is a beautiful question, and one that is very much a part of the public discourse these days, as we see articles and essays on the need for all of us to be more open-minded and willing to "get outside our own bubble."

There are many questions in this book that can serve as tools to help shift your view and your thinking in various ways. They are based on theories of critical thinking and "debiasing," as well as common sense. But they won't help at all unless you are 1) willing to develop a habit of asking such questions and 2) humble and flexible enough to adjust your thinking based on what you learn from asking those questions.

As for dealing with the final (and formidable) enemy of questioning, time, we'll consider various ways to carve out more time for thoughtful self-questioning. But to bring the power of questioning to bear on your decision-making, creativity, and relationships, questioning must become an integral part of those activities—woven into the processes of making decisions, working on creative projects, or engaging with people. That means we must slow down some of these activities and processes. In a rushed world, where everyone is under pressure to "get it done," asking people to slow down is asking a lot.

But I think most of us do manage to find the time for something if that something is considered important enough. So in the end, the problem of finding the time to ask more questions comes down to this question: *Is it really worth taking the time to do it?*

Why is questioning now more important than ever?

Having strong questioning skills has always been important. But in a time of exponential change, it's a twenty-first-century survival skill. From an individual career standpoint, continued success will depend on having the ability to keep learning while updating and adapting what we already know. We must continually invent or reinvent the work we do every day. None of this is possible without constant questioning.

In the same way that individuals in this dynamic work environment will be forced to keep inquiring and learning in order to survive and prosper, organizations must do likewise. Even the most established, successful businesses are in a state of upheaval now— brought on by technological change, globalization, and the other forces reshaping just about every industry in the modern business world and having a similar impact on nonprofit organizations, government agencies, and schools at all levels.

Talk to executives heading up hundred-year-old operations, and some will confide that they don't know what's coming next—and that their tried-and-true business approaches and methodologies are not working as well as they once did. "We have to rethink almost everything we're doing," one CEO told me.

She added that many people at all levels throughout the company are now under pressure to change their established ways of working—and some are quite uncomfortable with that. Having become used to thinking of themselves as experts of their domains, they are now being asked to adopt fresh approaches and new ways of thinking. Rather than just managing and maintaining, they're expected to innovate and create.

It's not an easy adjustment to make, but all of us (whether we believe it or not) are creative. However, we may need help in bolstering our creative confidence and developing new ways of seeing potential creative opportunities—and then getting to work on them.

An underappreciated quality of questions is that the right ones can be quite *propulsive*—as opposed to having the assumed effect of slowing things down or paralyzing us with doubt. If I'm feeling uninspired, the right question can open up a new avenue of thinking. If I'm feeling "stuck" and ready to give up on a creative project, questioning can be used to talk myself down from the ledge. If I'm having trouble determining whether my idea is good and where it might need help, questioning can guide the necessary analysis or be used to solicit feedback from others.

The demand for creativity is so great today—both in the business world and outside of it—and there are so many opportunities and venues to bring your ideas to fruition. In doing so, you can advance your career and improve the quality of your life (doing creative work makes you happier and healthier, research shows). Most important, you may be able to bring creative solutions or an inspiring vision to a world very much in need of both.

Can questions bridge the gap between us?

Elie Wiesel once observed: "People are united by questions. It is the answers that divide them."

Those "answers"—often just opinions dressed up as certainties—seem to be dividing us more than ever these days. And yet we continue to have a deep and powerful need to connect with others. A growing body of research shows that human connection is central to leading a happier, more meaningful life.

Increasingly, we turn to technology as a means of generating more connections. But *more* is not necessarily *deeper*—and when it comes to life-enriching connections, deeper is better. In the effort to forge deeper, more meaningful human connections, one of the great, under-appreciated tools available is the low-tech question.

On the most basic level, questions help us understand, and empathize with, other people. When you ask someone else a question, you are showing interest and providing an opportunity for that person to share thoughts, feelings, and stories. The better the question, the more it invites such sharing.

When we're close to people and know them well (a spouse, family members, a business partner, a lifelong friend), we tend *not* to ask them questions. A powerful change can occur in these relationships when we shift away from advising, criticizing, opining—and toward the direction of asking and listening. That shift to "asking mode" can even transform adversarial relationships—the kind that are tearing much of our society apart these days at town halls and holiday dinners.

The challenge is to reach out with questions that open avenues for conversation, rather than provoke yelling. To quote the radio interviewer and expert questioner Krista Tippett: "It's hard to transcend a combative question. But it's hard to resist a generous question. We all have it in us to formulate questions that invite honesty, dignity, and revelation."

Because questioning is such an effective tool for connecting with others, the ability to question well *should* be seen as a critical leadership skill. But this raises a question that is much debated these days: *Can a leader embrace uncertainty, ask questions, admit vulnerability—and still be seen as a strong and confident leader?*

This much is certain: The challenge of leading, in almost any area, is becoming more complex and demanding. In the past, being a leader meant you'd attained a certain level of expertise and authority in a field or within an organization. Thus, you were seen as the one who could confidently tell others what to do. But in a time of rapid change, the leader who claims to have all the answers is apt to lead people off a cliff.

The more visionary and proactive leaders of today and tomorrow must be able to identify and then challenge the assumptions that may be limiting the potential of a team, an organization and perhaps an entire industry. The questions and inquiry techniques in the Leadership section of the book can help readers become "questioning leaders" in their own domains.

At the same time, questioning is an essential part of being able to identify and choose good people to lead us. If we're not asking the right questions, we may not know who to believe, what sources of information to trust, and how to make sensible choices in a confusing world.

What if the future of democracy depends on questioning?

In one of his last interviews, just months before his death in 1996, the astronomer (and great champion of questioning) Carl Sagan told the interviewer Charlie Rose: "If we are not able to ask skeptical questions . . . to interrogate those who tell us something is true, to be skeptical of those in authority . . . then we are up for grabs for the next charlatan, political or religious, who comes ambling along."

Two decades later, Sagan's words ring truer than ever. But in this age of "alternative facts," the question is, *Do we even know how to ask those skeptical, interrogatory questions Sagan talked about? And when we do ask such questions, are we willing to accept information that may conflict with our existing views?*

To do the former and latter together is to engage in critical thinking. The psychologist and critical-thinking expert Daniel J. Levitin believes that these are difficult times to make sound judgments because the sheer amount of information coming at us puts a strain on our ability to evaluate it. "We've become less critical in the face of information overload," Levitin says. "We throw up our hands and say, 'It's too much to think about.'"

When that happens we can end up making important decisions based on emotions or "gut reactions" rather than evidence or logic. To improve our decision-making capabilities, we need to sharpen our critical thinking. And to do that, we must arm ourselves with a set of critical questions—*and* be willing to consistently ask and thoughtfully consider those questions before rendering judgment.

FIVE ALL-PURPOSE QUESTIONS FOR BETTER THINKING

- *How can I see this with fresh eyes?*
- *What might I be assuming?*
- *Am I rushing to judgment?*
- *What am I missing?*
- *What matters most?*

By employing this type of questioning, we can do what Carl Sagan called "baloney detection"—the dismantling of false claims and slanted arguments from politicians, advertisers, or biased news sources (a skill needed more than ever in a world where the "baloney" is in abundance, and often well-disguised). Despite the best attempts to vet and filter unreliable information, we will likely be swamped with it from here on out—so we're going to have to rely on our built-in baloney detectors, which run on questions.

We should think critically about many of the decisions we make, not just political and consumer choices. Whether we accept a job offer, take a risk on a new venture, or opt to pursue a new calling, the same kind of rigorous thinking and questioning is needed. And while most of our everyday personal decisions may not be as subject to manipulation by outside influences—"fake news" isn't trying to sway your career choices, for example—those decisions are subject to a distorting influence that comes from within: our cognitive biases. To make better decisions in all aspects of our lives, we must be aware of those biases and subject them to rigorous questioning.

The next section lays out a strategy and sets of questions for doing that. Through questioning, we can more accurately assess risks, overcome irrational fears, and figure out what's in our long-term best interests. We can detect baloney and ferret out phonies. We can begin to clarify what matters most to us and identify passions to pursue. We can do all of that by making better decisions, and we can do *that* by first asking better questions about those decisions.

PART I

Questions for Better
DECISION-MAKING

Why should I question my own decisions?

Every day we are confronted with questions that cry out for a decision. Some of the questions are relatively insignificant: *What should I have for breakfast? Shall I read this news article or skip to the next?* Others are more important: *Should I take on that new project? Talk to my boss about a problem that has come up at work? Is it time for our family to start looking for a new house?*

It is perfectly natural, and reasonable, to want to answer such questions as soon as possible. Why waste time being indecisive? Whether you're trying to decide on what to wear or whether to take that new job offer, the clock is ticking. There's often no "right" answer—or if there is one, who knows what it might be? And so, we figure, there's no point overthinking it—might as well choose what feels right in the moment or, to put it another way, "go with your gut."

One can justify this approach by pointing out that a number of top business leaders are known for making critical decisions by relying on "great instincts"—or so the glowing profiles in the business press tell us regularly. The "gut" truly became hip after Malcolm Gladwell's popular 2005 book, *Blink*, which told stories of split-second, instinctive decisions that turned out astonishingly well.

But a growing body of research has concluded that our instincts—our natural tendencies to think or react in certain ways when faced with a decision—aren't as trustworthy as we might believe. We're subject to inherent biases, false confidence, irrational risk aversion, and any number of decision-making pitfalls. Katherine Milkman of the University of Pennsylvania's Wharton School, who has researched and written extensively on decision-making, says: "The science simply doesn't support the value of following your gut—in fact, it supports exactly the opposite approach to decision-making." The psychologist and decision-making expert Daniel Levitin concurs: If you make decisions based on instinct, he says, "your gut is going to be wrong more than it is right."

So what can we do about that? When it comes to important decisions, we can put less trust in feelings and more in evidence. We can seek input from outside sources and differing perspectives—to try to see past our own biases and limited views. We can generate more options to choose from when making a decision (which experts say is a key element in arriving at better decisions). We can also factor in our innate tendencies to be overly cautious or too focused on short-term benefits, and strive to make decisions that are bolder and more forward-looking.

But we can't do any of that unless we're willing to think about—and ask questions about—the decisions we make, as we're making them. In this section, we'll look at why you should question your decisions (or at least some of them) and which questioning strategies seem to be most effective. We'll consider how you can use self-questioning to make more balanced decisions as well as make more courageous ones to help overcome fear of failure. And we'll see that asking the right questions can even help with the biggest decisions—such as figuring out where your passions lie, so that you can decide which goals and dreams to pursue.

As for the smaller decisions—choosing the right coat to wear or the best route to work this morning—not every choice made during the course of the day must be subject to rigorous questioning. People do, after all, have to get things done. Mike Whitaker, author of *The*

Decision Makeover, advises that rather than spending time analyzing small decisions, "have fun with them." Use them as an opportunity to be spontaneous or creative. *Ice cream for breakfast?* Go with your gut.

But the decisions that matter—in your business or your career, in personal relationships or financial investments, in the voting booth—are worthy of more thought. This brings us quickly to one of the problems of decision-making: Many of us don't particularly *like* to think about difficult decisions. The process can be uncomfortable and unsettling.

Hard decisions demand that we make a choice in the midst of uncertainty; they force us to confront the unknown. Fortunately, the question is a tool designed for this precise situation. Questions enable us to "organize our thinking around what we don't know," says Steve Quatrano of the Right Question Institute, an inquiry research group.

Think of your innate questioning skills as a flashlight and the decision ahead of you as a dark room. Each question illuminates a new area (and the better the question, the more light it casts). As we confront the various unknowns surrounding a tough decision, each question—*What am I really trying to decide here? What's most important? What critical information do I have and not have?*— enables us to see a little more clearly, and helps us to step forward in the face of uncertainty.

Questions can also make it easier, even fun at times, to do the hard work of thinking about a decision. A question is an invitation to think. It can be almost irresistible: Ask yourself an interesting question and you've given your mind a puzzle to solve. And when making important decisions, the more invitations we give ourselves to think, the better—because there are strong forces pulling us *away* from thinking at all.

IT SEEMS WE are wired to make quick, instinctive decisions. Blame it on our jungle ancestors. Daniel Levitin notes that our skill sets developed to make quick judgment calls based on limited information—such as a rustling in the leaves. And when we follow those instincts while making decisions, it can lead us to respond more quickly than is necessary.

It isn't easy to convince people to slow down, think more, and spend time gathering and weighing evidence before deciding. "It's going against evolution," Levitin says. "We developed our cognitive sets to deal with a world that was much simpler," in terms of the amount of new information and the pace of change. This resulted in "a fixedness in the brain," he adds, "and it doesn't serve us well today when we're making decisions."

We're also a bit lazy, cognitively speaking. In their research on decision-making habits, the professors Katherine Milkman, Jack Soll, and John Payne concluded that humans resort to snap judgments because "we're cognitive misers—we don't like to spend our mental energy entertaining uncertainties."

Whatever the reason, it's time to ask: *Why are we making decisions as if we're still in the jungle?* We may have deadlines to meet, but we don't have lions charging at us. There's usually time, particularly with important decisions, to give them thought. In modern life, we're more apt to face decisions that are less about surviving immediate dangers and more about navigating a complex world while trying to be more productive and happy in our lives. And unlike our ancestors who often *had* to rely on hunches, we have a wealth of information (too much, it sometimes seems) at our fingertips that can help inform our decisions.

If we don't use the available time and tools to make better decisions—if we opt *not* to think deeply or question vigorously—that, in itself, is a decision. And it's not a good one.

When making decisions, we are prone to falling into "a raft of traps," according to the researchers John Hammond, Ralph Keeney, and Howard Raiffa. In their writings on decision-making, they cite a number of those traps, including:

- Fear of the unknown, which can skew decisions toward playing it safe (this is why the researchers say it can be hard to resist "the magnetic pull of the status quo" when making a decision about a possible change)

- A tendency to focus on the wrong information (that article you read in the paper this morning can have far too much influence on a decision you make this afternoon)
- Overconfidence in our own forecasts
- An inclination to favor information that confirms our preexisting assumptions and biases

Consider how these tendencies might impact a decision: Let's say my company offers me a higher-paying position if I relocate from New York to run the new Seattle office. Immediately, my "status-quo bias" is causing a bad feeling in my gut. (*Change is dangerous; who knows, there may be deadly predators lurking in the bushes of Seattle.*) Also, a friend told me recently that he once spent a few days in Seattle and didn't care for it. Besides that, I feel pretty certain (nobody's said anything, but I *feel* it) that I'll be running the New York office before long. Just to be sure about my decision, I do ten minutes of research via a quick Google search on Seattle—lots of articles pop up, but I end up reading a travel writer's rant about the city being too crowded and coffee obsessed. I don't even like coffee—that clinches it.

In that scenario, I fell into all four of the traps described by Hammond, Keeney, and Raiffa. While I might end up feeling that I have good grounds for my Seattle decision, it's actually based on an irrational fear, an overconfident prediction, and a couple of random personal opinions that are not my own. That doesn't add up to much—though such input can *feel* like a lot at the time we're making decisions.

When we make snap judgments, we're relying on a limited or distorted view of a situation while thinking we have a more complete and accurate view. Based on his research of this phenomenon, the psychologist Daniel Kahneman developed a name (and acronym) for it: "What you see is all there is," or WYSIATI. We form a story in our heads based on what little we know, without allowing for all we do *not* know, Kahneman explains.

Interestingly, Kahneman's research found that some people *are* able to make good snap judgments in certain situations, but only because they know more than most about that particular situation (usually based on past experience). As Kahneman points out, a chess master, for instance, may have reliable gut instinct when deciding on a move—because there is so much experience from similar past decisions to draw upon. So on the question *Should I rely on my gut instinct when making decisions?*, the scientific view is that you should do so only if you're a chess master or someone with similarly prolonged, specific experience making decisions repeatedly in a particular situation.

Most of us aren't like the chess master—though we may think we are. "Overconfidence arises because people are often blind to their own blindness," Kahneman writes. They "sincerely believe they have expertise, act as experts and look like experts." But all the while, "they may be in the grip of an illusion."

Rather than ask, *Should I trust my gut instincts?*, the better question is, *How can I override those instincts?*

And this brings us to a central premise of this book and especially this section: As you're making decisions, you can attempt to override instincts, avoid that "raft of pitfalls," and become less "blind to your own blindness" simply by asking more questions. If, as Kahneman suggests, we make poor decisions because of our limited field of view, then *what if we could open up a wider view— using our questioning flashlight to do so?*

Why do I believe what I believe? (And what if I'm wrong?)

The first thing to do with that flashlight is turn it on yourself. The path to better decision-making begins by questioning one's own beliefs, biases, and assumptions. It's something people rarely do—and it's certainly not easy to do. (There are some biases that are likely to remain invisible to us no matter how hard we search for them.) It may be more difficult than ever in these "echo chamber" times. Today, if one is predisposed to believe something or hold a certain view, it is easier to seek out information that confirms that view while avoiding information that challenges it. Facebook's newsfeed algorithm steadily feeds confirmation bias by exposing people to news and information that mostly aligns with their established preferences.

When the Nobel Prize–winning physicist Arno Penzias was asked what led to his success, he explained that he made a daily habit of asking what he called the "jugular question." Penzias said, "The first thing I do each morning is ask myself, 'Why do I strongly believe what I believe?'" Penzias felt it was critical to "constantly examine your own assumptions." And this is important to do whenever making decisions—because our assumptions and preconceived notions can greatly influence decisions (assuming, and the tendency to want to confirm our assumptions, is one of the four "decision traps" cited previously).

To take a more holistic view of your own assumptions about a particular issue you're deciding on, break Penzias's jugular question into three parts—the "What?," the "Why?," and the "What if?" The first part involves simply trying to identify some of your biases or assumptions. The initial question to ask yourself would be: *What am I inclined to believe about this particular issue?* For example, returning to my "job offer in Seattle" scenario, this initial question can help uncover feelings and assumptions I might have about Seattle, about the challenges of moving to a new location, about working in a startup branch office, and so forth.

Moving from "What?" to "Why?," we return to Penzias' original question—which tries to get at the *basis* for whatever feelings or beliefs you might have on this subject. By thinking about this (and perhaps researching or talking to others about it), we can begin to see if the belief or gut feeling holds up to scrutiny. We may realize that it has little evidence to support it. It may be a viewpoint that made sense once but not anymore (this is such a common problem that the author Daniel Pink recommends regularly asking, *What did I once believe that is no longer true?*).

In questioning why you believe what you believe, don't overlook the "desirability bias," which, researchers are finding, is quite powerful (perhaps even stronger than the much-discussed "confirmation bias"). To figure out what your desirability bias is on any given issue ask yourself this simple question: *What would I like to be true?* Going back to your decision about whether to take a job at Company X, you may have a strong gut feeling or belief that you'll thrive at Company X because you'd *like* that to be true. (Optimism is fine, but too much wishful thinking can crowd out critical thinking.)

After considering "What?" and "Why?," move to "What if?"—as in, *What if my beliefs or assumptions on this issue are just plain wrong?* In exploring this possibility, there's a simple and effective strategy you can use: Think of whatever you believe about a particular issue, and then consider the possibility that the opposite might be true. Richard Larrick, a Duke University professor and a leading researcher on the subject of ".debiasing," says that the "consider the opposite" approach "consists of nothing more than asking oneself, 'What are some reasons that my initial judgment might be wrong?'" Larrick says this question works because "it directs attention to contrary evidence that would otherwise not be considered."

ASK THESE FOUR QUESTIONS TO CHECK YOUR BIASES AND BELIEFS

- *What am I inclined to believe on this particular issue?* Start by trying to articulate your beliefs/biases.
- *Why do I believe what I believe?* The "jugular question," per Nobel Prize–winning physicist Arno Penzias, forces you to consider the basis of those beliefs.
- *What would I like to be true?* A "desirability bias" may lead you to think something is true because you want it to be true.
- *What if the opposite is true?* This question is inspired by "debiasing" experts and Seinfeld's George Costanza.

All of which means that there is at least some scientific basis for the "Opposite George" strategy once employed by the *Seinfeld* character George Costanza. In a 1994 episode of the show, George (with advice from Jerry) has an epiphany: Since his gut instincts had always seemed to lead him astray in the past, he decides that, henceforth, he will do the opposite of whatever he's inclined to do in a given situation—in other words, let "Opposite George" take over.

In the show, automatically going against his instincts works wonders for George's dating life and career. But in a real-life situation, the "consider the opposite" strategy is not meant to provide a clear and reliable solution; rather, it's designed to open up your thinking to possibilities beyond your first impulse. The opposite choice *might* turn out to be a good option, but it could also show you that your first instinct was correct—or, perhaps, you'll realize the best path lies somewhere in between.

Am I thinking like a soldier or a scout?

In order to be able to question your own thinking—so that you can make room for other ideas and views that might conflict with yours—you must be "humble enough to admit that you don't know something or that you might be wrong about what you think you know," says Daniel Levitin. This goes against a natural tendency in many people to defend what they believe. When trying to consider multiple perspectives, evaluate evidence, and make thoughtful decisions, that tendency to be defensive can get in the way.

To illustrate this point, Julia Galef, cofounder of the Center for Applied Rationality, offers up a clarifying metaphor in the form of a beautiful question. Galef suggests we ask ourselves this question: *Am I a soldier or a scout?* She explains that there is a very different mindset for a soldier as opposed to a scout. A soldier's job is to protect and defend against the enemy, whereas the scout's job is to seek out and understand. These two distinct attitudes can also be applied to the ways in which all of us process information and ideas in our daily lives. "Making good decisions is largely about which mindset you're in," Galef says.

The mindset of a scout (or any type of explorer) is rooted in curiosity. As Galef notes, "Scouts are more likely to say they feel pleasure when they learn new information or solve a puzzle. They're more likely to feel intrigued when they encounter something that contradicts their expectations. And scouts are grounded: Their self-worth as a person isn't tied to how right or wrong they are about any particular topic."

In other words, scouts have "intellectual humility," to use a term that has been popularized in the past few years by a number of articles, blog posts, and books (and also because the Google executive Laszlo Bock publicly announced that one quality the company looks for when hiring is intellectual humility).

Defined as "a state of openness to new ideas, a willingness to be receptive to new sources of evidence," intellectual humility is seen by one of its champions, author and University of Virginia professor Edward Hess, as the key to thriving in days ahead. We can't compete with artificial intelligence unless we humans keep learning, experimenting, creating, and adapting, Hess says. And we can't do any of that unless we assume the lifelong role of humble inquirer. As Hess declares in the title of his book, "Humility is the new smart."

If the "old smart" was about getting high grades, knowing more right answers, and not making mistakes, the "new smart" is measured by one's ability to keep adapting. But to do that, Hess says, we must avoid being overly invested in our own ideas and expertise. "I must decouple my beliefs from my ego," Hess explains. "I must be open-minded and treat my beliefs as hypotheses to be constantly tested and subject to modification by better data."

Though humility is often associated with meekness, Hess says we should think of it as "being open to the world." "I've got to overcome my reflexive ways of thinking—my ego, my fears, my fight or flight responses," and in that regard, it can be seen as courageous. If we embrace intellectual humility, he believes, it can help with everything from innovation to civil discourse because "it's no longer about who's right—it's about what is accurate."

Overcoming the desire to "be right" takes a conscious effort, it seems. The venture capitalist Christopher Schroeder says he uses the following question to

---

QUESTIONS TO TEST YOUR "INTELLECTUAL HUMILITY"

- *Do I tend to think more like a soldier or a scout?* A soldier's job is to defend, while a scout's purpose is to explore and discover.
- *Would I rather be right, or would I rather understand?* If you place too much importance on being right, it can put you in "defense" mode and close off learning and understanding.
- *Do I solicit and seek out opposing views?* Don't ask others if they agree with you—ask if they disagree and invite them to say why.
- *Do I enjoy the "pleasant surprise" of discovering I'm mistaken?* Finding out you were wrong about something needn't be cause for shame; it's a sign of intellectual openness and growth.

remind himself to keep an open mind: *Would I rather be right or would I rather understand?*

"If you're adamant about being right," Schroeder says, "you lock yourself in your own echo chamber—and that can cause you to make bad decisions." Another venture capitalist I spoke to said he uses a question similar to Schroeder's when deciding whether or not to fund a startup entrepreneur—except that instead of asking the question of himself, this VC tweaks the question and uses it to evaluate the candidate under consideration: *Is this someone who would rather be right or would rather be successful?* He tends to put his money on the latter.

The rationale is that if an entrepreneur is overly concerned with being proven right about his original idea, it may make it harder to bring the idea to market—because the person could be resistant to modifying the idea or reluctant to admit and correct mistakes in the original business plan. This VC had found through experience that successful entrepreneurs were more open to feedback and willing to be proven wrong—and thus were able to learn, adapt, and improve their idea or offering.

Clearly, the "need to be right" can affect more than just business decisions. It applies to politics, too—wherein people may be loath to admit their vote for a candidate was a mistake, despite strong evidence to suggest that. And in personal relationships, it can keep arguments and feuds going far too long. There's no doubt that pride plays a big part in all of this: It feels good to think you're in the right and to be told by likeminded others that, yes, you're right and you've been right all along. But it doesn't do much to improve learning, understanding, decision-making, or to promote progress in general.

"If we really want to improve our judgment as individuals and as societies," Galef says, we should endeavor to change the way we feel about being right—and being proven wrong. "We may need to learn how to feel proud instead of ashamed when we notice we might have been wrong about something, or to learn how to feel intrigued instead of defensive when we encounter some information that contradicts our beliefs," she says. Galef has her own version of the "need to be right" question; she advises people to ask them-selves, "What do you most yearn for—to defend your own beliefs or to see the world as clearly as you can?"

If you can commit to striving for the latter, then you're in a posi-tion to begin making decisions with a more open and informed mind.

Why should I accept what I'm told?

But being open to new information doesn't mean you should accept it without question. Having turned that questioning flashlight within, it must also be shined on claims, viewpoints, and evidence you encounter. As you consider and evaluate that information, in an effort to make a reasoned decision or judgment about it, you're engaging in critical thinking.

The term "critical thinking" can sound both musty and nega-tive. "It's a terrible name," says the critical-thinking expert Neil Browne, not least because it fails to engage young students who need to learn how to employ this type of thinking. (Browne muses that since it requires an agile, flexible mind and an ability to slice apart false arguments, perhaps "ninja thinking" might be a more appealing term.)

When it comes to making decisions or arriving at a judgment, the critical (or ninja) thinker strives to do so based on solid evidence while trying to remain objective and fair-minded. It takes some effort to engage in open-minded critical thinking instead of just assuming and accepting. But the good news is that mastering some of the basic steps of critical thinking is not hard. It's really just a matter of asking a few fundamental questions—though you must know which questions are most useful in a given situation and be willing to take the time and trouble to ask them.

What are those questions? You'll find different "critical-thinking" questions on different lists, but according to Browne and other authorities on the subject, a good question to start with is the "evidence" question, which is used to try to determine the substance behind any new information you're encountering. A critical thinker presented with any sort of claim—whether it's coming from a product salesman, a politician, or a news story—habitually asks, *What is the evidence behind this claim and how strong is it?* That may lead to a subset of more specific evidence questions, such as, *Does this evidence come from a solid source? Is there an agenda behind it?*

Answering these questions may require some digging to find out if, for example, the source of information has a strong track record for telling the truth or whether that source may have a special interest in advancing this particular claim. (In terms of the latter, always ask, *Cui bono?*—Latin for "Who benefits?")

Going back to my "relocate to Seattle" scenario, I was basing my decision in part on random opinions (my friend, a travel post I found on Google). I would have been wise to question that evidence. (*Does it represent the views/experience of more than these two people? How much time did these two people spend in the city, and how well did they really get to know it?*)

Sometimes the problem with information is not what is there, but what's missing—whether it's a news story with insufficient reporting or a sales pitch that leaves out important details. Thus, a critical thinker should always ask, *What are they not telling me?* when offered potential solutions that may neglect to mention side effects, hidden costs, and potential negative consequences.

When people are trying to persuade you, they may use flawed reasoning that suggests you should believe A because of

---

USE THESE FIVE QUESTIONS TO DETECT B.S.

- **How strong is the evidence?** Critical thinking starts with demanding that there be substance behind any claim. A subset of "evidence" questions might include, *Does this evidence come from a solid source? Is there an agenda behind it?*

- **What are they not telling me?** Sometimes the problem with information is not what is there, but what's missing—whether it's a news story with insufficient reporting or a sales pitch that leaves out important details.

- **Does it logically follow?** When people are trying to persuade you, they may use flawed reasoning that suggests you should believe A because of B.

- **What is the opposing view?** To avoid "weak-sense critical thinking," be willing to seek out an opposing side of the issue you're deciding on—and try to consider it with an open mind.

- **Which of the conflicting views has more evidence behind it?** Go with the side that has more weight.

B, or they may promise that if you do A, then B will surely result. Critical thinking questions are designed to root out "logical falla-cies" that may be based on faulty assumptions or, worse still, may be tricks designed to lead you to a false conclusion.

An excellent resource for identifying common logical fallacies is Carl Sagan's "baloney detection kit," originally published as part of his 1996 book *The Demon-Haunted World: Science as a Candle in the Dark.* (Sagan's writing on critical thinking has gained renewed attention, in part due to being featured on Maria Popova's popular *Brain Pickings* blog.) As part of his kit, Sagan offered a list of twenty tricks that critical thinkers should always watch for, including argu-ments that rely on authority (*I'm the president, so you should believe me*), false dichotomies (*You're with us or against us*), and "slippery slope" arguments (*If we take this seemingly reasonable step, it will surely lead to something much worse*).

Since one of the keys to critical thinking is fair-mindedness—which requires a willingness to consider multiple perspectives—critical thinkers are trained to ask, *What's the other side of this issue?* The idea is to get in the habit of always considering an opposing view of the issue or claim at hand.

When trying to consider the "other side," keep in mind that it can also be useful to ask, *Is there actually another side?* ("There is not another side to the question of whether we really landed on the moon," Daniel Levitin points out. "We did.") If there is another side, consider both sides together and ask, *Which of the conflicting views has more evidence behind it?* In the end, one may still be left with a judgment call—as in, "I have three strong reasons to believe one side and one reason to believe the other; I'll go with the stronger case."

Does my critical thinking have an agenda?

An interesting point about critical thinking: If you bounce back and forth between political blogs on the left and on the right, you'll notice something peculiar. On both sides of the political divide, people talk about critical thinking regularly, often to complain that there is a troubling lack of critical thinking in today's world. But each side tends to think the *other side* is suffering from this problem. "Those other people" are the ones falling prey to propaganda, not asking skeptical questions, and failing to make sound political judgments.

This is not a new phenomenon. The late Dr. Richard Paul, a university professor who helped launch the Foundation for Critical Thinking in the 1970s, studied a common behavior that he labeled "weak-sense critical thinking," in which a person might be adept at applying the basic tools and practices of critical thinking— questioning, investigating, evaluating—but would be inclined to do so for the sole purpose of confirming an existing view. You might say such people are critical thinkers with an agenda.

Bowling Green College's Neil Browne has also studied weak-sense critical thinking and he points out that people doing this often don't recognize that their reasoning and judgment may be skewed. "It is very common for someone to believe, 'Those who disagree with me are biased, but I am not,'" Browne says. "It is one of the biggest obstacles to critical thinking."

So if we think of a critical thinker merely as "someone who asks critical questions," we're missing a very important piece. By this definition, all of the partisan political hacks are critical thinkers, as are climate-change deniers and flat-earth believers.

Clearly, to be a "skeptical questioner" is not enough to qualify one as a critical thinker, particularly if the skepticism runs only in one direction. Critical thinkers must be flexible enough to consider and question all aspects and all sides of an issue, including—and perhaps especially—the side they are inclined to favor.

What if this isn't a "yes or no" decision?

Because critical-thinking questions help in weighing evidence and evaluating between conflicting options, they can be particularly useful when making binary decisions. *(Should I accept this offer?*

Believe that story currently circulating on the Internet? Trust that candidate?) But a lot of the important decisions we face are not "yes or no" or "A versus B" choices—or at least, they shouldn't be.

A binary decision is an answer to a closed question. We may choose to frame a decision in binary "yes/no" or "either/or" terms because it limits the choices we must consider; it makes it easier to decide. In his research, Daniel Kahneman found that "people who face a difficult question often answer an easier one instead, without realizing it." A difficult question might be: *I'm having problems with my boss at work; how might I address that?* An easier question would be: *Given the problems I'm having with my boss, should I quit my job—yes or no?* The first question could be answered countless ways and requires some creative thought; the second can be answered quickly, in the heat of the moment.

But that easy "yes or no" decision closes down a whole range of possibilities. In decision-making—at least at the initial stages of thinking about a decision—having *more* options to consider is generally a good thing. A decision can be no better than the best option under consideration, according to the aforementioned researchers Milkman, Soll, and Payne. They point out that people have a tendency to "frame decisions as a yes or no question instead of generating alternatives." The brothers Chip and Dan Heath, authors of the book *Decisive,* concur that "the first villain of decision making—'narrow framing'—is the tendency to define our choices too narrowly, in binary terms."

So then: *How do you open up more options?* Simple: Ask yourself to do so.

If you can reframe that "yes or no" choice by changing it from a closed question to a more open-ended one, it can profoundly alter the decision you're making. The closed question, *Should I quit my job—yes or no?*, becomes more open-ended by turning it into a "How?" or "What?" question, such as: *How might I improve my situation at this job? What possibilities might exist between quitting or doing nothing?*

The point is not to avoid making a hard decision—you still may end up quitting the job—but to open up more possibilities to consider before making that decision. Of course, you don't want to drown in too many choices, but Milkman, Soll, and Payne suggest generating at least three options for any decision. If your business is trying to decide about expanding, the three options might be something like: 1) *We could open a new branch* 2) *We could expand but do so within our existing branches* 3) *We could decide not to expand at all.* Those options might be based on projecting scenarios that range from rosy to lousy. As you're generating options, consider three possible outcomes or scenarios that might result from this decision by asking: *What is the great, the good, and the ugly?*

When trying to come up with three options to decide upon, the consultant Paul Sloane suggests

---

USE THESE FIVE QUESTIONS TO OPEN UP POSSIBILITIES

- *How can I "open up" the question to be decided?* We have a tendency to make binary decisions (yes/no, either/or), which limits options. Trying using open-ended questions (What are the best ways . . . ? How might I . . . ?) to frame your decision.
- *What is the great, the good, and the ugly?* When making decisions, try to choose from at least three options. Do this by projecting three different potential outcomes or scenarios—one very positive, one moderate, and one negative.
- *If none of the current options were available, what would I do?* Imagine that the existing options you're deciding between suddenly have vanished; this forces you to try to come up with additional possibilities. Upon returning to reality, you can weigh your newly-imagined options against the existing ones.
- *What is the counterintuitive choice?* Include one option that goes completely against the others; you probably won't choose it, but it stimulates unconventional thinking.
- *What would an outsider do?* You can get an actual outsider to help answer this—or just try to look at the situation the way an outsider might.

---

that the third option you generate should be an unusual one that runs counter to the others. So as you're thinking of possibilities, ask: *What is the counterintuitive option?*

Sloane offers this example: You are considering firing Fred, who has been underperforming. Option 1 is to fire him; Option 2 is to put him in a training course to try to shape him up; Option 3 is to give Fred a promotion! That third option may seem offbeat, but Sloane explains that "it is deliberately included to stimulate and provoke your thoughts to consider something unconventional."

If you're having trouble generating additional options, here's a trick suggested by the Heath Brothers, based on their decision research. Whenever you're trying to decide between existing choices, try asking yourself the "vanishing options" question—*If none of the current options were available, what would I do then?* This question forces you to consider alternative possibilities by temporarily removing existing ones.

What would an outsider do?

One of the most important jobs questioning can do to aid in decision-making is to remind us to step back and try to see the decision from a different perspective. Katherine Milkman, the Heaths, and other decision researchers (all influenced by Kahneman's groundbreaking work) reference the common problem of having a "limited view" of the issue at hand because we're too close to it.

A simple yet effective way to adopt a fresh perspective is by asking: *If my friend had to make this decision, what advice would I give?* The "advice" question is championed by many decision experts, including author and Duke University–based psychologist Dan Ariely, who explains that, strange as it might seem, we give more sensible advice to others than we give ourselves.

Why would we do that? The Heath Brothers point to research showing that "our advice to others tends to hinge on the single most important factor," as it should—but when we're thinking about ourselves, we get caught up in too many large and small concerns. Or as the Heaths put it: "When we think of our friends we see the forest. When we think of ourselves, we get stuck in the trees."

Another odd but apparently effective self-distancing technique: Try asking yourself about a decision by using the third person—for example, I might ask myself, *What should Warren do in this situation?* (instead of *what should I do?*). The psychology professor Ethan Kross has found that this can lead to cooler, more rational thinking because it allows us to see ourselves and the situation from an outside perspective. Kross points out that superstar athletes like LeBron James sometimes are mocked for speaking to and about themselves in the third person ("LeBron is going to be ready come

Thursday's game," LeBron might say). But LeBron is right about this, Kross says. When talking to ourselves, there can be a method to the madness.

To get even more distance from yourself, try asking about the decision from *someone else's* perspective—as in, *What would Warren Buffett do if faced with this decision? (Or for that matter, LeBron James?)* The "outsider" whose perspective you adopt could be someone who has no connection to the issue you're deciding on, or someone who might have only a slightly different perspective.

A famous story in the business world involves the cofounders of Intel, Andrew Grove and Gordon Moore, who, early in the company's history, had to make a critical decision about whether Intel should abandon an existing core product in order to shift in a new direction. Grove posed the question *If we got kicked out and the board brought in a new CEO, what do you think he would do?* That question helped create the distance they needed to see the situation more impartially. A new CEO, they reasoned, would not have an emotional investment in the old product and would base the decision on what made sense going forward. Thus, Grove and Moore decided to abandon the old strategy—and it proved a wise decision, as evidenced by Intel's subsequent success.

In trying to "take an outside view" on a decision, you can speculate about what an outsider might decide, as Grove and Moore did. You can also consider the experience of others who've had to make a similar decision (by finding and questioning such people or relying on case studies involving situations similar to the one you're facing). Another option is to turn to an advisor or consultant, who may have experience working with others who've made similar decisions; the consultant herself also provides the perspective of an outsider.

Be forewarned: Taking an outside view can sometimes result in a complete reframing of the decision in question. The consultant Dave LaHote of the Lean Enterprise Institute shared a story of being brought into a company that was struggling with how to reform its sales approval process. The current process had multiple levels of approval and took two weeks before a sale could go through.

Realizing that was too slow, the company's leaders became fixated on streamlining the approval process so that it took two days instead of two weeks. But as an outsider, LaHote saw things differently: He considered the situation and then asked why they needed the approval process at all. When faced with this unexpected question, company leaders began to examine the rationale behind the process—and found that it wasn't justifiable. They needed to "step back from the process and see it objectively as I did," LaHote says.

HAVING CONSIDERED THE many questions that can help inform a good decision, at some point you must stop asking questions and just decide. How does one know when that time has arrived? The venture capitalist Schroeder says: "In decision making, you're always navigating between gathering enough information and gathering too much." As to how much is enough, here's an interesting formula from Amazon CEO Jeff Bezos: "Most decisions should probably be made with somewhere around 70% of the information you wish you had. If you wait for 90%, in most cases, you're probably being slow."

But getting to 70 percent usually doesn't happen in a "blink." Decisions should not be rushed, for any number of reasons—not least of which is that people tend to make poor decisions under pressure. When faced with an important decision, it's worth asking, *Does this decision have to be made now?* and *Is this the right time to decide?* It's been shown that there are times when we should avoid making decisions—when we're tired, stressed, or just anxious to "get this thing over with!"—because we're more apt to decide based on emotion or impulse.

When you've decided to make the decision, try to make it twice—once, and then again a day or two later. People may be reluctant to second-guess themselves, but if a decision is a solid and considered one, it should hold up. One way to test the soundness of the decision is to consider these two questions: *Is it possible to shoot holes in this decision?* and *If I had to defend this decision at a later time, how would I do so?*

Taking the time to question decisions doesn't mean you should waffle on them or postpone making a final call. When people put off deciding for too long it can eventually result in having to make the decision at the last minute, under pressure. The author and business consultant Todd Henry says a common problem he encounters is that people put off making decisions because of uncertainty—and it keeps them from moving forward with their lives or businesses. He recommends we routinely ask ourselves: *Where in my life right now am I living under the fog of indecisiveness?*

There are some decisions we may avoid making because there is great uncertainty surrounding them or because the stakes are so high (or both). To help in such circumstances, we need to ask "courageous" questions—designed to provide just enough clarity and confidence to enable us to take a leap into the void.

What would I try if I knew I could not fail?

As decision makers, we seem to veer from being overconfident and willing to "go with our gut" to being terrified that if we make the wrong choice, the business will collapse, the career will stall, and "we'll end up dead and broke on the side of the road," in the words of Khemaridh Hy.

Hy has become a student of the effects of fear on decision-making in work and life, though he came to this endeavor via an unusual background as a high-flying investment banker. The son of immigrant parents who instilled in him a fierce work ethic, by his early thirties Hy had become one of the youngest managing directors of the BlackRock's hedge fund. But he felt restless and dissatisfied. He consulted a life coach who eventually posed this question: *What are you so afraid of?*

When he really started to think about that question, Hy says, he realized that fear was a driving force behind his need to keep earning more money and attaining higher levels of success in the financial world. No matter how much money he made, he was still afraid of ending up broke. He also feared that he'd die before he could leave his mark on the world. And he worried he'd fail to live up to expectations of others.

Hy left his job—"to consider these kinds of questions, you need the time and space to be able to think," he says—and began to write a blog about his fears and anxieties and how he was learning to understand and cope with them. The blog quickly became popular, first in the banking world—"all these young, successful finance guys would write to me saying, 'You touched on something I've never thought about,'" Hy says—then in the tech sector. Hy's blog, podcast, and Snapchat messages became so popular that CNN dubbed him "an Oprah for millennials."

While his writing covers all manner of tips on finding fulfillment and meaning in life, Hy remains particularly focused on fear. "That angst is everywhere," he says—and it can influence or even determine many of the choices we make, leading us in directions we might not really want to go and keeping us from enjoying our everyday lives as much as we should.

What Hy says is backed up by the research on decision-making, which suggests that an outsized fear of negative outcomes—also known as the "negativity bias"—can lead us to make choices that may not make sense or be in our best interest. The negativity bias can be rooted in something that we experienced in the past that has a disproportionate influence on our current thinking and behavior; psychologists point to the case of people continuing to choose to drive instead of fly long after the 9/11 tragedy. (All that extra driving in an attempt to stay "safe" led to an increase in car crashes.)

But those fears can also be traced to a more distant past—and to dangers that have nothing to do with our modern-day lives. Adam Hansen, coauthor of the book *Outsmart Your Instincts*, explains that those "jungle instincts"—the same ones that can cause us to feel we must react and decide quickly—can also push us in the direction of risk avoidance.

In the jungle or in other life-and-death situations, avoiding risk may make sense, but in business, in one's career, or even just in terms of living a full life, it can severely limit possibilities. Hansen, a creative consultant for companies, says that in the business world, the negativity bias can have a paralyzing effect. "It keeps companies stuck in place because they are afraid to try anything new or bold. It brings innovation to a halt."

How can questioning help with something as primal and powerful as fear?

To begin with, questioning can help us identify the fears that may be influencing decisions and behaviors. "It can be hard to figure out what you're really afraid of," says Hy. "But often, once you do identify it and verbalize it—for instance, the fear that I'll end up broke or dead or both—you can start to come to grips with it."

Phil Keoghan, a lifelong adventurer and fear conqueror who hosts the television series *The Amazing Race*, agrees that asking probing questions about one's fears is a good starting point for overcoming them. Keoghan has coached people to help them conquer a range of fears (from the fear of heights to the fear of sharks), and he says he often begins by asking: *What is your earliest memory of this fear? How do you react to it? What has it kept you from doing? How might things change if you were able to overcome this fear?* In dissecting the fear, "we talk about the irrationality of it—and about real versus imagined risks," he says.

Notice Keoghan's last two questions focus on the positive benefits of overcoming a fear. The life coach Curt Rosengren points out that it's critical to emphasize the *Why?* when trying to overcome fears—as in, *Why would I want to do this thing or make this choice, even though it scares me?* "Rather than focusing on what you are going to do (the thing inducing the fear), focus on the positive energy of the desired outcome," Rosengren advises. That outcome may be a personal benefit or it might involve having a positive impact on others. Either way, when the answer to *Why am I doing this?* is about making a difference, "that inspires you and pulls you forward"—and it becomes easier to move past the fear.

When you're deciding on a possibility that makes you uneasy, focus on the positive feelings associated with taking a risk. Adam

Hansen suggests clients ask themselves: *Within this scary possibility, what excites me?*

But it's also important to examine the negative feelings that may be associated with taking a risk—which can be based on legitimate concerns about what might go wrong if you pursue a risky possibility. Rather than avoiding thinking about these, it's generally better to come right out and ask: *What is the worst that could happen?*

That's a familiar question and a fairly basic one—but that doesn't make it any less valuable. The question is a favorite of not only professional risk managers but coaches and psychologists as well. And though it may seem like a negative question because it evokes worst-case imaginings, as long as it is paired with a more positive follow-up question—*And how would I recover from that?*—it can actually end up lessening your fears and giving you the confidence to take on the risk.

The author and entrepreneur Jonathan Fields notes that often when we think about failure, "we do so in a vague, exaggerated way—we're afraid to even think about it clearly." But before embarking on a high-risk challenge, if you visualize what would actually happen if you failed—and what you'd likely have to do to pick up the pieces from that failure—this can help you realize that, as Fields says, "failure in any endeavor is rarely absolute. There is a way back from almost anything, and once you acknowledge that, you can proceed with more confidence."

"COURAGEOUS" QUESTIONS TO OVERCOME FEAR OF FAILURE

- **What would I try if I knew I could not fail?** Start with this favorite Silicon Valley question to help identify bold possibilities.
- **What is the worst that could happen?** This may seem negative, but the question forces you to confront hazy fears and consider them in a more specific way (which usually makes them less scary).
- **If I did fail, what would be the likely causes?** Do a "premortem" on a possible failure, listing some of the potential causes; this tells you what pitfalls to avoid.
- **. . . and how would I recover from that failure?** Just thinking about how you would pick up the pieces if you did fail tends to lessen the fear of that possibility.
- **What if I succeed—what would that look like?** Now shift from worst-case to best-case scenario. Visualizing success breeds confidence—and provides motivation for moving forward.
- **How can I take one small step into the breach?** Consider whether there are "baby steps" that could lead up to taking a leap.

The scientist and decision-making expert Gary Klein is a proponent of using "premortems" (doing a postmortem in advance) to envision what a potential failure might look like, so that you can then consider the possible reasons for that failure. To put the premortem into question form, you might ask: *If I were to fail, what might be the reasons for that failure?* Decision researchers say using premortems can temper excessive optimism and encourage a more realistic assessment of risk. Here again, the main benefit of thinking about failure in advance is that it tends lessen the fear and uncertainty surrounding possible failure; if you can begin to envision it, you may see it's not necessarily catastrophic and that there are ways to respond if it actually happens.

While you're envisioning the possibility of failure, be sure to consider the opposite, as well, by asking: *What if I succeed—what would that look like?* Jonathan Fields points out that this question is important because it can help counter the negativity bias. Fields recommends visualizing, in detail, what would be likely to happen in a best-case scenario. The reality may not live up to that, but that vision can provide an incentive strong enough to encourage taking a risk.

That still doesn't make it easy to actually move forward with a high-risk decision or course of action. The consensus among those who've studied and worked on overcoming fear seems to be that questioning, envisioning, and advance planning can take you only so far—at some point, there's no substitute for action. (The person with a fear of water inevitably must enter the water.) But even at this action stage, there is a useful question to ask: *How can I take one small step into the breach?* Phil Keoghan finds that when he's coaching people on overcoming fears, he develops a plan that starts with small steps and limited exposure to the source of the fear. For someone conquering a fear of heights, he logically starts with going to the top of a low structure before moving to a higher one.

A similar strategy can be used with almost any high-risk venture. In business, concerns about introducing a new product can be eased by starting with a limited introduction of a low-cost "beta" version of the offering before diving in with a full-scale rollout of a finished product. Almost any business trying to be innovative today has to become practiced at asking two questions: *How can we generate more ideas?* and just as importantly, *How can we quickly and inexpensively test those ideas?* Knowing how to answer the second question makes it feasible—and less risky—to pursue the first.

ONE OF THE powerful things you can do with a question is use it to temporarily shift reality. The question *What would I try if I knew I could not fail?* is a great example of a reality-shifting question, and it's one I've been sharing with audiences for the past few years. I'm not the only fan of it—it's been a popular question in Silicon Valley ever since a similar version was quoted in a 2012 TED Talk by Regina Dugan, a technologist who has worked with Google and DARPA. But the question goes back way before that: More than four decades ago, the American pastor Robert H. Schuller used it in inspirational sermons and books.

A reality-shifting question can permit us to see the world through a different lens. "In order for imagination to flourish, there must be an opportunity to see things as other than they currently are or appear to be," explains John Seely Brown, a technologist and futurist who works with the Deloitte Center for the Edge. "This begins with a simple question: What if? It is a process of introducing something strange and perhaps even demonstrably untrue into our current situation or perspective."

By asking *What if I could not fail?*, we create a mental landscape in which the constraint of failure is removed. It's actually quite common and effective to use questions to remove real-world limitations and constraints as a means of encouraging people to think more boldly and imaginatively. For example, product developers sometimes use the hypothetical question *What if cost were not an issue?* in order to temporarily remove practical limits on thinking. Once the cost restraint is set aside, it allows for a much wider exploration of ideas.

Of course, in the real world, constraints do exist: Budgets are limited, and the possibility of failure is very real. The ideas that emerge during the "What if I could not fail?" stage of thinking may have to be tempered or even discarded later. But—just as with the technique of "considering the opposite," discussed earlier—the point is to open up more possibilities (in this case, bolder and riskier ones) for consideration.

An interesting variation of the "What if I could not fail?" question was explored in the *New York Times* by the writer Ron Lieber. He shared the story of Daniel L. Anderson, who'd grown bored with his real estate job in Reno and was trying to decide between an offer for a "safe" job in Houston and a riskier one in San Francisco. As Anderson was grappling with the decision, a mentor asked him the question: "What would you do if you weren't afraid?"

Anderson said that question "caused me to re-examine my situation to make sure I wasn't doing what was easy and comfortable," adding that he also thought of stories his mother had told him about retired friends with regrets. "I didn't want to be that person," he said. He ended up taking the riskier San Francisco job, where he's now thriving. As for that "safe" job offer he turned down in Houston? It was "from a company named Enron."

What would "future me" decide?

Our natural aversion to change and risk sometimes steers us away from choices that could improve our lives. But what if we were encouraged to make bolder choices—would we then be happier? The economist Steven Levitt wanted to find out, and conducted a study involving people in the midst of trying to make a difficult decision. The subjects each agreed to abide by the results of a coin flip in making their choice—if the coin came up heads, they'd say yes to the job offer, marriage proposal, or whatever they were considering.

Six months later, Levitt interviewed the subjects and found the heads ("yes") people were significantly happier than the tails ("no") people. What does it tell us? Reporting on the study in the *New*

York Times, columnist Arthur C. Brooks came to this conclusion: Left to our own devices (without a coin toss to guide us), "we say 'no' too much when faced with an opportunity."

Brooks goes on to make the point that these days, risk-averse behavior is "everywhere, particularly among young people." Case in point: Brooks points to data showing that people under age thirty today are much less likely than their counterparts in the past to relocate for their careers. In other words, when faced with the question *Will you pursue this opportunity or would you rather stay put?*, we're apt to give in to the status quo bias.

But what if we reframed that question, enabling us to consider the same decision from a different perspective—seeing it from the future, looking back?

A story shared by Julia Galef of the Center for Rational Thinking shows how examining a decision in this way can help us break free of the status quo bias. A friend of Galef's was offered a job that would amount to a $70,000 pay increase but initially was reluctant to take the offer because it required that he move to a distant location. Then Galef's friend changed his perspective by asking himself this question: *What if I already had the job in that location and was offered a chance to move back closer to home—but with a $70,000 pay cut? Would I accept that?*

Framed that way, his answer was no—which suggested to him he should take the job (and he did). So why did a simple reframing of the question have the effect of making the offer seem more attractive? According to Galef, her friend's initial reluctance to accept the offer was based on a common aversion to change. However, once he envisioned a future scenario in which he'd already *made* the move, he realized it was probably worth doing.

A question that enables us to envision a future scenario—in order to help with a present-day decision—could be thought of as a "crystal ball" question. Such questions are worth asking because we have a tendency to focus too much on the here and now. This inclination toward short-term thinking causes us to focus on immediate preferences while ignoring long-term aims and consequences.

One way to counter it is to try to imagine how we might feel about something in the future. "Good decision-making is tied to our ability to anticipate future emotional states," says Ed Batista, an executive coach who teaches at Stanford University. "We need to vividly envision ourselves in a future scenario."

So if, for example, an opportunity comes your way and you're trying to decide whether to take it, consider this question shared by writer Rob Walker: *If I look back years from now, will I wish that I'd made a change when the opportunity was ripe?* If you can imagine how "future you" might feel about this, it can help guide you toward the better long-term decision.

Which option will allow me to evolve and flourish?

Keep in mind that "future you" is likely to be quite different from "present you." This is part of what makes long-term decision-making challenging. "Human beings are works in progress that mistakenly think they're finished," says psychologist Dan Gilbert. His studies show that people vastly underestimate how much they will change over the next ten years, in terms of their values and preferences.

When faced with a decision that has long-term implications— joining a new organization, moving to a different area, changing career tracks—an overarching question to consider is: *Which option will allow me to evolve and flourish?*

If we think about this question in terms of, say, joining a new company, it encourages looking beyond the more immediate incentives (such as a pay hike) in order to consider growth opportunities and other future benefits. Writing in the *New York Times*, Adam Grant offered several more targeted questions that help answer the broader question cited above.

According to Grant, if you want to find the company that's right for you, one of the most important things to determine is: *Can the little person rise to the top?* In that company's lore, there should be stories of people going from secretary or elevator operator to top executive positions. That tells you this is a place where "future you" can rise up. A related additional question suggested by Grant: *Can I shape my destiny and have influence in this organization?* Getting promoted up the ladder is only part of what might fulfill "future you"; having a real say in what happens at that company is just as important.

At the same time, it's good to know if this new company is a place where you can learn, experiment, create—because those are the activities that will help you evolve and advance. Grant boils it down to this question: *How will the boss react to mistakes?* You can find the answer by digging into stories of how the company and its leaders have reacted to past failures. Grant references a famous IBM story involving an employee who made a mistake that cost the company $10 million. The employee figured IBM chief Tom Watson would fire him, but Watson's response was: "Fire you? I just spent $10 million educating you."

In trying to project whether you'll be able to develop and grow at a company, start by asking, *How have others at this company added new skills and expanded responsibilities?* And don't overlook the social component of work— it is a large and often underrated factor in job happiness, says workplace expert Ron Friedman, founder of ignite80. Friedman suggests trying to find out, *How does the organization encourage "connectedness" between employees?*

QUESTIONS TO ASK BEFORE TAKING THAT JOB

- *Can the little person rise to the top?* Seek the proof in the form of multiple stories of people who were able to make that climb.
- *How does the organization react to mistakes?* This will determine whether you can experiment and grow. (Another way of asking: *Will I be punished for exploring?*)
- *Can I have influence in this organization?* Find out whether people at all levels have a say.
- *How have others here added to their skills?* Another key determinant of whether you'll be able to evolve.
- *Does this place encourage camaraderie?* The social aspect of work is more important than most think.
- *Will I enjoy the "small pleasures" of my daily routine?* Being happy in your job hinges on the little things you'll be doing every day.

Some companies do a much better job than others at promoting a sense of camaraderie.

Interestingly, there's a tendency to care *in the present* about issues such as whether your job offers a chance to do interesting work and spend time with people you like. But research shows that we don't seem to think any of that will be important to us *in the future*, says Ayelet Fishbach, professor of behavioral sciences at the University of Chicago. Which leads her to ask: "Why are people fully aware that present benefits are important in their current job, and yet expect not to care about those benefits in the future?" Fishbach wonders, "Why, for example, does a student who cannot sit through a boring two-hour lecture think she would be satisfied by a boring but well-paying job?"

Fishbach attributes this tendency to a basic human failure to think about the future in realistic terms. Her advice: "Make sure you choose a career or project that you enjoy pursuing" and that offers the kind of "small pleasures in your daily routine" that often end up being a big part of what creates job satisfaction.

How would I later explain this decision to others?

When making decisions for the long term, think of each important decision as a chapter within a larger story, advises Joseph Badaracco, a professor of business ethics at Harvard Business School. Then, ask yourself the following: *How does that chapter fit with the larger narrative?*

Badaracco says that for a decision to make sense in that larger context, it should tie in with long-term goals and purposes. And when making such a decision, also be cognizant of obligations, relationships, and values, he adds. Badaracco recommends asking the question, *What are my core obligations?* (to an organization, customers, community, family), so that you can assess whether the decision serves those interests, too.

Lastly, he offers this "crystal ball" question as way to figure out whether you'll be able to live comfortably with this decision: "Imagine yourself explaining your decision to a close friend or a mentor—someone you trust and respect deeply. Would you feel comfortable? How would that person react?"

While you of course want to avoid making decisions that "future you" (and "future others" who may depend on you) will regret, often the biggest regrets are the decisions that erred on the side of safety and caution. Going back to Levitt's study and those people who said yes to a bold decision because of a coin flip (and ended up being happy they did), I would suggest an alternative to a random coin toss. Instead use a weighted question designed to push you a little more in one direction than the other: *If I'm generally better off saying yes to bold decisions, why not say yes to this one?* Framed this way, the question puts more of a burden on the "no" side.

If you are going to err on the side of "yes" when making decisions, there are a couple more questions to keep in mind, including: *If I'm saying yes to this, what am I saying no to?* This question, shared by the executive coach Michael Bungay Stanier, is intended to remind you of the "opportunity cost" of any decision. If you choose to do X, you may miss out on doing Y. It shouldn't keep you from saying yes to X, unless Y is actually better *and* likely to happen. Mostly, this question reminds us to be careful about saying yes to things that aren't really worthwhile—because it may later cost us the opportunity to do something better. (Ask yourself the question when tempted to fill all the empty dates on your calendar with any halfway-decent opportunity that comes along.)

If you're following the "err on the side of yes" approach, this doesn't mean you should say yes lightly or out of obligation. In particular, this can be an issue when deciding how to respond to an invitation. We often default to yes, just to be polite—then regret it later when the event arrives.

There's a way to check, in the present, to see if you're likely to regret saying yes to an invitation—it involves another "crystal ball" question, this one offered up by psychologist Dan Ariely. He calls it the "cancel-elation" question. When someone invites you to do something, ask yourself: *How would I feel if I accepted that invitation—and then found out it had been canceled?* "If you feel elation, you don't want to do it," Ariely says. "You're doing it out of obligation or discomfort with saying no."

A final thought about deciding with the future in mind: Memorable experiences are worth a lot to "future you"—perhaps more than cash bonuses and other short-term benefits that won't last. Writing in the *New York Times*, Carl Richards posed this question: "What if putting experience first makes us happier, more fulfilled, more creative and more memorable people?" Richards then went on to answer his own question by pointing to research suggesting that, in fact, rich and memorable experiences do improve our lives in all of those ways mentioned.

The experiences you say yes to now will be the stories that are remembered and shared by "future you." Which brings us to one more "crystal ball" question, shared by the author and consultant John Hagel, who suggests that whenever you face a decision between two diverging paths, ask yourself the following: *When I look back in five years, which of these options will make the better story?* As Hagel explains, "no one ever regrets taking the path that leads to the better story."

What is my tennis ball?

If certain types of questions can help bring a fresh perspective to a decision or a problem, how might we apply this tool to one of the greatest challenges we all face—identifying or clarifying a sense of purpose in our lives?

These days, we're urged to "follow our passions"—but what if you're not sure which one(s) to follow? This can be an issue not only for those starting out in a career but also for some who are established, even highly successful yet feel unfulfilled. It's easy to find oneself on a path determined by others or by circumstance (e.g., the job offer or project that comes along unexpectedly and is too good to turn down, and then becomes a career). Whether you're starting out or considering a possible change in direction, you can use targeted questions to try to get a better sense of what you're meant to do.

Before looking at some of the questions designed to identify your true passion in life, it's worth considering a contrarian question: *Should I even be asking, "What's my passion?"* Some feel that the "passion" question can do more harm than good. "Young people get paralyzed by the idea that 'I'm going to find this thing I'm meant to do,'" says author Cal Newport. "Passion is not something you follow. It's something that will follow you as you put in the hard work to become valuable to the world." Newport's advice: Pick a career that seems interesting (and leave passion out of it); then focus on becoming good at that thing, and eventually it may become your passion.

Similarly, the author Elizabeth Gilbert says she has stopped advising people to "follow your passion" because it creates pressure for those who may have no idea what their one true calling might be—if there even is one. Gilbert now advises people to "follow your curiosity"—which may lead you to a passion (or many different ones).

Still, there is something to be said for identifying a pursuit or goal that can provide direction, motivation, and focus. Drew Houston, cofounder of the tech startup Dropbox, has observed that the most successful people "are obsessed with solving an important problem, something that matters to them. They remind me of a dog chasing a tennis ball." To increase your chances of happiness and success, Houston advises, you must find your tennis ball—"the thing that pulls you." Identifying what that "tennis ball" is can have a clarifying effect on many other decisions and choices that come along—because you can now ask, in effect, *How does this help me in the pursuit of my tennis ball?*

There's no simple formula for figuring out what your particular tennis ball is, but there are three categories of questions you can ask: about your own strengths or assets; about your natural interests; and about the ways in which you might contribute to something larger than yourself.

The "assets-based" question is fairly simple and straightforward: It boils down to, *What are my signature strengths?* The psychologist Martin Seligman, who has conducted research on this topic at the University of Pennsylvania's Positive Psychology Center, says you can identify these qualities by thinking and even writing about specific times when you've been at your best, then inquiring more deeply about those successful episodes: *What personal strengths did I display when I was at my best? Did I show creativity? Good judgment? Kindness?* Seligman says that as you begin to figure out what you're good at, the next challenge is to figure out how to deploy those strengths.

A more playful way of thinking about this is to ask: *What are my superpowers?* The idea behind this question from renowned business consultant Keith Yamashita is to "unpack the combination of personality traits and aptitudes you bring effortlessly to any situation." If you're having trouble listing your powers and strengths, check out Gallup executive Tom Rath's popular "StrengthsFinder 2.0" program, with its menu of thirty-four traits. Having identified your strengths, you'll be in a better position to make the most of what you already have going for you.

Once you've inquired about what you're good at, ask yourself what you're naturally interested in—the two may overlap, but not necessarily. Sometimes, we may not be all that aware of what truly engages us until we examine our own activities and behaviors from a detached perspective. The idea is to become "an anthropologist of your own life," says coach and *Essentialism* author Greg McKeown, who recommends asking yourself: *When was I truly happy and why? What activity or theme do I keep coming back to?* and *When do I seem most like myself?*

This can include not only present activities, but past ones as well—going back to childhood. The psychologist Eric Maisel recommends asking, *What did I enjoy doing at age ten?* After drawing up a list of favorite childhood activities, "see what still resonates with you today. And then it's a process of updating those loves. You may have loved something that doesn't even exist now, or doesn't make sense in your life now— but you may be able to find a new version of that."

Another way of determining where your natural interests lie is to ask yourself: *What makes me forget to eat?* Forbes columnist Mark Manson has picked up on this idea, which derives from the work of psychologist Mihaly Csikszentmahalyi on "flow" (people who enter a state of creative flow while working tend to lose track of time and everything else not related to the work they're doing at that moment). Manson shares that in younger days, he would forget to eat while playing video games— then he later found that he experienced that same level of immersion when writing. For other people, that feeling may come when teaching, solving problems, or organizing things. "Whatever it is, don't just look at the activities that keep you up all night," Manson says, "but look at the *cognitive principles* behind those activities . . . They can easily be applied elsewhere."

LOOKING BEYOND SKILLS and natural interests—and beyond yourself—one can study the larger world and ask the question: *What is needed and how might I help?* The journalist David Brooks writes about the difference between people who pursue the "Well-Planned Life," which emphasizes individual agency, and those leading the Summoned Life, who are inclined to ask, *What are my circumstances summoning me to do? What is my most useful social role?* This theme was addressed in an essay written for college graduates by the psychologist and *Grit* author Angela Duckworth, who advised readers not only to "move toward what interests you" but also to "seek purpose." So rather than just asking what you want to do with your life, Duckworth recommends asking: *In what way do I wish the world were different? What problem can I help solve?* She adds: "This puts the focus where it should be—on how you can serve other people."

The goal of improving people's lives may seem rather grand, but as the author Daniel Pink points out, it can manifest itself in more modest ways. "You can think of Purpose with a capital P," says Pink, which might involve feeding the hungry or solving the climate crisis. "I also think there is another kind of purpose with a small p," he adds. It can be measured by asking, for instance, "If I didn't come into work today, would things be worse?" You can use the following two questions to distinguish between the two different types of purpose: With "capital P" Purpose the question is, *Am I making a difference?* With "small p" purpose the question is, *Am I making a contribution?* Pink notes that both types of purpose are worthwhile and meaningful; the latter may be more attainable than the former.

Whether you're trying to find a new business opportunity or identify a possible lifelong pursuit, if you want to tackle a truly ambitious beautiful question—one designed to help you find the ultimate tennis ball—consider this one: *How might I apply my signature strengths to a pursuit that is of natural interest to me and helps others?* By addressing all three "passion" elements—strengths, interests, purpose—it can help guide you to something that both engages you and enables you to use your gifts to make a difference.

But even if you do find an opportunity that seems to answer that question, Cal Newport has a warning: It still will have its hardships and downsides. The tennis ball won't always taste good. Newport observes that people tend to think once they find a pursuit that fits their idea of a calling or passion, it's going to be easy after that. But he has seen some of his students quickly give up on interests and potential careers as they discover that it's hard to master anything. "They find that 'I'm not automatically good at it, so it must not be my passion.'"

Considering how hard it is to do anything worthwhile, perhaps a good question to keep in mind is this off-color one, shared by Mark Manson: *What is your favorite flavor of shit sandwich?* As Manson explains, "Everything sucks, some of the time . . . So the question becomes: What struggle or sacrifice are you willing to tolerate?"

If you've tried asking all of the preceding questions and still have not found your tennis ball, perhaps what's needed is not another question but rather a definitive statement—one that sums up who you are and what you mean to achieve in this life. If that seems like something that would be difficult to produce, it's actually not—you just have to ask yourself, *What is my sentence?* This question was once posed by journalist and Congresswoman Clare Booth Luce to President John F. Kennedy. Luce told Kennedy "a great man is a sentence"—meaning that a leader with a clear and strong purpose could be summed up in a single line (e.g., "Abraham Lincoln preserved the union and freed the slaves"). Daniel Pink, an admirer of Luce's question, points out that it can be useful to anyone, not just presidents.

In trying to figure out your sentence—which could also be thought of as a personal mission statement—try asking, *How would I like to be remembered? What matters most to me? What change would I like to create?*

For many people, finding purpose—chasing the tennis ball—is tied to creativity, which is the focus of the next section. If you've decided to pursue a more creative life (and there are strong reasons to say yes to that decision, as we'll see), there are many penetrating questions that can help with the challenges of figuring out what to create, how to motivate yourself to get started or keep going, how to determine if your work is good and how it can be improved, and how to keep evolving and staying fresh in your ongoing creative pursuits.

These questions apply to the individual working in solitude or to the group trying to create and innovate together. They pertain to works of art that aspire to express an original thought, as well as inventive products that aim to change a business or the way people live. And they are relevant whether you tend to think of yourself as "creative" or not.

PART II

Questions for Sparking *CREATIVITY*

Why create?

Some years ago, David Kelley, founder of one of the most successful consulting firms in the world, took a day off work to visit his daughter's fourth grade class, where he served as a guest-teacher that day. While at the school, he received a call from his doctor, who told him he had been diagnosed with throat cancer. It was advanced, and it was serious; Kelley, fifty-six, was given about a 40 percent chance of surviving.

Upon learning the news, one of the first people he called was his brother Tom—who'd shared a bedroom with David growing up and who, all these years later, worked alongside him as a partner at their company, IDEO. Tom was in Brazil at the time, just finishing a business presentation, when he got the call. He immediately flew home to be with David.

They saw each other nearly every day for the next six months as David battled through chemotherapy treatments and surgery, which proved successful. Toward the end of this period, with his prospects brightening somewhat but his future still uncertain, David told Tom that he was grappling with a large question: *What was I put on this earth to do?*

He'd already built a great business, had a loving family, a beautiful house. But when he thought about some additional way that he might leave a lasting impact, Kelley arrived at this beautiful question: *How can I help as many people as possible rediscover their creative confidence?*

The Kelley brothers decided to work on this question together, with their efforts picking up momentum as David made a full recovery from his cancer. Through teaching, coauthoring the book *Creative Confidence*, delivering a TED Talk, and creating online courses, they began to put forth a philosophy about creativity that had three core principles behind it:

1. That creativity is essential to business and career success—and that, in Tom's words, "creativity has a way of spilling over into your whole life," making it more fulfilling and productive.

2. That each of us is creative—though many of us have been conditioned, in the years since childhood, to believe we're not. During their years teaching university courses and working with employees and clients at their firm, IDEO, the Kelleys had seen, firsthand, that if you could instill in someone a sense of "creative confidence"—a belief in one's own ability to generate creative ideas and bring them to life—you could unlock that person's creative potential.

3. That there are ways to surface creative ideas and develop them by following certain steps and behaviors. By following this process, creativity could be summoned as needed, and hence one didn't have to wait until "an angel of the Lord appears and tells you what to do," as David puts it. The Kelleys use the term "design thinking" to describe the IDEO approach to generating creative ideas and bringing them to life. I think of it as "applied questioning"—because much of it revolves around asking specific types of questions at each stage of the creative process.

These three ideas—that creativity matters to all of us; that we're all capable of being more creative in our work (and our lives); and that there are basic steps we can take to stimulate our creativity and guide it toward productive results—are the focus of this section. By asking yourself questions, you can address all three of these issues. Moreover, questioning can help with many of the challenges associated with creativity, including: finding an original idea; overcoming creative blocks; figuring out when and where your creativity can flourish (even in the midst of abundant distractions); knowing how to improve, finish, and "ship" creative work; and finding ways to continually evolve so that your creative work doesn't grow stale.

The questions that can help inspire and nurture your own creativity are, like the decision-making questions in the previous section, designed to help shift perspective at critical moments—enabling you to see creative opportunities (and challenges) in a new light. But they're also meant to help in navigating the ups and downs of creating—and to provide an occasional boost to the "creative confidence" that, as the Kelley brothers note, is within all of us, whether we realize it or not.

While most of the questions to follow will address the "how" of creating, I tend to think it's wise to begin with "why." Making the commitment to be creative is a major undertaking. *Why be creative?* There is an abundance of great creative work out there already. *Why add to the pile?* There's no way of knowing if your creative work will be financially rewarding, or even whether it will be liked by anyone, including yourself. *Why take the risk?*

Considering these questions at the outset can help you decide in favor of creativity—and that decision, in and of itself, can have a surprising effect. The psychologist Robert Sternberg studied successful creative people and found that, at some point, they'd made a conscious decision in favor of being creative. Sternberg concluded that, "without the decision, creativity will not emerge." In light of Sternberg's findings, perhaps the first question any of us should ask about creativity is: *Am I willing to decide in favor of it? And if so, why?*

There are many potential answers, but here is a good one to start with: Even if your creative work never goes beyond the room where you labor over it, it can have a highly positive impact—on you.

Research has shown that just doing one creative task, no matter how small, can add to your happiness and increase your sense of well-being. As the productivity author Phyllis Korkki puts it, "Creativity is yoga for the brain."

Psychologist Mihaly Csikszentmihalyi discovered something akin to this in his extensive research on creativity. He found that when people become fully engaged in a project that pushes them to the limits of their imagination and capability, it's a one-of-a-kind feeling. Csikszentmihalyi observed: "The excitement of the artist at the easel or scientist in the lab comes closest to the ideal we all hope to get from life—and so rarely do."

When we create, we rule the universe—or at least a tiny part of it. The prolific poet and author Kwame Dawes says, "I write in what is probably a vain effort to somehow control the world in which I live, recreating it in a manner that satisfies my sense of what the world *should* look like and be like." As he creates, Dawes is "trying to capture in language the things that I see and feel, as a way of recording their beauty and power and terror, so that I can return to those things and relive them. In that way, I try to have some sense of control in a chaotic world."

The "sense of control" associated with creation is also cited by Gina Gibney, the artistic director of a New York–based dance company. "In life, we experience so much fragmentation of thought and feeling. For me, creating art brings things back together." Gibney says the early stages of her creative work tend to be "deeply reflective and informative." But it's the experience of marrying all the disparate elements together into a form—"distilling and shaping movement, creating a context, working to something that feels cohesive and complete"—that she finds intoxicating.

In his research, Csikszentmihalyi observed that deep creative work not only provides a highly satisfying experience during the process but also offers an added bonus: Something is (hopefully) produced from that work that can then be shared with others—"leaving an outcome that adds to the richness."

As Kwame Dawes puts it, "I want to somehow communicate my sense of the world—that way of understanding, engaging, experiencing the world—to somebody else. I want them to be transported into the world that I have created." The dance director Gibney thinks of the end product of her creative work (in her case, a live performance) as "a kind of gift." She sees this as "the most meaningful aspect of my work."

As it enables us to bring new and potentially valuable ideas and creations into the world, creativity can offer benefits beyond personal satisfaction to the creator. Being creative can make you more successful professionally. This extends beyond the arts into business, and covers a wide range of occupations and activities.

"In the twenty-first century, what the market values is the ability to produce something rare and valuable," says the author and consultant Cal Newport. An entrepreneur's success is often based on the ability to find and develop creative ideas. In more established organizations, leaders and managers may thrive if they can envision and enact creative solutions to that organization's problems. Even the lowest-level employee has the potential to rise up by suggesting an imaginative new way to do a job.

To some extent, this has always been partly true (and part myth: Through the years, countless employees with creative ideas have been told, "Just do your job"). But it's truer now because businesses today are under great pressure to innovate in order to keep pace with rapid change and increased competition. And that innovation often comes from the ability of people working for the company to think of and develop new ideas, products, processes, and solutions.

If you can create, you are now more likely to be in demand. For example, creativity was never thought of as a leadership skill in the past but recent surveys rank it as a top skill of business leaders. The value of creativity in the workplace will only accelerate in years ahead. As technology eliminates many noncreative jobs, the remaining opportunities will mostly go to those who are capable of creating.

Given the benefits, why would anyone *not* decide in favor of creativity? According to Kelley and other creativity experts, it's not so much a conscious decision. What keeps people from being more creative is that they don't believe they have it in them.

Where did my creativity go?

The most common wrong question to ask about your own creativity is *Am I creative?* David Burkus, author of *The Myths of Creativity*, has found that one of the primary myths is what he calls the "breed myth"—the notion that some are naturally creative and others are not. As Burkus notes, scientific findings do not bear this out. "We can't find anything in the research that suggests there's a 'creativity gene,'" Burkus says. Nevertheless, "we talk about creativity as if it is a gift from the gods when it's actually available to everyone."

Burkus and others point to the high levels of creativity demonstrated by many people when they're children, which show that creativity *is* in us. And while it's true that many kids who freely imagine, draw, build, and experiment seem to do less of those things as they get older, this suggests that instead of asking, *Am I creative?*, we might better ask, *Where did my creativity go?*

Many have suggested that schools train creativity out of students, though social pressures play a role, too. "As you get older, you become more aware that not everyone loves your crazy ideas," Burkus says.

The author Brené Brown found about a third of those she interviewed could recall a "creativity scar" from when they were younger—a time when they were told their creative work wasn't good enough. The discouragement may even come from friends and family members trying to offer good advice along the lines of, "Don't waste your time on artistic pursuits when you could be focused on something more practical."

Eventually, Burkus says, the negative feedback becomes an accepted truth—and it may even become a handy excuse. "If you can say, 'Well, I'm not one of those creative people,' it lets you off the hook. You don't even have to try."

That's an attitude David Kelley says he often finds among clients visiting his firm, IDEO, or students coming to the classes Kelley teaches at Stanford University. People arrive insisting they're "not creative," Kelley says. "And we know it's not true, because they end up doing amazing things in the class." To build confidence, Kelley encourages students to start by doing small creative exercises—drawing stick figures, building something simple—and work their way up to more demanding projects.

In the process, Kelley reassures students that whether they can draw well, for example, is not a measure of their creativity; that's a specific skill, which can be developed over time. Creativity, on the other hand, is not a skill but a "mindset" or a way of looking at the world. And we all have the ability to look at something—a problem, a subject, a situation, a theme—and bring forth our own ideas and interpretations.

Just as asking the right questions can inspire creativity, asking the wrong ones—questions rooted in faulty assumptions—can inhibit creativity. To avoid

IF YOU WANT TO BE MORE CREATIVE, *STOP* ASKING THESE 6 QUESTIONS

These are wrong questions that people often ask about creativity. Read the answers below—then stop asking them.

- *Am I creative?* If you're human, you are creative. There is no "creativity gene" that some have and others lack. It's a gift that is available to everyone.
- *How creative am I?* It's difficult to measure or answer this (and besides, it's not a competition). Better to rearrange the question and ask: How am I creative? You will likely find many answers to that question.
- *Where will I ever find an original idea? (Hasn't everything been thought of already?)* You don't have to create from whole cloth; almost every new idea consists of fragments of existing ideas. And the fragments are everywhere.
- *Where will I find the time to create?* Start by turning off your iPhone (unless you use it to create).
- *How can I come up with an idea that will make money?* Don't begin with the outcome in mind. Find and develop a worthy idea; the money will follow (maybe).
- *Where do I begin?* You don't need a perfect starting point. To quote the composer John Cage, "Begin anywhere."

taking the risks associated with trying to do creative work, people will sometimes raise questions at the outset that seem designed to talk themselves out of trying.

Before even starting on a creative endeavor, people may become anxious about how their efforts will be received by others and whether those efforts will pay off in the end. In so doing, they focus too much on the outcome, rather than on the work itself. For example, those who ask *How can I find an idea that will make a lot of money?* (or even an idea that will "touch the hearts of millions") should consider that it's very difficult to know at the start what the outcome of your creative efforts will be. In his research on creativity, the psychologist Dean Simonton found that even experienced creative people had trouble predicting whether their individual projects would be successful—creators are simply bad at knowing what will be a hit, Simonton says. However, the successful ones overcome that by just forging ahead and creating. Through sheer productivity, the occasional and sometimes surprising successes tend to emerge.

If you're trying to decide whether to pursue a project and want to make sure you're doing it for the right reasons, ask yourself, *What if I knew at the outset that there was no possibility of fame or fortune from this work—would I still want to do it?*

Fear of getting started—of taking that first step on a creative endeavor—is also a major obstacle, the Kelleys say. This fear is expressed in many ways, but three questions, in particular, tend to be used to avoid actually doing something creative. Beware of the three "where"s: *Where will I find the time?*; *Where will I find an original idea?*; and *Where do I begin?* We'll get to the "time" issue in due course, but as for the last two, the short answers are: 1) everywhere and 2) anywhere. A longer answer follows.

What if I go looking for problems?

In thinking about where and how to find an original idea, consider two recent breakthrough ideas that have met with great success and acclaim: the popular Nest thermostat and the hit Broadway show *Hamilton*. One is a consumer product, conceived by a designer named Tony Fadell. The other is a work of performing art, dreamed up by the playwright and hip-hop musician Lin-Manuel Miranda. Both are highly original: No one had ever before seen a household device quite like the Nest or a play like *Hamilton*. So how did Fadell and Miranda "find" these two great ideas?

Fadell didn't have to search for his idea—it was staring him in the face. Most of us pay little attention to thermostats, but Fadell has a designer's eye and couldn't help noticing that every house he stayed in had an old-fashioned one—that looked like "an ugly beige box from the 1990s"—prominently displayed on the wall. They not only looked bad, they were also hard to use and, from a technology standpoint, behind the times. Fadell wondered: *In an era of sleek smartphones, why are thermostats still so dumb?* He began to envision a new kind of thermostat that combined stylish looks with smartphone compatibility. When the product was introduced in 2011, it sold out immediately—and within two years, it became the industry leader.

As for playwright Miranda, his idea was waiting for him in a bookstore, then followed him to the hotel pool while he was on vacation. He bought Ron Chernow's biography of the founding father Alexander Hamilton to have something to read during his travels, but as he began reading it, something clicked for him.

To quote the designer Saul Bass, creativity arises "from looking at one thing and seeing another." Miranda looked at the story of the immigrant Hamilton and, as he explained later, saw a larger story about immigration in America. (Miranda's own father had migrated to New York from Puerto Rico.) And in the character of Hamilton—a rebel, a prolific writer, and a man prone to feuds—he found parallels to modern-day rappers like Tupac Shakur. Before long, Miranda was writing hip-hop songs about Hamilton, and the songs eventually led to a musical that became an instant phenomenon.

So what do the origin stories of the Nest and *Hamilton* have in common? They show that the source of creativity usually isn't a bolt from the blue, as people tend to think. It is more likely to be something right under our noses. *Hamilton* and the Nest also are examples of "smart recombinations"—which result when someone takes existing elements or ideas and combines them to create something new and original. Fadell combined a thermostat with the design and functional elements of the iPhone; Miranda married the life story of Alexander Hamilton (as presented in Chernow's biography) with elements of hip-hop, a classic Broadway musical, and other influences.

To be inspired by things that already exist in the real world— that are all around us, waiting to be noticed and then reimagined in a whole new form—is the way most original creations come into existence, notes *Myths of Creativity* author David Burkus. But that's not the way we tend to think about creativity.

Burkus cites the "originality myth"—the notion that creativity must come from completely original ideas or sources—as one of great misconceptions about creating. "Almost all new ideas are combinations of preexisting ideas," he says. He points to the iPhone as a prime example—in 2007 Steve Jobs combined elements of the cell phone, Blackberry, camera, and iPod into that highly original combo package.

This kind of creativity comes naturally. Our brains are wired to make such connections and combinations, and we shouldn't feel guilty about it. "What is at issue is not the fact of 'borrowing' or 'imitating,' of being 'derivative,' being 'influenced,' but what one does with what is borrowed or derived," wrote the neurologist and author Oliver Sacks in his essay "The Creative Self." It's all for the good, as long as the borrower "compounds it with one's own experiences and thoughts and feelings," and "expresses it in a new way, one's own."

For those who aspire to create, this should come as a relief. There is nothing more paralyzing than trying to think of a "great idea" by going into a quiet room and attempting to conjure something from nothing. But if we don't have to create ideas from whole cloth, then the prospect of coming up with new ideas is less daunting. There are sources of inspiration all around—an abundance of raw material that we can begin to study and play with, even if we're not quite sure how we might want to reshape it.

If we embrace that concept, it provides a partial answer to the question of *Where do I find an original idea?*—you're apt to find *potential sources* of an original idea anywhere and everywhere. However, those sources, as you find them, are often in the form of other people's ideas, so they can't be yours (at least not if you aspire to be original, creative, and ethical). The magic seems to happen when creators like Fadell and Miranda look at existing ideas and are inspired to think of something related yet entirely different.

Why is it that some of the raw materials we encounter inspire us, and others don't? And can we seek out the ones that do? To some extent, there's an element of randomness involved. Miranda has commented that on his fateful visit to the bookstore, he might have just as easily purchased a biography of Truman. (It's hard to imagine a hip-hop musical coming from that.)

But it does seem that inspiration is more likely to come from particular types of influences, suggesting we might be wise to guide ourselves in the direction of those. Not surprisingly, we tend to be inspired by what interests us, or to put it in stronger terms, what stirs something in us. But there must also be room to take that interesting thing and improve it, adapt it, or transform it, based on a personal vision.

Fadell was interested in the thermostat but also envisioned something much better. Miranda was intrigued by the story of Hamilton, but immediately wanted to transform it into something that fit with his own vision of what the story might be. You could say that both Fadell and Miranda were intensely dissatisfied with what they encountered. They focused on what was missing, what might be. They wanted to introduce complications.

Another way of thinking about this, then, is that when you're looking for an idea, you're not really looking for just an idea, per se—you're looking for a problem.

"It is the discovery and creation of problems . . . that often sets the creative person apart," according to Csikszentmihalyi and fellow social scientist Jacob Getzels. They found in their research that the most successful artists tended to take an existing situation and look for ways to rework it. They were less apt to try to solve problems in a straightforward way by following instructions. The "problem finder" goes looking for trouble. The creative process can encompass both finding (and even making) the trouble, as well as fixing it with a creative solution.

Problem finding runs counter to the notion that creative people should be trying to think of ideas that emerge as fully formed solutions. It suggests the ideas and solutions will come (hopefully) along the way, but the *problem* is the starting point. Problem finders look at the world around them, focus in on something in particular—a situation, an existing creation, a theme—and inquire

TO FIND YOUR BIG IDEA, ASK THESE QUESTIONS

- **What stirs me?** To find a "problem" that's worth devoting your creative efforts to solve, start with a high interest level—meaning it touches on something that matters to you.
- **What bugs me?** Frustration is the starting point for many innovations and creative breakthroughs.
- **What's missing?** Whereas the previous question may focus on existing problems or inadequacies, this one focuses on the absence of something—a product that doesn't exist but should, a need not addressed, a perspective that is underrepresented.
- **What do I keep coming back to?** Pay attention to recurring themes that keep coming up in your work or even in your conversation. It may be a sign that your big idea is trying to find you.
- **What is ripe for reinvention?** It could be a product but also a classic story, a theme, or a genre.

deeply about it: *What is lacking here? What is happening that doesn't make sense? What is the story that is not being told? How might the whole thing be reinvented or turned upside down?* And the most critical question: *Why might I want to take on this problem and make it my own?*

Miranda was stirred by the Hamilton story because themes within it—pertaining to immigration, the power of words, and more—resonated deeply with him. "Something about it just grabbed me," he told an interviewer.

The feeling must be strong, but it doesn't have to be positive: You can be stirred by a problem because it bothers you to the point of being unacceptable. When asked about the source of his creativity, Fadell focuses on the word "frustration," adding: "I look at the world, and different products, and say, 'What's wrong with this product? Why doesn't [a better] product exist?'" In the case of the thermostat, he was frustrated that this device that was so important to people—it is used constantly and relied on for the basic need of staying warm—had been under-designed and unchanged for so long.

So many of the innovation stories that have emerged in recent years from Silicon Valley involve someone who was frustrated by an everyday problem and then applied creativity to the problem— first introducing complications, then arriving at a solution. Netflix, Airbnb, Warby Parker, and many other startups originated in this way. IDEO's Tom Kelley says frustration is such a rich source of creativity and innovation that all of us should try to tap into it by creating our own "bug lists"—documenting all the things encountered in everyday life that seem in desperate need of improvement—and then referring to that list regularly as we're searching for creative endeavors to tackle.

It's important to pay attention to and capture whatever moves us—whether it's something that bugs us or stirs the imagination. To keep those valuable thoughts from disappearing, the Kelley brothers recommend "capturing ideas systematically." David Kelley keeps a whiteboard and marker in the shower. Tom never goes anywhere without his trusty notebook. But it's not enough to just write down ideas and thoughts—you also must go back and review them, regularly. At the end of each week, Tom asks, *What were my most creative ideas this week?* The answers are there in his notebook.

The Wharton School psychology professor and author Adam Grant does something similar, but with a slightly different system. Grant collects ideas in a notebook, and at the end of each week he transcribes the notes into a Word document. "Then, once a month, I'll review all my idea notes," he says. "It's so telling when I've written down the same idea two or three times. If I was excited by it multiple times, that's a really good sign."

Indeed, when an idea or thought keeps coming up in your life or work, it might be worth asking yourself: *Is this a problem that is trying to find me?* Sometimes a theme may follow you around without your being aware of it. The novelist Dennis Lehane says that he "didn't recognize it until about my seventh book, but in every single one is the question of 'What is family? How do you define family?' Is family through blood or is it family through choice?"

By asking, *What do I keep coming back to?*, we can begin to identify ideas and themes that are already there, waiting to be noticed. We can tap into an even greater source of creative possibilities if we can somehow see what *isn't* there—and perhaps should be.

What is the world missing?

The difficulty with finding problems is that we often have trouble seeing them as problems, or noticing them at all. Like Fadell's thermostat, problems are everywhere, inviting us to inquire about them and go to work on them. But when the thermostat is right in front of you—and so familiar that you pay little attention to it—the problem may go unnoticed.

How do we become better at seeing potential creative opportunities that are all around? Tom Kelley believes it's a matter of looking at the world around us more closely. The goal is to see the familiar—which could include not only products we use but also the ways we do our jobs, the people around us, or even the path we routinely travel to get to work—as if seeing it for the first time. When David Kelley teaches design students at Stanford about problem finding, he sometimes takes them to a familiar place—such as a gas station, airport, or hospital—and instructs them to spend time quietly watching what happens in those places. Invariably, they notice details they'd never been aware of before.

TO SEE THE WORLD DIFFERENTLY, ASK

- *What might I notice if I were encountering this for the first time?* Apply this "fresh eye" approach to your job, the people around you, your everyday path to work.
- *What if I stand on the desk?* Not necessarily to be taken literally, but try changing the angle from which you view things.
- *What is in the background?* Try to focus on that which is usually obscured or ignored.
- *What here would fascinate a five-year-old?* Or a ninety-year-old?
- *What would Seinfeld be amused by?* Use a comic observer's eye to look for inconsistencies.
- *What would Steve Jobs be frustrated by?* Use an innovator's eye to notice inadequacies.

The simple reason most of us don't notice the details of what's going on around us is that we "stop looking too soon," says Tom Kelley. It's not just a matter of how long we look but where we focus as we're looking.

Stanford University business professor Bob Sutton, who has written extensively about the power of observation, says that in order to see more, we must "shift our focus from objects or patterns in the foreground to those in the background."

Sutton says that when trying to shift your view, it can be helpful to step back from everyday routines and habitual behaviors. And it can be useful to ask questions that help shift your perspective. One question to ask about anything you're trying to observe more closely is, *What might I notice about X if I were seeing it for the first time?*

Another variation of the question (with the same goal of trying to access a novice perspective) is: *How would a five-year-old child see this object or situation? What would the child be likely to notice?* Kelley recommends yet another perspective—that of the traveler or visitor. "When you're traveling you notice every detail because you're trying to figure out a world that is foreign to you," he says. So when taking that familiar path to work in the morning, ask: *How would a traveler see this?*

Listening is as important as looking. When trying to "find problems" in business, keep in mind that "customers are *always* beautifully, wonderfully dissatisfied," according to Amazon founder Jeff Bezos. They will find the problems that exist within any business offering, and they are inclined to express that dissatisfaction in some way. But if no one at the business is listening, the problem will remain "unfound." (In general, businesses are not great at problem finding: One study found 85 percent of companies surveyed admitted they had trouble diagnosing their own problems.)

Even the solo artist or author can find new problems to pursue by paying attention to feedback from "customers." Adam Grant acknowledged that his recent book *Originals* was inspired in part by discussions with, and questions from, the readers of his previous book. Hence, creativity coach Todd Henry suggests: "Look at your work and ask, *When am I most resonant? What are people responding to in my work?*"

If there is a single go-to question for problem finding, it may be this: *What is missing?* Central to most problems is the lack of something. Fadell could easily see what was missing from the thermostat (style, programmability, functionality), but it isn't always that apparent. What is missing may be something that doesn't exist yet and must be imagined. The story of Alexander Hamilton, it turned out, was missing a hip-hop beat. It took a wild imaginative leap on Miranda's part to figure that out.

Any business offering products or services should be asking *What is missing?* on a consistent, ongoing basis. And you shouldn't necessarily ask by actually asking. As IDEO and others have found, sometimes it can be more effective to quietly observe people who are using a product or service in order to see where they may be having trouble. It's a way to actually see what's missing, in action.

But *What is missing?* also applies, in a different way, to artistic creations. Whereas the entrepreneur may be inquiring about what is missing (or lacking) in the existing world, the artist may be focused on what the world is "missing" in terms of what we're all failing to see—a perspective or a side of the story that the larger world is unaware of or misunderstands. If the artist can identify that gap, she has found a good problem.

Why should this be my problem?

Just because you've found a problem (or it has found you), does that mean it's the right problem for you to pursue as a creative endeavor? Grant says that when he's deciding on a creative project, "The first thing I ask is, *Do I look forward to thinking about this topic?* I can get interested in a lot of things, and often the initial energy is due to the fact that new things are always fun. So I ask myself, *Will I want to commit to this six months or a year down the road?*"

When asking the question *Will I still love this problem tomorrow?*, factor in the likelihood that there will be frustration and failure along the way—which means you'd better have enough passion for this project to withstand that.

Grant says the second big question he asks is, *Can I make a unique contribution here?* "I used to just say yes to anything where I thought I could be helpful," he says. "Now I want to figure out, *What am I adding that somebody else couldn't?*"

Similarly, Fadell asked, at the outset of the Nest project, *Is this a challenge that I can apply my skills to?* His previous experience as a top designer at Apple made him an ideal person to undertake the creation of an Apple-like thermostat. Likewise, Miranda had an unusual combination of talents and experience (Broadway meets hip-hop) that perfectly prepared him for the *Hamilton* project.

Another question to ask is about "ownership" of the problem. It may be a great idea, but are you the only one who has staked it out? Can you own it? If you discover that others are pursuing a similar opportunity, that doesn't necessarily mean you should abandon it, but it does raise another question: *If others are pursuing the same idea, what's my twist? How might my approach differ from others?*

Finally, there is the question of potential impact. *What is the upside if I do solve the problem?* Early on, Fadell asked himself two questions relating to this: *Will it [the Nest] make a difference? And is it a great business?* One question focused on the positive effect the product might have on people's lives, which Fadell figured could be significant. The other tried to gauge whether the commercial need was big enough to support a substantial business.

The numbers Fadell gathered on the size of the thermostat market indicated there was a business there. All of this was based on the assumption that the product could be made and made well—a best-case scenario.

> **BEFORE COMMITTING TO AN IDEA, ASK**
>
> - *Can I own this problem?* The best kind of problem is the one that you, alone, have noticed. But if others are pursuing it, then the question becomes: What is my special twist?
> - *What can I bring to this that others can't?* This is not so much about the approach you have in mind (that's your special twist), but more about your talent, perspective, expertise—and how all of that can enable you to make a unique contribution to this creative challenge.
> - *Will I still love this problem tomorrow?* This is a "crystal ball" question: It requires you to try to envision how well the subject, and the work itself, is apt to keep you engaged and enthused over time.
> - *What is the potential upside?* Not to be confused with trying to predict hard outcomes (Will I make a million bucks on this idea?), but rather trying to envision the positive impact this project could have in a best-case scenario.

While there was, of course, a chance Fadell might not be able to make the product he envisioned, he wanted to know that if he *did* succeed, the impact would be considerable.

Notice that Fadell's questions weren't focused on outcomes such as the money he might make. That money certainly did come eventually—in the form of a $3 billion acquisition of Nest by Google—but Fadell's early "crystal ball" questions focused more on the creation's potential effects on people and on the industry.

When you've found your problem and have decided to take ownership, here's a small thing you can do that can make a big difference: Phrase your overall challenge as a beautiful question you can ask yourself. If you are trying to create a thermostat with the appeal of an iPhone, ask: *How might I create a thermostat as appealing an iPhone?* Framing a challenge as a question can help initiate the flow of ideas—because your mind (including your subconscious mind) can't resist trying to answer a question that has been posed.

This is true not only with product innovations but with artistic creations as well. The author Amy Tan has said that when she can frame the idea she's working on as a question, it provides "a focus" that can guide her through the creative process.

Upon taking ownership of the Hamilton "problem," Miranda began to immerse himself in research on the man and his life. He read whatever he could find, including Hamilton's letters. He talked to Chernow and other experts, and traveled to the places where Hamilton lived and wrote. He even went to the actual dueling grounds where Hamilton died. In doing so, Miranda was providing his creative mind with raw materials to connect.

Research feeds creativity, says Kyung Hee (KH) Kim, an education professor at William & Mary who has been researching creativity for the past twenty-five years. Before you generate new and original ideas, "you have to develop your expertise in one specific area so you can have a lot of material" to draw upon, she says.

It may seem that sudden "Eureka!" insights have come out of the blue, but "they don't come into existence from nothing," notes psychology professor John Kounios of Drexel University. "Your ability to make new connections is limited—or empowered—by the amount of knowledge you have. So if your goal is to be struck by new ideas, you first have to do the relevant homework in whatever field you hope to be innovative."

While doing research, focus on "Why?" questions to try to gain a better understanding of the problem or issue at hand. *Why does this problem matter? Why does it exist in the first place? Why hasn't someone solved it already? Why might that change now?*

These questions don't just apply to business innovations. You can use a similar "Four Whys" approach to dig into the motivations of a fictional character, for instance: *Why does this character matter? Why is he frustrated? Why hasn't he done something about that? Why might he be ready to do something about it now?* The actress Laura Linney has said that when she first gets a role, "I read the script and ask, 'Why?' until there's no more 'Why?' to ask."

Having asked the "Why?" questions and gathered the various bits and pieces of

---

ASKING THESE "FOUR WHYS" WILL HELP YOU UNDERSTAND ANY PROBLEM

- *Why does this problem matter?* Use research to clarify what is at stake by digging deeper into who is affected and how. Consider the significance of that, in terms of overall effect and future ramifications.
- *Why does the problem exist?* Try to get to the root causes that put this problem into motion. (This may necessitate additional "whys" to get all the way down to the root.)
- *Why hasn't it been solved already?* This will make clear the obstacles you are up against (and may uncover past efforts that hold lessons).
- *Why might that change now?* What are the conditions and dynamics that might bring about a desired change?

---

research, what often follows is a creative incubation period—a time when those bits and pieces come together to form insights. It's a stage that demands deep thought and focus—as well as an environment conducive to that. You can't do this type of work just anywhere; incubation requires a nest, or better yet, a shell.

Where is my tortoise shell?

John Cleese, the great British comedian and one of the original creators of Monty Python's Flying Circus, has had a successful second career as a creative coach to business leaders. A few years ago, while watching one of Cleese's creativity talks, I was struck by his insistence that any creative person who wants to actually create must regularly escape to what Cleese called a "tortoise enclosure"—a quiet, secure place where one can be alone with one's imagination. Cleese advised going into that shell for a designated period of time—and, he said, "you mustn't come out until the time's up."

Inspired by this, I set out, at the time, to find my own tortoise enclosure and ended up in a windowless, stone-walled, subterranean room that soon became known as the "cave." I co-rented the space—located in the cellar of a Victorian mansion—with a few other writers, and we worked out a schedule so that each of us could have solitary confinement time in the cave. Once inside, there was no possibility of texting or tweeting (forget Wi-Fi—the place barely had air), and we were forced to stop reading other people's writing or talking about our own—which left nothing to do but write.

Heeding Cleese's advice, I designated a set amount of time to remain in my enclosure each time I visited (usually four hours), and only after the time was up would I return to daylight. If it sounds like a form of self-punishment, it may have felt like that occasionally—but more often it was a wonderfully immersive experience, and a productive one. I wrote a full book there in less than a year, as did a fellow cave dweller, the author Joseph Wallace. (Wallace, who was working on an apocalyptic thriller, later joked with me, "The world really could have ended outside and I probably wouldn't have known it.")

It may seem that the place where you create is incidental and that creativity can happen anytime, in any place. But creativity generally requires the creator's focused attention—and that is under siege today by forces that endlessly distract. There has never been a greater need for a shell, a cave, or some other form of refuge. So after asking, *Why do I want to create?* and *What might I want to create?*, be sure to ask: *Where will I actually be* able *to create?*

The answer is not the same for everyone. My cave probably wouldn't work for *Dilbert* creator Scott Adams, who says he does his best work in close proximity to the buzz of a crowd, such as in a coffee shop.

But wherever it is, the place where you create must allow for focus. "Focus is the new IQ," says Cal Newport, author of the book *Deep Work*. As Newport notes, the enemy of focus is distraction—and it has reached epidemic proportions. Newport and others have observed that distraction is built into social media technology—with much of it designed to "hijack the executive attention network in the brain," which enables us to focus and control our attention. The writer Andrew Sullivan observed that "the tiny cracks of inactivity in our lives . . . are being methodically filled with more stimulus and noise," and we "are only beginning to get our minds around the costs," as digital addiction affects everything from personal relationships to productivity at work.

It poses a particular threat to creativity. Constant interruptions can keep you from concentrating—which is, of course, a necessary part of creating. And the steady influx of messages, emails, and tweets provide a tempting alternative to actually doing creative work. The truth is, most of us would much rather answer another email than face the blank page. We *want* to be distracted. As the designer Stefan Sagmeister puts it, "It is easier to react than to create."

While a conversation is growing about the issue, digital distractions aren't going away, so we all must develop our own ways of coping—and protecting our opportunities to think and focus. Here is a good question to start with, shared by the writer Matthew Crawford: *What if we saw attention in the same way that we saw air or water, as a valuable resource that we hold in common?* This then leads to a second question, *How might I begin to protect this precious resource?*

To do so, Cal Newport suggests we flip the ratio of online time versus disconnected time. "Instead of taking breaks *from* digital media, we should allow ourselves occasional breaks to indulge in it," he says. In other words, get into the habit of asking the reframed question, *When should I take a break to connect?*

For those who can't bring themselves to disconnect completely, blogger Khe Hy recommends asking the question, *If I must be connected, how can I at least reassert control?* Hy came up with his own "hacks" to cut down on digital dependency and "preserve my ability to do focused work." Among his tips: Create different and long passwords for each social media account and for your iPhone (the idea is to create a log-in barrier that at least slows you down); turn off all notifications; disable your Facebook newsfeed; batch your email inbox (so that email is delivered in bunches, say, three times a day); convert your iPhone screen to grayscale (it's not nearly as addictive without the colors, Hy insists); and, if all else fails, he advises, "go for airplane mode."

Without that stimulation, will you end up bored? Perhaps—but that can be good for your creativity. Recent studies have shown that bored people tend to come up with more ideas. Boredom leads to daydreaming, which is associated with creative epiphanies. We actually don't do *enough* daydreaming these days, the psychologist Sandi Mann says, because "we try to extinguish every moment of boredom in our lives with mobile devices." (It's "like eating junk food," she adds.)

IF YOU CAN'T FIND THE TIME TO BE CREATIVE, ASK YOURSELF THESE FIVE QUESTIONS

- *If I began to see my attention as a precious resource, how might I better protect it?*
- *How can I shift from a "manager's schedule" to a "maker's schedule"?* The former tries to fill every hour with appointments; the latter is designed with multi-hour, uninterrupted blocks.
- *Am I pruning the vine?* If you're juggling many projects and pastimes, consider cutting back lesser ones to provide more time for the primary ones.
- *What if I trade the morning news for the "morning muse"?* The morning can be a prime time for creative thinking, so skip the morning news and march straight from the bed to the tortoise shell.
- *Instead of taking breaks from social media, what if I reverse that?* Spend more time disconnected and think in terms of taking breaks to social media.

When is my prime time?

According to John Cleese, having a shell that limits interruptions is not the only requirement to foster creativity. For the creative person to be truly productive, he says, you must create "barriers of space and time."

Significant blocks of time are needed for deep creative work. How much time depends on the individual; I tend to work in blocks of no less than three and a half hours. (I actually need three hours of uninterrupted work time, but it takes a half hour to finish preparing my tea and shuffling papers—the writer's equivalent of clearing one's throat.)

Having this amount of time devoted to solitary thinking and creative work may seem like a luxury that busy people can't afford. The Silicon Valley venture capitalist and essayist Paul Graham has written about the difference between "the maker's schedule" and "the manager's schedule." Graham says makers need multi-hour blocks of time to be creative, while managers believe things should transpire more quickly, in half-hour to one-hour blocks. That's because makers are making, and managers are having meetings. Or to return to Sagmeister's idea, makers are creating, while managers are reacting. One takes more time than the other. If you aspire to do more "making" (creating), consider the question, *How can I shift from a manager's schedule to a maker's schedule?*

It's not easy to do. Many of us automatically fill our calendars in the style of a manager—with many short blocks, devoted to specific tasks, meetings, phone calls. Any part of the calendar not filled is considered "empty" and we seek to fill those spaces with more tasks and appointments. But the psychology professor and author Dan Ariely points out that when we do this, we leave no time for deep creative thinking. "You open your calendar and you see a blank space and that seems like it's the wrong thing," he says. "The reality is, blank spaces are the spaces where you're supposed to do the most meaningful work." It's all those other things filling up the calendar that should be seen as expendable. So the challenge is: *How can we resist the urge to fill in the blank spaces?*

You must make a conscious effort to "prune the vine," says creativity coach Todd Henry. He notes that just as a winemaker must prune some good fruit so that better fruit can get the needed resources, creative professionals must cut back on activities and new projects that may interfere with deep work on primary projects. "If we're squeezing all the white space out of our lives by filling it with activity, if we're not pruning and saying no to things on occasion, then we're not going to have the space we need to innovate or think,"

Henry says. "We're not going to have those moments of serendipity or those insights that are just hanging there."

When scheduling creative time, another question to be addressed is: *When is my creative "prime time"?* Again this is an individual matter. To determine what times of day you seem to be most productive, Daniel Pink, the author of *When: Scientific Secrets of Perfect Timing*, suggests giving yourself a "flow test." This involves looking for a pattern as you keep track of your most creative periods each day. Once you know when your creative prime time is, Pink says, try to restructure your day to take advantage of these peak periods.

Often, it comes down to a binary "morning versus night" question: *Am I a lark or an owl?* For those who answer "owl," just be aware that you may be missing out on what seems to be a particularly fertile period of creativity for many artists. One study of successful painters, writers, and musicians found that 72 percent of them did their best work in the morning.

And there may be good reason for that. As neurological research shows, amazing things are going on in the subconscious of your brain—mental connections are being forged, ideas are constantly forming and transforming. Your unconscious mind comes alive when you're sleeping and dreaming. So what better time to tap into its creative power than when you're just waking up?

Back in the 1930s, the writing teacher Dorothea Brande wrote a persuasive argument for doing creative work in the mornings, when we're in the midst of the "waking dream." As Brande put it: "To have the full benefit of the richness of the unconscious" you must begin your creative work "when the unconscious is in the ascendant." In the mornings, Brande advised, get up a half hour earlier than usual and—"without talking, without reading the morning's paper"— begin to write. This advice can be extended beyond writing to any creative endeavor: Get up, go someplace quiet, and start thinking and capturing ideas. Try to take advantage of what Brande calls the wonderful "twilight zone between sleep and the full waking state."

Even before getting up from the bed, you can maximize that awakening period by summoning what Tom Kelley calls the "snooze muse." When your alarm clock goes off, hit the snooze button and instead of going back to sleep, use that ten minutes to think specifically about whatever creative project you're working on.

What if you go into your tortoise shell at the appointed time, close the door, plant yourself in your chair and . . . nothing happens? Actually, this is not a "What if?" scenario—it's reality. The initial moments (or even the first hour) of going to work on a creative project tend to be the hardest, and the temptation to abandon the shell can be overwhelming. So a question to ask is, *How can I fight through that initial period and not give up?* It can help if your tortoise shell is away from home—forcing you to travel (even if it's just a few blocks) to get there, which makes it less likely you'll leave after ten minutes.

In general, the idea is to make it more difficult to escape. Being locked in a prison cell would do the trick, but short of actually getting arrested, you might consider asking, *How can I put myself in creator's jail?* This may call for timers, locks on the door, and stern rebukes from those willing to stand guard.

A point may arrive at which it becomes counterproductive to stay in the shell (or the jail cell) when nothing is being produced. The writer Elizabeth Gilbert sets a time limit, using a kitchen timer, on her imprisonment—forty-five minutes. "No matter what happens at the end of this 45 [minutes], you are free," she tells herself.

"There's something about knowing that you get to leave that takes away a gigantic portion of the anxiety." Gilbert confides. "Usually what happens is that I spend about 37 minutes unhappy and watching the clock. But somehow, always right towards the end when you know you don't have to do it anymore, you find something."

When I'm doing my writing, I find myself pushing out the escape period further, to at least an hour and a half. And even then, it's not so much a full release as a furlough—perhaps a half-hour walk in the free world, then a return to the shell. In any case, if you're going to put yourself in creative "jail," work out those details in advance: *What is my early release time? Shall I offer myself a brief furlough?*

Leaving the shell for occasional breaks (the furlough system) can help when you're struggling to produce. There are good reasons we sometimes have epiphanies while taking a walk or going for a drive instead of when we're in a room wracking our brains. In searching for ideas, the mind sometimes needs room to roam. Scott Barry Kaufman, a professor at the University of Pennsylvania who studies creative thinking, says that "if you let your mind wander and think about other things, you have a higher chance of coming up with an insight than if you're exerting all your effort and energy on the task."

So when you're stuck, think of the tortoise shell as portable—get up and take a walk. Almost as good as a walk is a drive, a shower (the "idea in the shower" moment has become a cliché with good reason), mowing the lawn, or washing the dishes. Tending the garden is a favorite of many artists, reports creativity expert KH Kim. And then there are more unusual diversions: The rock musician Michael Stipe of REM composed songs in his head (including the hit "Losing My Religion") while wandering through a maze.

What these various activities have in common is that they're mindless, repetitive tasks that allow you to think without being conscious that you're thinking. What one needs, according to Scott Adams, are "distractions that don't distract." So, to find your own ideal version of that, ask: *What activities distract me a little but not too much?*

When leaving the shell in search of stimulating inspiration, do so judiciously. There seems to be a fine line separating what is "stimulating" (from a creative standpoint) and what is "distracting." Going to a movie, for example, is more likely to distract you from your own creative thoughts as you give yourself over to someone else's. (The same is true of going on social media.) A creatively stimulating environment exposes you to inspiration, yet still leaves room for you to think about your own ideas. And—best-case scenario—it may result in you connecting someone else's ideas to your own. A number of places can provide this kind of stimulation, such as a bookstore or a library. Creative advertising legend George Lois suggests this foolproof option: Go to the museum. "Museums are custodians of epiphanies."

Notwithstanding the occasional need for early releases or furloughs, there is something wonderful about being in your own tortoise enclosure. It is a time to escape from "the cacophony in which it is impossible to hear your own voice," as author William Deresiewicz says. It's a time of being "unplugged," when you can feel as if you're plugging into your best self—the one who imagines, reasons, connects, builds. And yet, you need to be prepared to encounter moments of death and destruction.

Am I willing to kill the butterfly?

It always begins the same way for the novelist Ann Patchett: An idea for a new book begins to form in her head and it is "a thing of indescribable beauty." She feels certain it will be the greatest book she, or anyone else, has ever written. All she need do "is put it down on paper and then everyone can see this beauty that I see." And so, when finally she can no longer put off doing so, "I reach up and pluck the butterfly from the air. I take it from the region in my head and I press it down against my desk, and there, with my own hand, I kill it."

She doesn't want to kill it, Patchett writes, but the only way to bring to life an actual novel is to first capture that vision fluttering in her mind and pin it down on the page. When she does that, "everything that was beautiful about this living thing—all the color, the light and movement—is gone."

Patchett's marvelous description of the painful early stages of her writing process, which appears in her book *This Is the Story of a Happy Marriage*, should resonate with just about anyone who has tried to create something that began as a beautiful, seemingly perfect idea. The actual, tangible creation rarely measures up to the vision. The disparity can be especially great in the first stages of trying to give form to an idea, when efforts to produce something may be clumsy and misguided. It can be dispiriting—so much so that Patchett believes it's the reason why many people never are able to write the "great novel" that is in their heads. "Only a few of us are going to be able to break our own hearts by trading in the living beauty of the imagination for the stark disappointment of words," she writes.

So the question that must be asked upon beginning work on an idea is: *Can I live with this discrepancy between imagination and reality?* Or, to paraphrase Patchett, *If I can't create the thing I dream of, can I at least create the thing I'm capable of making?*

Patchett believes we can do so if we're willing to forgive ourselves for our own inadequacies. The initial stages of creating can be so humbling and frustrating that it can cause the creator to give up immediately or to stall indefinitely.

There may be a temptation to jump to another idea—a fresh butterfly, still untouched and perfect. Scott Belsky, head of the creative consultancy Behance and author of *Making Ideas Happen*, says that kind of butterfly-hopping keeps creative people from fully developing an idea. "A surplus of ideas is as dangerous as a drought," according to Belsky. "The tendency to jump from idea to idea spreads your energy horizontally instead of vertically."

In order to stop hopping, Belsky says, you must chart a clear course of action for each of your ideas—one that forces you to stay focused and keep taking next steps. Creative people tend to have a built-in resistance to organizational processes; we'd rather be dreaming up the next idea, which is why so many ideas never get past the dreaming stage to the "doing" stage. But Belsky maintains that every idea you're serious about should be treated as a formal work project. And to keep that project moving forward, constantly think about— and write down—the next "Action Steps" to be taken.

Staying with ideas takes discipline. There will be times when you get "stuck" and have trouble moving forward with an idea and times when you just feel sick of it. At these difficult stages of idea development, it's tempting to revert back to the more fun stage of idea generation. But as Belsky points out, anyone can come up with ideas. The question to ask yourself is, *Do I have what it takes to make the idea actually happen?*

Another question to consider when beginning to develop ideas is, *Who will hold me accountable?* Belsky recommends trying to build supportive communities around the ideas you're working on—which can help you through the rough spots. If you get stuck, you can ask for advice or ideas from the community. And if other people have an interest or stake in your project they're likely to encourage (pressure) you to keep going when you hit those occasional stopping points. Chris Baty, who heads National Novel Writing Month (NaNoWriMo), says, "Projects that you do quietly by yourself are much easier to abandon."

While it's important to prepare for a creative writing endeavor—by, for example, finding and setting up your workspace and compiling preliminary research—the act of preparing to create can easily become a stall tactic. The designer Bruce Mau shares a story about a writer friend of his who was about to embark on an ambitious new book. The writer "was always preparing to get started," Mau said, "always arranging his bookshelves and organizing his office" so that everything would be exactly where he needed it to be as he began working on the book. Only trouble: He never did get started.

If you find yourself engaged in lengthy preparations—taking crash courses, reading all the books and articles you can find on the subject at hand, amassing your files—be sure to ask yourself: *Am I rearranging the bookshelves?* The point is to train yourself to recognize when you are using excess preparation to delay the scary inevitability of facing the blank page, the empty canvas, or the white computer screen.

IF YOU'RE HAVING TROUBLE GETTING STARTED ON A CREATIVE PROJECT, ASK THESE SIX QUESTIONS

- *Am I chasing butterflies?* Meaning you keep thinking of new ideas instead of moving forward with an existing project. To develop an idea, you must pick one butterfly and pin it down.
- *Who will hold me accountable?* Share your idea with someone—and schedule a series of small deliverables.
- *Am I rearranging the bookshelves?* This refers to the act of "preparing to create." It may involve setting up a workspace, taking lessons, or doing research—each of which is fine until the point it becomes a stall tactic.
- *How can I lower the bar?* Instead of trying to begin with greatness, be willing to start off with something merely okay or even bad.
- *What if I begin anywhere?* If you're stuck trying to think of a beginning, start in the middle, at the end, or somewhere in between.
- *Can I make a prototype?* Find some way to give rudimentary form to your idea (outline, rough sketch, collage, beta website).

It's a tricky dilemma because of course you may need to do research on a creative project as you're getting started. But research in the Internet era can go on forever. There's always more to investigate. Scott Sonenshein, author of the book *Stretch*, says that if we get in the habit of asking, "What can I do with what I have?," it enables us to "bypass the paralyzing trap of waiting to get more in order to do more."

Rather than trying to do exhaustive research upfront, it can be better to begin actual work on a project—even if you must do so with limited knowledge—sooner, rather than later. Ask, *What small first step can I take to give form to my idea?* In design terms, this is known as prototyping and it can take many forms: by doing a rough sketch, an outline, a summary written in one page, a quickly made website. Any of these can serve as a starting point.

What if I allow myself to begin anywhere?

The designer Mau says that the most common lament he hears from young people trying to start a creative project is, "I don't know where to begin." And Mau often responds by sharing a favorite quote from the maverick composer John Cage: "Begin anywhere." Cage's advice applies to anyone creating anything. Don't get hung up on finding the perfect starting point—the brilliant opening sentence, the stirring musical prologue. Begin with whatever you have right now; even if it's a partial idea, an incomplete or flawed prototype, or the middle of a story that has no beginning or end. Ask, *What if I allow myself to begin anywhere?*

Authors have been known to begin a book with a single phrase, quote, or description of an image that pops into their heads, emerging from somewhere in a story they haven't dreamed up yet. My favorite example involves the book editor turned author William McPherson, who began work on his first novel because of an image that came into his mind while walking to work one day—that of a woman practice-swinging a golf club. "I saw it with such clarity and intensity that I couldn't get it out of my head," he said. So he wrote up a description of that vision—and it became the starting point of his acclaimed 1984 novel, *Testing the Current*.

As McPherson discovered, if you can capture that fragment of an idea floating in your mind by writing it down, sketching it, giving it form in some way, then there is something upon which to build. Whether it comes from the middle or the end of the story, it is, nonetheless, a beginning.

If beginning *anywhere* works, so can beginning *badly*—that, too, is a start. The first effort to give form to ideas doesn't have to be good. It will likely be revised or maybe scrapped altogether as you keep working. IDEO's Tom Kelley suggests this starter question: *What if I lower the bar?* Give yourself permission to start with something rough, imperfect, maybe even lousy.

Kelley cites a favorite scene from the indie film *Ruby Sparks* in which a writer suffering from creative block is advised to just begin writing anything. "Can it be bad?" the writer asks. When told yes, he starts writing whatever nonsense comes into his head. But quickly he starts changing and improving what he wrote, turning it into something good.

This often happens in real life, says the neuroscientist Robert Burton. If you shift to the "editor off" mode of your mind "and you're willing to write anything, without regard to whether it will work or not, new ideas will emerge," Burton explains.

How do I get "unstuck?"

In the early stages of the creative process—and later ones, too—one of the best ways to get "unstuck" is to use questioning to try to access various perspectives on whatever you're creating. Adam Grant says he uses this technique when working on a new book or research project.

"Often, I'll ask myself, 'Who would look at this problem from a different angle?'" says Grant. "And I have in my head a group of people whose thinking I admire for its originality, so I'll try to run whatever I'm working on through their vantage point."

When he does this exercise, Grant sometimes tries to see through the lens of people who might have a particular connection to the issue at hand. But he also tries to tap into the perspectives of a "standard set of original thinkers I admire," he says. "Some of my favorite research projects have started with asking, *What would Lincoln think in a situation like this?*"

Grant also tries to time-shift his own perspective: "Another question I use is, *If I would have tried to tackle this problem ten or twenty years ago, how would I have approached it differently?* Then I'll mentally time travel forward as well and ask, *If I were to imagine future me, ten or twenty years ahead, how do I imagine I'd look at this problem differently?* The past one helps me shed assumptions I'm making. I like to go 'past' first, then 'future.'"

Another creativity-starter technique involves trying to think of "wrong ideas" at the outset of a project. The creative workshop leader Tom Monahan uses an approach called "180-degree thinking" in which "you start out making something wrong and then see if you can turn that bad thing into something good," Monahan says. In the exercise, you might ask yourself, for example, *What if I tried to create a car that is unable to move? Or an oven that can't cook?*

This upside-down process forces your mind out of its usual patterns of problem solving and creative thinking. And in so doing, it can spark ideas and insights that might not have surfaced otherwise. By purposely starting wrong, you may end up with ideas that are more interesting—and therefore more "right."

The beginning point of a creative project isn't the only time people get "stuck." The midway stages can be even more hazardous. At that point, the early enthusiasm may have waned and yet the end is nowhere in sight.

In his study of the creative process, Adam Grant describes five stages that tend to trigger different emotional responses in the creator. The energized, optimistic feeling at stage 1 ("This is awesome!") is followed by a more realistic stage 2 ("This is tricky"). Then comes the dreaded stage 3 ("This is crap"), followed immediately by stage 4 ("I'm crap"). If the creator somehow crawls out of that pit, they work their way to stage 5 ("This might be okay."), and finally arrive at completion, stage 6 ("This is awesome!").

To overcome the dangerous third and fourth stages, Grant recommends using self-questioning to challenge these exaggerated negative feelings—and design the questions to point yourself toward a rational examination of evidence and past experience. "The first question I would ask myself is, *Have I ever solved a problem like this before?*" Unless you're a novice, you probably have evidence that you've done it before, which suggests you can do it again.

Grant adds, "Another question I ask is, *Have other people with my motivation and ability been able to accomplish something remotely similar?* I know a lot of people who've written books. You think about all the people you know who are managing to do things with similar difficulty or scope—and if they can do it, I can probably pull this off, too."

If you can work your way through the difficult middle stages of creativity, confidence and enthusiasm tends to return as you draw close to completion. Indeed, finishing up a project—and adding those final tweaks and polishes—can be so satisfying that you might not want it to end. Moreover, you may be reluctant to bring your finished work out of the tortoise shell—and into the outside world.

Am I ready to "go public"?

For a number of years, I reported on the advertising industry, covering some ad agencies known for their creativity and some known for making more predictable, unexciting ads. I noticed that at the less creative agencies, people tended to more closely guard their ideas, keeping them in locked drawers as long as possible, fearing that someone in the next cubicle might copy an idea and take credit.

But at the more creative agencies, such as the renowned TBWA\Chiat\Day, ideas were posted on the wall soon after they were first scribbled on paper. The longtime creative director of the agency, Lee Clow, felt that a good idea should be able to withstand scrutiny—and that the creator of the idea would likely benefit from having others comment on it and offer suggestions. As for people stealing each other's ideas? Clow explained that it was actually harder to steal an idea once it had been posted on the wall because everybody knew who put it up there. Besides, at TBWA\ Chiat\Day nobody wanted to steal ideas—they were having too much fun coming up with their own.

For most creative people in any field or discipline, I think the TBWA\Chiat\Day model is the better one to follow with regard to creative work that's finished or even partially finished. Get it out of the drawer and on the wall, in full view of others. Take standard precautionary measures (if it's appropriate and relatively easy to copyright it, why not?), but don't hold back work out of fear that someone will steal the idea—or criticize it.

The author and marketing guru Seth Godin has a word he uses often and persuasively, and that word is "ship." As Godin sees it, too many people are unwilling or unable to share their projects, dreams, and creations. They are leery of putting their ideas out into the world to see what will happen. They are afraid to ship.

And that fear is understandable. "Shipping is fraught with risk and danger," Godin has written in his long-running blog, *Seth's Blog*. "Every time you raise your hand, send an email, launch a product or make a suggestion, you're exposing yourself to criticism." If you ship, Godin adds, "you might fail. If you ship, we might laugh at you." But it's the chance you must take as a creative person because, as Godin puts it, "Real artists ship."

And the most successful ones tend to ship often. In today's intensely competitive marketplace, the more ideas and creations you put out there, the better your chances of breaking through. Creativity researcher Dean Keith Simonton, who has conducted studies on successful creative people, says, "Creativity is a consequence of sheer productivity. If a creator wants to increase the production of hits, he or she must do so by risking a parallel increase in the production of misses . . . The most successful creators tend to be those with the most failures."

In order to be able to ship often, you must be willing to ship early. Mark Zuckerberg of Facebook says, "We have the words 'Done is better than perfect' painted on our walls to remind ourselves to always keep shipping." Zuckerberg refers to the "Hacker Way" of creating things, which involves "quickly releasing and learning from smaller iterations rather than trying to get everything right all at once."

For the tech companies, this is not a new philosophy. Guy Kawasaki, who was responsible for marketing the Apple Macintosh when it was introduced in 1984, says the company could have held back and kept trying to make the product perfect, "but if you wait for ideal circumstances . . . the market will pass you by." So Apple didn't wait: "Revolutionary means you ship and then test," Kawasaki says. "Lots of things made the first Mac in 1984 a piece of crap—but it was a revolutionary piece of crap."

Do I want to be done or do I want to improve?

Just as important as being willing to accept failure is the willingness to accept feedback. The authors Douglas Stone and Sheila Heen, who work with the Harvard Negotiation Project and are coauthors of the book *Thanks for the Feedback*, point out that most of us have a built-in resistance to feedback. We have a strong need "to feel accepted, respected and safe—just the way we are *now*," according to the authors. So of course, we can handle positive feedback, telling us our work is fine, *as is*—but critical feedback is another matter.

USE THESE QUESTIONS TO GET HONEST, USEFUL FEEDBACK ON YOUR WORK

- *Am I coming across?* Use feedback not to change your basic idea, but just to see if it's being expressed clearly and understood.
- *What do you like least about this?* This question requires some courage to ask, but it's important because it gives permission to offer honest criticism. It also focuses on where the biggest problem(s) may lie.
- *And what else?* Also known as the "AWE" question (more on this in part III). It is designed to extract additional criticisms and often yields deeper insights.
- *What would you suggest I try?* Good feedback usually tells you what's wrong or missing but may not offer a solution. Use questioning to pull that out of the feedback giver.

However, as Adam Grant points out, "The only way to improve is to get negative feedback—so if you decide not to seek out criticism you're resigning yourself to stay at your current level of skill. Which to me is depressing."

Grant points out that people working on a creative project often are overly focused on finishing it—and they may worry that critical feedback will force them to have to go back to the drawing board. But this means they're focused on the wrong question, Grant says: "The key question is not 'How can I get this project done?' but rather, 'How do I make it better?'" And in terms of the latter, feedback is essential.

In trying to convince his students to be more open to feedback, Grant sometimes asks them: *Is your goal to stay at your current level of skill, or to improve?* When the question is framed that way, he says, almost everyone opts for improvement—and feedback.

One way to condition yourself to become better at accepting feedback is to think of it as a gift—which, in fact, it is, Tom Kelley points out. The feedback giver has invested her time and effort to help you to produce the best result. If the feedback is given honestly, from someone you trust, then ask yourself: *Why am I resistant to simply accepting this gift?* (As Kelley points out, you're not obliged to agree with or comply with feedback suggestions—merely to accept them with gratitude and an open mind.)

In finding the right people to provide feedback on your work, seek out those whose opinions you respect and who are entirely on your side. Ask yourself, *Who are my trusted advisors?* When you've come up with a handful of candidates, "create your own advisory board," Kelley says. The earlier you can get work to your "advisory board," the better; their early input may help you avoid wasting time polishing and tweaking something that actually needs reworking.

Be honest when asking for feedback. "If you know that feedback will meet resistance or dismissal from you, then ask only for positive thoughts," says the writer Kwame Dawes. It may be that all you want "is encouragement to continue—if so, then say that."

On the other hand, if you truly are interested in critical feedback—which is the most valuable kind—then ask for it explicitly. Mike Birbiglia, a veteran stand-up comedian and director of the film *Don't Think Twice*, writes that when he sought out feedback on his own film, "I'd get my friends all drunk on pizza and then ask them hard questions like: *What do you like* least *about the script?*"

Birbiglia adds: "I've learned that harsh feedback, constructive feedback, even weird random feedback, is all helpful, if you know the essence of what you're trying to convey."

How do you figure out when to listen to other people—and when to listen to yourself? The children's book writer Laurel Snyder says she was once asked this by a young girl and Snyder "was utterly stumped" by the question. There's no easy answer, but when the feedback giver is suggesting that you make significant changes to your work, ask yourself the following: *Is the feedback suggesting that I alter my vision or merely improve upon the execution?* Be wary of the former and more receptive to the latter.

To this point, Birbiglia shares a feedback tip he learned from the director Ron Howard: When Howard tests rough cuts of his movies with audiences, "he doesn't do it to be told what the movie's vision should be, but to understand whether his vision is coming across. If not, he makes changes." In other words, Howard knows what he wants to say but he's open to feedback on whether he's conveying it clearly enough. One of the most important feedback questions to ask is not, *Is my idea good?* (trust your own instincts on that), but simply, *Am I coming across?*

Feedback often is not prescriptive. According to Pixar executive Ed Catmull, "A good note says what's wrong, what's missing, what makes no sense." It's focused on the problems, not the solution. But if you are open to suggestions on specifically how to fix problems or make changes, ask for it: *I was wondering about how to improve X or Y—what would you suggest I try?* To return to Kelley's earlier point, you don't *have* to follow feedback suggestions, so there's little downside in getting as much input as possible from trusted sources.

Feedback experts Stone and Heen believe it's important to approach feedback on your work with "confidence and curiosity."

They also suggest that immediately after you receive feedback, you should evaluate and even grade your response to it—you can do this by asking yourself, *How well did I take that feedback?*

How do I stay "en route"?

After you've found a problem worth pursuing, retreated to your shell, managed to begin anywhere, survived the middle "suck stages" of creativity, responded to feedback, and, finally, "shipped" your completed work out into the world, what ultimately happens next to that work may be out of your hands. But whatever comes of it, no matter—a new problem is out there waiting to be found, as the creative cycle begins all over again.

As you continue to produce new creative work over time, a new challenge emerges: how to remain inspired and make sure that work stays fresh. According to those who've been on the creative journey for a long time, the best way to stay inspired is through constant reinvention.

Back in the mid-1990s, a then-young comedian Jon Stewart interviewed a then-aging comedian George Carlin, and Stewart asked Carlin what motivated him to keep creating original material and changing his act. In other words, why not just coast on his reputation and his existing comedy routines? Carlin explained that "an artist has an obligation to be *en route*—to be going somewhere. There's a journey involved here and you don't know where it is going—and that's the fun. So you're always going to be looking and seeking and trying to challenge yourself. It keeps you trying to be fresh, trying to be new."

Carlin was known for regularly throwing away all of his current material and starting with a blank page. He never stopped searching for new topics and trying out fresh approaches. His daughter, Kelly Carlin, said she believes that her father's willingness to continually "begin again" is what enabled him to stay relevant and popular in his fifties and sixties—a rarity among comedians. "It can be terrifying to let go of past successes, but he trusted that whatever got him there in the first place was going to get him to the next good thing."

To keep moving away from what you know is good for your creativity, research suggests. In fact, the more we stay in one place—the more mastery and expertise we gain in one domain—the worse for our creativity. "As expertise goes up, creative output tends to go down," the *Myths of Creativity* author David Burkus says. It's not that experts don't come up with new ideas, Burkus says—it's just that because of all their experience, they're often "better at coming up with reasons why a new idea won't work." Bottom line: To remain creative, you must think and behave like a novice, always discovering.

A creative person who remains "en route" is exposed to more diverse ideas and more varied influences—which can end up providing richer source material for those mental connections and "smart recombinations" that form new ideas.

How can you keep moving away from what you know? The easiest way is to follow your curiosity. The author Elizabeth Gilbert, in a talk extolling the benefits of "the curiosity-driven life," shares a wonderful analogy involving jackhammers and hummingbirds. According to Gilbert, people who behave like jackhammers focus obsessively on one thing, drilling deeper and deeper. Those who are more like hummingbirds follow their curiosity as they "move from tree to tree, from flower to flower . . . trying this, trying that."

So: *Should a creative person be more like a hummingbird or a jackhammer?* It probably depends what stage you're at in your work. Curiosity can be a wonderful source of creative inspiration, constantly leading you to new ideas. But it can also work *against* you in terms of getting the work done. If curiosity is unfocused (or, to use the term applied by researchers, "diversive"), it can keep you endlessly bouncing from tree to tree, idea to idea, subject to subject, never digging too deep on anything because you're quickly distracted by something else. On the other hand, focused (or "epistemic") curiosity can lead you to want to know more and burrow deeper on a single fascination.

To be both productive and unpredictable in your creative work, you need extended periods of focused curiosity—drilling into one project until completion—followed by occasional flights of diversive curiosity that can lead you to something completely new and different. The key is in knowing when it's time to shift from one mode to the other. During the course of a creative career, there may be a need to periodically ask: *Is it time now to be a jackhammer—or a hummingbird?*

It's not easy to fly away from work that has been successful—in fact, it can be scary. Bono, the lead singer of the band U2, described the feelings associated with U2's effort to move from one style of music to another back in 1990. "You have to reject one expression of the band first before you get to the next expression," he said. "And in between, you have nothing. You have to risk it all."

But the creators who manage to stay interesting and relevant over the long haul seem to be quite comfortable in that "in-between" territory. Bob Dylan may be the master of this type of creative reinvention; he has been "en route" for half a century. One of his biographers, Jon Friedman, notes that the journey has taken the onetime folk singer from early "finger-pointing songs" to introspective tunes to electric rock. Next, Dylan conquered the country genre, returned to rock and then back to message songs, with a detour along the way to sing about becoming a born-again Christian.

"To reach a new generation of music fans, he reinvented his approach to performing," Friedman points out. Instead of going out on the road every year or two, he launched "The Never Ending Tour," playing one hundred shows a year around the world, "even showing up in minor-league baseball fields." To quote Todd Haynes,

USE THESE QUESTIONS TO KEEP YOUR CREATIVE WORK FROM GETTING STALE

- *How can I keep moving away from what I know?* To avoid becoming a "comfortable expert" in your work, follow your curiosity.
- *Is it time to be a jackhammer—or a hummingbird?* The hummingbird keeps landing in new places; the jackhammer drills deep in one spot.
- *What am I willing to abandon?* To keep work fresh, you must give something up: reliable material, proven methods, familiar turf.
- *How might I "go electric"?* Like Dylan at Newport, a creative person should recognize that the times are a-changin' and embrace new styles, tastes, forms, and technologies.
- *Where is my petri dish?* To experiment with your work, you may need to find a place where you can do so safely.

director of a 2007 film about Dylan, "The minute you try to grab hold of Dylan, he's no longer where he was."

Perhaps the most memorable transformation occurred early on in 1965, when Dylan famously plugged in an electric guitar at the Newport Folk Festival—to boos from an audience that wanted him to keep performing the folk songs that had made him a star. It may have seemed a risky move at the time, but it enabled Dylan to transition from the fading folk genre to the burgeoning electric rock scene.

Every once in a while, one should ask, *How might I go electric?*—as a means of considering whether it might be time to adapt your work to new tastes, formats, and technologies. The late novelist Ursula K. Le Guin did just that when, at age eighty-one, she started her own blog. It gave her a chance to reach a new audience, try her hand at a new medium, and stay current.

That new medium also provided a place for Le Guin to experiment with her writing—because there are things you can try out on a blog that you can't do in a book. Which brings up one last point to keep in mind when thinking about how to stay "en route." In order to ensure that your creative work evolves over time, you may need a place to try new approaches and experiments. Ask yourself, *Where is my petri dish?*

The question is a favorite of the business consultant Tim Ogilvie, who maintains that companies should designate areas where people can separate themselves from the everyday pressures and politics of the workplace in order to explore radical new ideas and approaches. (The company's petri dish may take the form of an in-house innovation lab.) But Ogilvie's question applies to individual creators as well, who may need to find a low-stakes project or platform—or a stage with a smaller audience—where they can work through attempts to try something new.

When experimenting, it can be useful to have lab partners. The Kelley brothers note that a creative support network can help you explore new possibilities and provide feedback on experimental efforts. "Spearhead a creative confidence group that meets once a month," they suggest.

And when you convene meetings of that group, bring along and share some of the creativity questions from this section. While most are designed as questions to ask yourself, they also can be effective when creative people ask them of one another—or when the questions are considered and discussed collectively by a group.

If you don't know enough people to form a creative confidence group, then you may need to work on connecting with other like-minded souls. The next chapter explores ways to use questioning to widen your circle and deepen your relationships.

PART III

Questions to Help
CONNECT WITH OTHERS

Why connect?

Five decades ago, Arthur Aron and Elaine Spaulding, a pair of psychology students at the University of California at Berkeley, shared a kiss one day in front of the main study hall and immediately fell in love. The experience led to a mutual fascination not only with each other (they're still together and now married) but also with the mysteries of love itself. At the time, Aron was looking for a subject on which to base a research project and thought, *Why not do a study on romantic love?* With help from fellow researchers, including Spaulding, he set out on a journey that led him to try to answer this question: *How might we, in a laboratory setting, find a way to create instant intimacy between strangers?*

He brought pairs of strangers into his campus lab and tried to get them to like, or possibly even love, each other. Gradually, Aron discovered a powerful force that seemed able to produce the desired effect: not a love potion, but a well-crafted and strategically designed series of questions. Aron would give a list of the same questions to each member of the participating pairs. The partners would then take turns asking each other the questions and responding.

Some questions were more effective than others. Through trial and error, Aron was able to determine the ones that best helped participants share personal information and gradually begin to feel a greater mutual appreciation. He eventually came up with thirty-six questions, to be used sequentially. The list began with more superficial queries (e.g., *Who would be your ideal dinner guest?*) and then built to much more personal questions probing deep feelings about hopes, regrets, dreams, core values. When trying to build a connection with another person, Aron discovered, "you don't want to share too much, too fast . . . What works best is back-and-forth self-disclosure that increases gradually."

When people questioned each other in this way, the results were surprising—even to Aron. Most of the pairs of strangers came out of the session with highly positive feelings for each other; one couple later married. Aron's research, and his thirty-six questions, gradually began to gain notoriety in the science world.

Then Aron's thirty-six questions went viral in early 2015, when a *New York Times* writer penned a story with the irresistible headline: "To Fall in Love with Anyone, Do This." In the article, writer Mandy Len Catron recounted her own experience trying out the thirty-six questions with a college acquaintance. The result caught her by surprise. "Because the level of vulnerability increased gradually, I didn't notice we had entered intimate territory until we were already there," Catron wrote. She and her college pal did, indeed, fall in love, and are still together.

Meanwhile, Aron has continued to study ways in which his list of questions—tweaked and adapted for varying circumstances—might be able to create closeness among people in all kinds of situations and relationships. *Could the questions be used to rekindle a spark among long-term couples who'd grown a little too used to each other?* Yes, they could, Aron found (though he learned that, in this case, it worked better if a couple took the test with another couple, and they all shared questions round-robin style). *Could the questions strengthen the relationship between people who might have less in common—and might even be adversarial in some cases?* To test this, Aron had police officers share questions with citizens in their community. And he also ran the question experiment with pairs of people of different races.

In most cases, the experiments resulted in building a stronger bond—more warm feelings, greater respect—between the members of each pair. But they had an even greater impact, Aron learned: If he could get two people from different groups to like each other more, those feelings extended to the overall group. The person who shared questions with a police officer was then apt to respect *all* police more. Likewise for those who exchanged questions with someone from another race.

What makes certain questions so powerful when it comes to building stronger relationships between people? When formulated and asked the right way, questions can do a few key things, Aron says. "First, just by asking, you're showing that you care about the other person. Second, the question encourages that person to reveal something about themselves. And then that creates an opportunity for you to respond to what they are revealing."

QUESTIONS SHOW INTEREST, create understanding, and build rapport. Those are three strong legs upon which a relationship can be built and supported. It's no accident that people with jobs that require them to quickly establish trusting relationships—therapists, coaches, hostage negotiators—rely on questions as a primary communication tool. These professionals are trained to ask certain types of questions (usually more open-ended ones that invite a fuller response) in particular ways.

As former head of the counterintelligence behavioral analysis program at the FBI, Robin Dreeke's job was to quickly establish rapport and gain the trust of operatives and potential sources of information. His work revolved around knowing precisely how to ask a question so that it encouraged someone to open up, cooperate, and reveal sensitive information. The wording of his questions mattered greatly, he says, but just as important was his attitude while asking the questions. *Am I genuinely interested in the other person? Am I able to put my ego aside and suspend all judgment? Am I prepared to truly listen, as opposed to just acting as if I am listening?* "If you don't do all of these things, it can undermine the rapport you're trying to build with your questions."

The good news is that none of the techniques used by Dreeke and other "professional questioners" are all that technical. Anyone can use them well if they remain mindful of *what* they're asking and *how* they asking it *as* they're asking. In this section, we'll consider various general techniques and approaches, but we'll also focus on specific questions—to ask others and yourself—that are designed to strengthen relationships both new and old.

Most of us have been using questioning to connect with people around us since childhood. In fact, as with most things question related, we were probably doing it better then than we are now as adults. Children come to realize, at an early age, that a question is a means to engage with the people around them and to draw information out of them. It greases the skids of communication and gives people a sense of what they should say back to you. (All you need do is answer the question.) Kids seem to understand intuitively that the question is not only a tool for gathering information but also for breaking the ice.

Over time, we begin to use that questioning tool less in social interactions—and to the extent we do use it, we often misuse it. Some of the more common misuses: We ask rote, incurious questions out of habit (*How are you?*); we ask questions that are really just critical statements in disguise (*What were you thinking?*); and we express opinions or dispense advice in the form of questions (*Why don't you just do this?*). These types of questions may fill dead air or provide the self-satisfaction that comes with "venting," but they don't contribute much to the building of relationships. They don't show true interest, don't create understanding, and don't build rapport.

To get better at asking the kinds of questions that do forge deeper connections with the people around us, we need to do a few things: endeavor to ask "authentic" questions rooted in curiosity; try to suspend judgment and withhold advice as we focus more on inquiry; take a small risk by being willing to ask open-ended, "deeper" questions (even of people we may not know very well); and be willing to listen carefully and follow up on what we're hearing with questions that gently probe a little deeper.

THIS IS AN interesting time to talk about "connecting" with other people because, clearly, the word has taken on a new meaning in the age of LinkedIn, Facebook, and other forms of highly connective social media. A "connection" now may refer to a loose tie between people who, often, have never met and know little about one another. Initial contact comes in the form of generic invitations to connect or "friend" or follow. The reflexive response is to tap "accept" or "ignore," or, in the case of Tinder, to swipe left or right. This new connectedness made possible by technology has its advantages, to be sure—never has it been so easy for someone to provide impressive numerical evidence of one's "popularity."

But research suggests that if we truly want to be happy, we need more of that old-fashioned direct human contact, particularly as it reaches a level of closeness that might be termed "companionship." Various studies, including the landmark Grant Study, which followed a group of Harvard men for decades to track their happiness, point to a powerful correlation between the warmth of your relationships and your overall health and happiness in old age. (Author E. M. Forster had it right, it seems: "Only connect!")

People who have companionship are not only happier and healthier, but they also are likely to have a greater sense of "meaning" in their lives, according to the findings of *The Power of Meaning* author Emily Esfahani Smith. This is true in terms of closeness to family and friends, but it also extends to the workplace, studies show. For many—and for millennials in particular—having friends at work is critical to being happy at work and is considered more important, even, than the size of the paycheck.

When it comes to friendship, less may be more. A handful of intimate, deep relationships are worth more than five hundred "friends" on Facebook, at least in terms of producing the kinds of life-enriching benefits Esfahani Smith is talking about. But "connecting" face-to-face can be harder than connecting online. When meeting new people in person, there's more discomfort, more in-the-moment pressure to get the words, the tone, and the timing right. We need an icebreaker, social lubricant, and an empathy app, all in one.

Questions can fill that role—and many of us do, in fact, use questions to establish contact with others, including people we've just met. However, at critical moments of introduction or reintroduction, we tend to rely on generic, superficial questions—*How are you? How's it going? What's new?* These rote questions lack the ingredients—genuine interest, curiosity, and wonder—that tend to invite a more meaningful answer. A rote question often evokes a rote answer followed by an echo of the original rote question ("How are you?" "Fine. How are *you?*"). Instead of providing a good starting point, it is more apt to be a conversation stopper.

What if we go beyond "How are you?"

Chris Colin and Rob Baedeker noticed this and wondered, *Why do we go around asking each other such pointless questions?* Colin, a writer, and Baedeker, a sketch comedian, coauthors of the 2014 book *What to Talk About*, were interested in questions that could get a conversation going, and help the participants to remain more engaged. They found that good conversation takes planning. "When it comes time to exchange words with another human being, we find we're all sort of empty-headed," Colin says. But it can help if you come armed with the right questions. "A good way to get beyond small talk is to ask open-ended questions that invite people to tell stories, rather than give bland, one-word answers." Colin adds: "Curiosity has to be at the heart of your heart when you talk to someone. The kind of curiosity that works best is a curiosity for stories."

To tease out others' stories, some of the questions Colin and Baedeker came up with are specific ("How did you get to this party tonight?") but others are expansive ("What are you most passionate about?" and "What problem do you wish you could solve?"). These provide a better alternative to the standard "What do you do?" question, for a number of reasons. Not only is *What do you do?* a rote, superficial question, but it's also understood as *What do you do for a living?*, and thus forces a person to talk about their job when they may have more interesting stories to share (and may not even have a job at present).

Colin and Baedeker recommend putting a twist on more standard questions. Instead of *How was your weekend*, try *What was the best part of your weekend?* Instead of *Where are you from?*, try *What's the strangest/most interesting thing about where you grew up?*

THINK OF COLIN and Baedeker's approach as the "open up and go deep" questioning strategy. Take questions that are closed, meaning they call for simple factual or yes or no answers (*How long have you lived in Boise?*

QUESTIONS TO ASK INSTEAD OF *HOW ARE YOU?*

- **What's the best thing that happened to you today?** This can be adapted to ask about this week, the weekend, etc.

- **What are you excited about in your life right now?**

- **What are you most looking forward to at this gathering?** This one is good for conferences and other social events.

. . . AND INSTEAD OF *WHAT DO YOU DO?*

- **What are you most passionate about?** This is a great way to shift from a job (which may be boring) to interests.

- **What problem do you wish you could solve?** This shifts from present realities to larger goals and possibilities.

- **What did you want to be when you were growing up?** This question invites a story about growing up and the road that led to the present.

Six years. *Do you like it?* No.) and make them more open-ended, calling for a more individualized answer (*What brought you to Boise? What's the most enjoyable thing about living there?*). To make those open-ended questions even deeper, try crafting the question so that it is asking for more of a feeling, an experience, a story. (*What was it like when you first moved to Boise? What's the single weirdest thing that ever happened to you there?*)

There's a tendency to think we shouldn't ask "deeper" questions of people we don't know very well. Not so, says writer Tim Boomer, who believes we should be asking just such questions when we meet people on the job, at cocktail parties, even on a first date. Boomer noticed how awkward it was when people on dates tried to talk about superficial things like their commutes or the weather. This raised a couple of questions in his mind: "Why did being with a stranger so often mean we couldn't immediately talk about meaningful things?" and "Why can't we replace small talk

QUESTIONS TO MAKE SOMEONE LIKE (OR EVEN LOVE) YOU

- *What would constitute a perfect day for you?*
- *If you could change anything about the way you were raised, what would it be?*
- *What does friendship mean to you?*
- *How do you feel about your relationship with your mother?*
- *When did you last cry in front of another person? And by yourself?*
- *What, if anything, is too serious to be joked about?*

From Arthur Aron's thirty-six questions experiment. For the full list, visit www.amorebeautifulquestion .com/36-questions.

with big talk and ask each other profound questions right from the start?"

He set out to answer his own question by going on a date and asking deep questions. (He later shared the results in an essay he wrote for the *New York Times*). On his deep-questions date, Boomer asked questions such as, "What work are you most passionate about?" and "What's the most in love you've ever felt?" As the questions went back and forth, "we laughed and we cried, and we learned nothing that would go on a résumé. Later, we kissed." Boomer says he has stayed away from small talk ever since, and he reports, "every date has turned into a real connection or at worst, a funny story." He's tried it in nondating situations as well, such as when he asked a colleague on a business trip, "Why did you fall in love with your wife?" The colleague was surprised by the question at first, but, Boomer recounts, "he thought about it for a moment and then told me something beautiful."

The thirty-six questions used in Arthur Aron's experiment are wonderful examples of open-ended, deep questions. They demand that the person on the receiving end actually think about the answer. They're also designed to be self-revealing; as such they serve to quickly illuminate where there might be common values, shared dreams and hopes, and other forms of compatibility. To varying degrees, this is one of the things we're trying to gauge when considering whether to deepen a relationship (whether it's with a friend, a coworker, or a romantic interest): *How compatible am I with this person, and is there potential for something deep and lasting?* The right questions reveal not just how you're getting along in the here and now, but how you might coexist in the future.

With that in mind, journalist Eleanor Stanford compiled a list of questions designed to be asked by two people considering marriage. One particularly interesting question—*Did your family throw plates?*—is intended to find out about "conflict resolution patterns" inherited from parents. Other questions on the list include: *What do you admire about me?*; *Can you deal with my doing things without you?*; and *How do you see us ten years from now?* (That last one can be made more specific by asking, *What do you envision as our ideal future?*)

One of the most practical premarriage questions comes from Mandy Len Catron (previously mentioned for her experiment with the thirty-six questions): *What would marriage offer us that we don't already have?*

THE "OPEN UP and go deep" questioning approach works in everyday family settings as well. We've all been in that situation where a parent at the dinner table asks, *So: How was everyone's day?* The answers typically run the gamut from "Fine" to stony silence. Two suggestions here: First, try asking the question individually. (It's hard for "everyone" to answer a question.) Next, try doing an open/deep tweak on that question, changing it to, for example, *What was the most interesting thing that happened to you today?* Depending on what you think your kids might respond to, "interesting" could be replaced with "weird" or "annoying."

Deborah Harmon, chief executive of Artemis Real Estate Partners, says that when she was growing up, during family dinners, her father would ask his children, *What was the most difficult problem you had today?* Next, he would ask them, *How could you*

QUESTIONS TO ASK YOUR SPOUSE INSTEAD OF *HOW WAS YOUR DAY?*

Sara Goldstein of Mother.ly came up with twenty-one questions; here are six of them.

- *When did you feel appreciated today?*
- *Will you remember any specific part of today a year from now?*
- *How can I make your day easier in five minutes?*
- *If we were leaving for vacation tonight, where do you wish we were heading?*
- *What made you laugh today?*
- *What do you wish you did more of today?*

have handled this differently? "Through his questioning," Harmon says, "he helped us become our own problem solvers." Similarly, Sara Blakely, the founder of Spanx apparel, was inspired when she was growing up by a question her father often asked at the dinner table: *What have you failed at this week?*

If you don't want to keep asking the same question (even a good one like Harmon's or Blakely's) at family dinners, and find it difficult to come up with new ones on the fly, consider using a question jar, a strategy recommended by Glennon Doyle, creator of the website Momastery. She got the idea from a schoolteacher who filled a jar with interesting questions from students in her classroom.

Doyle eventually began filling a jar of her own with questions at home. A few times a week, she and her children take turns pulling out a question during dinner. Sample questions: *If you were an inventor—what would you invent, and why? What was your first thought when you woke up today? Who in your class seems lonely? What do you think is the biggest challenge facing our world today?* (Doyle and teacher Erin Waters have come up with forty-eight altogether, which can be downloaded from the Momastery website).

According to Doyle, the questions are designed to unlock awareness on several levels, encouraging kids to think about themselves, other people, and the world at large. "Kids must become explorers of themselves first, and then their eyes open to other people in their lives," Doyle writes. "It's a process, teaching curiosity, awareness and compassion. This jar is a start."

How might I listen with my whole body?

As Arthur Aron explained, when you ask a question, you begin to show interest in the other person. But to show sustained interest—and to be able to meaningfully respond to whatever your question elicits—you must do more than ask questions. You must listen.

The act of listening is an underappreciated yet remarkably effective tool for building trust with just about anyone. Those who master it can strengthen friendships and family relationships, become a better colleague or boss at work, and can even be more successful at solving problems and creating business opportunities. Becoming a better listener also helps you to become a better questioner—in fact, listening is an essential ingredient of good questioning.

I learned that firsthand during my years as a newspaper journalist. I started out, as many journalists do, thinking that the key to conducting a good interview was to be armed with a strong list of prepared questions. I sometimes was so focused on asking the next question on my list that I didn't pay enough attention to what was being said at that moment. With experience, I learned that the questions you bring to an interview (or a conversation) can be very useful, but listening deeply to what's being said, and reacting to it, works better than following a script. Good interviewers learn that within each answer you receive may be the seeds of the next question you should ask—a follow-up question that digs a little deeper or teases out a few more critical details.

The same is true for nonjournalists trying to connect with, and possibly provide support to, a friend, family member, or coworker. Even if you're armed with great "starter" questions, those are only launching points. To deepen a conversation, you must ask questions that have been shaped by what you've just heard and learned. Borrowing the journalist's technique, you can use those questions to gently extract information that can be useful in sparking insights and solving problems. As the journalist Frank Sesno explains: "The simple act of asking, and of listening without comment or judgment" is powerful because it "invites a person to reflect and think aloud. It might even prompt a revelation."

But deep and active listening isn't easy. It requires breaking some of the poor listening habits that have become common—such as the tendency to nod as someone talks, while secretly thinking about what you'd like to have for dinner (or worse than that: to glance down at your iPhone while saying "Uh-huh . . . yeah, I hear you."). The author and business coach Cathy Salit observes that, "Increasingly, listening is a forgotten skill," and an endangered one, too—under siege from endless distractions and incoming messages. "And yet, listening to the people close to you—your team, your company, your sphere of influence—is more important than ever," Salit maintains. Precisely because there is so much "noise" out there, she says, we all must work harder than ever to listen.

Before engaging in important conversations, the first question to ask yourself is, *Am I ready to listen fully?* If the time isn't right—if you're distracted, tired, or so busy that you'll have to multitask during the conversation, put off the conversation until a better time. And being in the right place can be as important as finding the right time. "Your office space is a breeding ground for distractions. Email, ringing phones, smartphones and paperwork are like Kryptonite that can drain your power to listen," says the communications consultant Alison Davis. Find a quieter location where you can focus full attention on the conversation.

Another key question to consider up front is, *What does it mean to listen fully?* We associate listening with hearing, of course, but experts point out that it's more of a full-bodied activity. "Good listeners have a *physical, mental,* and *emotional* presence, and they know how to integrate all three," says Judith Humphrey, founder of the communications firm the Humphrey Group. It's worth noting that the Chinese symbol for listening incorporates the ear, the eyes, and the heart—a reminder that good listening really is a demanding activity.

What that symbol leaves out is the mind—which must be open when listening. Rather than thinking about whether you agree or disagree with what someone is telling you, the goal is to understand it, observes counselor Dianne Schilling. She recommends trying to "picture what the speaker is saying," so that it comes alive in your own mind. Even better than seeing it is to try to feel it. When someone is telling you about an experience or a situation they're dealing with, ask yourself: *What must this feel like?* At some point in the conversation, you may end up asking a version of this

Attentive listening

ears — eyes — undivided — heart

question directly to the other person—but first, start by using your imagination to try to empathize.

Listening with an attentive mind and open heart is signaled partly through body language—eye contact, turning toward the speaker, nodding, keeping your arms unfolded—and partly by way of verbal responses. Here is where the often subtle use of questioning can complement and support the act of listening. But what you don't say is also important: Staying quiet long enough to let the other person fully express themselves is key to good listening. And it can be very difficult to do. The temptation is to fill any opening (even if there is no opening) with opinions, statements, stories of our own.

Listening is not a competitive sport, though we sometimes treat it that way. As we listen we may be asking ourselves "wrong" questions that actually undermine listening: *What can I say in response to what I'm hearing that will show how clever I am? How can I top this story with one of my own?* But as we're thinking about these questions, we're not paying full attention to the person speaking. As FBI analyst Robin Dreeke points out, "The second that I think about my response, I'm half listening to what you're saying because I'm really waiting for the opportunity to tell you my story." Dreeke's advice: "As soon as you have that story or thought you want to share, toss it." Return your attention to the speaker.

As a reminder to talk less and listen more, try asking yourself the "WAIT question," shared by psychologist Ronald Siegel. "WAIT stands for *Why Am I Talking?*," Siegel explains, adding: "This simple question can help cultivate a reflective attitude" that restrains the impulse to interrupt and interject while listening to someone. Siegel considers the question to be a useful tool for therapists, but it also applies to all types of conversations, and even online interactions (the journalism professor Michael J. Socolow notes that if social media users got into the habit of asking the WAIT question "immediately before posting or retweeting, we'd all be better off").

It isn't easy to just shut up and listen because people are prone to "conversational narcissism," says Celeste Headlee, radio host and

ASKING THESE QUESTIONS WILL MAKE YOU
A BETTER LISTENER

- **Just to be clear, are you saying _____?** At key points, repeat back a paraphrase of what you've heard.
- **Can you explain what you mean by that?** This is a classic "clarifying" question used by interviewers to invite people to better explain themselves. (Tone is important: Go for curious, not puzzled or antagonistic.)
- **I imagine that made you feel __, right?** A variation of How did it make you feel? (which sounds too much like a psychiatrist's question).
- **And what else?** The "AWE" question may be the best way to draw out deeper insights—and keep you in listening mode.

author of the book *We Need to Talk.* We like to shift the conversation so that it focuses on ourselves. In an interview with the editors of *Heleo,* Headlee cites an example from her own life: A friend's father had passed away and tried to talk about it with Headlee—who then began to discuss her own experience of losing her father. Headlee didn't understand at first why her friend was put off by this. "I was just trying to be helpful. I was just trying to say, 'I know how you feel,'" she explains. She later came to realize that "I was interjecting my story of my own struggle, when it just needed to be about her." As Headlee puts it, "A conversational narcissist is the one that keeps taking the ball from the game of catch and not ever passing it back."

In describing the dynamics of a conversation, Mark Goulston, a psychiatrist and author of the book *Just Listen,* uses the analogy of a tennis match in place of Headlee's "game of catch." He says we fall into the habit of competing in conversation, thinking, "He scored a point. Now I need to score a point." Instead, Goulston advises, "think of it as a detective game, in which your goal is to learn as much about the other person as you can." Thus, instead of asking oneself, *How can I score a conversational point?,* a better question is, *How can I make sure I'm really hearing what this person is trying to say?*

There's a questioning technique for that—and it's so basic that you might underestimate its effectiveness. It's known as paraphrasing and should be done at various points during a conversation after the speaker has expressed a thought, particularly on an important or complex point. The listener repeats back what has just been said in the form of a question. (*Just to be clear, are you saying x, y, and z?*)

Salit notes that paraphrasing seems easy but is "is surprisingly difficult for the poor listeners of the world." It's effective for two reasons. First and foremost, it helps to ensure clearer communication. (You may have misheard what was said, or the person may have expressed it poorly on the first try.) But Salit points out that it provides the additional benefit of building agreement and trust between the speaker and the listener. It shows the speaker that you really are trying to understand them.

Former FBI hostage negotiator Chris Voss says that a shortened form of paraphrasing known as "mirroring" is a tactic that can help defuse tense discussions. It involves repeating several key words that have just been said, phrasing it as a question. For example, if someone said, "I feel as if nobody in this company cares about all the work I've done," you'd mirror that by saying, "Nobody in the company cares?" As Voss explains, the tactic encourages people to better explain themselves—and makes them feel as if they're being heard. The journalist Frank Sesno uses a similar technique that he calls an "echo question," which can consist of as little as one word. In the example given above, the echo question would be: "Nobody?"

One of the most effective follow-up questions consists of three simple words: *And what else?* Michael Bungay Stanier, a renowned executive coach (and another person I would categorize as a fellow questionologist), calls *And what else?* the "AWE" question, and considers it to be "the best coaching question in the world." By pushing people to go beyond top-of-mind answers, the question elicits more, and usually better, ideas and insights. It encourages the process of "thinking out loud" about a challenging subject. And by continually asking this question, the questioner can remain in a more supportive role. As Bungay Stanier notes, the "AWE" question can help to "keep 'the advice monster' at bay."

But he offers two caveats about the question. It must be asked with genuine interest. (If it is asked as nothing more than a rote question, then it becomes irritating.) And Bungay Stanier adds that it generally is most effective when asked three times in succession, but no more than that. By the third round, consider rewording the question slightly to: *Is there anything else?*—which invites closure.

The "AWE" question can be useful when talking to a friend or family member who's having a problem, but it's also a powerful tool in business—particularly for managers. In trying to diagnose a problem at work, it's not uncommon for managers to ask: *What's the issue here?* or *What's causing the problem?* But because people sometimes have trouble articulating a difficult or sensitive issue on the first try, it may take a couple of follow-up "AWE" questions before the real issue surfaces. Similarly, the question can be a tool for encouraging more creative thinking about solutions, as in: *What could we try in order to solve this problem . . . and what else?* or *What issues should our company be thinking about . . . and what else?*

Paraphrasing and simple follow-ups such as the "AWE" question are good for eliciting additional thoughts and greater clarification, but they may not get at deeper emotional feelings that people often have trouble expressing. To encourage the sharing of those feelings, Salit recommends using what she calls "empathetic listening": The idea is to try to identify the emotion a person is feeling and reflect it back in the form of a question.

She offers this example: "So, Bill, what I hear you saying is that you're angry with me because I haven't appreciated the lengths you've gone to in trying to win over our Latin American customers. Those efforts have caused you a lot of sleepless nights, time away from the family, and marital problems. Is that right?" Salit says, "This form of active listening is the hardest to undertake," but "if you've done it well, people will agree profoundly and powerfully with you."

It can be effective for a listener to try to read and play back the emotions of the person speaking. Goulston recommends using a question such as: *I'm trying to get a sense of what you're feeling and I think it's frustration. Is that correct?* This goes beyond paraphrasing—and may seem as if it borders on putting words in someone's mouth—but as long as you're paying close attention to what the speaker is trying to express, your clarifying question is likely to be helpful.

As the questioner helps put emotions into words, follow-up questions can be used to further clarify: *We've established you felt frustrated, but how frustrated were you? And what was the reason for that frustration?* As Goulston notes, if you're trying to work toward a solution, you may aim to arrive at: *What needs to happen for that feeling to feel better?*

Goulston refers to this as a form of listening and questioning that makes another person "feel felt"—to show that "you understand and accept how the other person feels and that you'd feel the same" if you were in that situation. "When people 'feel felt,' they feel less alone . . . less anxious and less defensive," Goulston writes, adding: "When you mirror what another person feels, the person is wired to mirror you in return . . . It's an irresistible biological urge, and one that pulls the person toward you."

An important point about listening: Some people (especially men, it seems) worry that taking on the role of listener may put them in a position of weakness or make them seem less interesting. Neither is true, communication experts say. It's counterintuitive, but according to research cited by Wharton's Adam Grant, we actually can be more persuasive, and therefore exert more power, when we act as "powerless communicators" who listen and ask questions. And as noted previously, people who listen and ask questions are showing interest—and "being interested makes you interesting," says Goulston.

What if I advise less and inquire more?

There is a human tendency that particularly gets in the way of good questioning—and it can adversely affect the way managers relate to employees, in addition to also having a negative impact on communications between family members, spouses, and good friends. To varying degrees, we're all guilty of doing it: giving advice.

Why are we inclined to advise others on what they should do? Michael Bungay Stanier believes it's "about certainty and control. When you're giving advice—even when you're not giving very good advice—you have high status. You're in control of the conversation.

You're the one with the answers. You get to be the person who is adding value. So you're feeling pretty damn good."

In contrast, he says, "when you ask questions, you're stepping into ambiguity and lower status. You may be empowering the other person, but in doing that you're disempowering yourself. I think because you're helping people, you win in the long term—but it doesn't feel like that in the moment."

Bungay Stanier says that people in leadership positions— managers on the job, but also the heads of households, too—may feel obliged to tell people what to do, to offer up a solution for every problem. But it seems to also affect close personal relationships. When we know someone very well (a spouse or best friend), it's easy to fall into the habit of giving advice.

And it isn't always a bad thing. Sometimes people actually need advice and you may be in a good position to offer it. "I don't say, 'Never give advice,'" says Bungay Stanier. "Just slow down the rush to advise people. Because the truth is, people's advice often isn't as good as they think it is."

One problem is that the advice giver may not know enough about what's going on in a situation—the history, the context—and may be trying to solve a problem that isn't the real problem. The advice giver has their own biases, experiences, and beliefs about how to deal with a given situation. The advice might make sense for them, but not necessarily for others.

Giving misguided advice to someone you know can end up damaging the relationship—assuming it isn't simply ignored. That is what many of us tend to do with the advice we're given (though it doesn't stop us from turning around and giving this unwanted gift to others).

What's the alternative? Rather than handing people what you think is "the answer," it's preferable to help them find their own answer, if possible—and one way to do that is through a combination of listening and asking questions that gently probe and guide. The model for this type of interaction is used by many life coaches, consultants, and especially therapists. Good therapists don't tell you what to do; they lead you on a path to figuring it out for yourself.

If you can help someone to think about a problem more clearly and gently guide them in the direction of possible solutions, you're leaving room for that person to arrive at their own insights and make their own decisions—so that they have more "ownership" of potential solutions.

This might be thought of as the "lead the horse to water" questioning strategy (based on the old chestnut "You can lead a horse to water, but you can't make it drink"). The mistake that advice givers make is to try to force water on the horse. Better to let the horse take those last few steps to the water, and if he's thirsty, he'll drink (and if not, maybe water isn't what the horse needs right now).

How can we use questions to guide the "horse" toward the "water"? By asking the ones that

---

SKIP THE ADVICE. ASK THESE SEVEN QUESTIONS TO HELP SOMEONE FIGURE IT OUT FOR THEMSELVES

- *What is the challenge that you're facing?*
- *What have you tried already?*
- *If you could try anything to solve this, what would you try?*
- *And what else?* (Repeat this two or three times, as needed, to surface additional ideas.)
- *Which of these options interests you most?*
- *What might stand in the way of this idea, and what could be done about that?*
- *What is one step you could take to begin acting on this, right away?*

---

can help someone sort through options—and see through what Hal Mayer calls the "fog." When people are dealing with a challenge, they may actually have their own ideas about what's causing the problem and possible courses of action, but they might need help organizing those thoughts into a coherent strategy. Mayer, executive pastor and leadership trainer at the Church at the Springs in Ocala, Florida, shares a great example of how, using only questions with not a word of advice, it's possible to help someone figure out what to do.

Mayer was coaching a woman who was trying to attract more volunteers to help in her parish. He started by asking her to set her goals (attract ten new volunteers). He next asked, *What have you tried?*, and she mentioned past efforts that had not worked. He then asked this question: *If you could try anything and money was not an object, what would you do to find new volunteers?* (Readers may recognize this as a variation of the "What if I could not fail?" question discussed in part II).

The woman came up with the idea of offering people $100 to volunteer. Mayer made note of that and asked, "What else?" With each subsequent idea she shared, he followed up by asking for another idea, and then another. When she ran out of ideas, he showed her the list of five ideas she'd come up with and asked: *Which one of these most interests you—which one would you like to discuss further?* She chose an idea about setting up a lemonade stand at which kids could hand out applications to volunteer.

Mayer then asked several practical questions about that idea: *How would you set it up? What would you need to get started? What problems might get in the way of this idea? What are the first steps you can take, right away?* By the time he was finished with the conversation—which took less than twenty minutes—the woman had a plan of action and was ready to begin in a few days.

As Mayer points out, he did not pass judgment on any of her ideas or try to tell her how to proceed. "All I did," he says, "was ask her questions to help her draw focus."

One of the important things Mayer did in the midway point of that conversation was to solicit multiple ideas (using the "AWE" question). The favorite idea, about the lemonade stand, wasn't the first or even the second idea mentioned by the woman. It had to be drawn out with follow-up questioning. When you're asking someone to talk about a challenge they're facing and how it might be addressed, the initial responses may be superficial or impractical. But generally, people will dig for deeper thoughts and better ideas if you use that powerful "AWE" question.

How am I guilty of the thing I'm criticizing?

About the only thing worse than giving people unsolicited advice is offering up criticism. According to *O, The Oprah Magazine* columnist

Martha Beck, if you're thinking of criticizing friends and family, "the professional consensus boils down to one word: don't." Beck points to research showing that "criticism wreaks havoc on trust and love" and may cause the recipient of the criticism to reflexively shift to "fight or flight" mode.

Moreover, Beck says, the instinct to criticize may be based on our own failings and frustrations. She recommends that before criticizing anyone, ask self-examining questions such as *What's motivating this critical urge?* and *How am I guilty of the thing I'm criticizing?* (Beck says that second question "never fails"—for instance, when we criticize people for being judgmental, we may be acting in a manner that is, itself, judgmental.)

It's also a good idea to consider whether the criticism you intend to offer is truly actionable or useful (otherwise, why bother?). And be honest with yourself about whether there's even a hint of enjoyment associated with offering the criticism. If so, you're doing it for the wrong reasons.

> **BEFORE YOU CRITICIZE SOMEONE, ASK YOURSELF THESE QUESTIONS**
>
> • *What's motivating this critical urge?*
> • *How am I guilty of the thing I'm criticizing?*
> • *How would I react if someone said something similar to me?*
> • *What positive result do I hope will come of saying this?*
> • *Am I deriving pleasure from criticizing?*

Criticism is sometimes disguised in the form of questions— e.g., *How could you do such a thing?* or *What were you thinking?* These "counterfeit" questions have the same negative effect as criticism because they *are* criticism, question marks notwithstanding.

Criticism is rampant in the workplace and is often expressed by way of counterfeit questions (*Why on earth did you do it that way?*) that are not truly seeking answers. But there is a need and a place at work for constructive criticism aimed at actually helping someone to do a better job or solve a problem. This can be done through a style of questioning designed to soften the edges and inject a more positive tone into questions. Known as "Appreciative Inquiry," it's an approach that emphasizes strengths over weaknesses and potential solutions over problems.

David Cooperrider, a professor at Case Western Reserve University and a pioneer of Appreciative Inquiry, says that critical questions tend to dominate workplace interactions. In business, we constantly ask, *What's the problem?*, *What's going wrong?*, *What is broken?*, *Who's to blame?* This type of question "is, unfortunately, the starting point of 80 percent of meetings in management," Cooperrider says. And he believes that when a company's questions are focused on problems and weaknesses, the organization may tend to become fixated on negative issues—rather than focusing on strengths and opportunities.

Using a more appreciative approach, a questioner would avoid asking, *What went wrong on this project?* and instead might say, *Take me through what happened on this project: What went well, what did you have problems with, and what can we learn from that going forward?*

Positive questioning becomes even more important when the tension is already high. When family feuds, workplace conflict, or political polarization create a situation wherein attempts to criticize someone or "correct" their views on an issue can make things worse, questioning can help—but it must be done carefully.

What if I replace judgment with curiosity?

Some years ago, the acclaimed playwright Lynn Nottage became interested in writing about what happens in a factory town as the jobs begin to disappear. She searched for a locale that might best encapsulate the changes and struggles of post-Industrial America, and settled on the steel town of Reading, Pennsylvania. But before writing about it, Nottage knew she needed to spend time there talking to the people of Reading face-to-face.

When she first went to Reading in 2011, she said, "I did not know anything about the city or anyone in the city—I was confronting it as very much an outsider." On the surface, she had little in common with the people she encountered there. Nottage is a female African American artist who leans to the left politically. Her interview subjects were mostly white working-class males. (One of them, she noticed, had white supremacist tattoos.) But as Nottage told the *New York Times*, "I like to replace judgment with curiosity. You tell me your story. I'm going to listen without interruption, and then decide what I think."

The people in Reading wanted to be heard. "It's surprising because I thought that there would be some resistance," said Nottage, "but I think so few people actually asked them questions, and asked them questions like, 'How are you feeling and what are you experiencing?' I found that people really sort of leaned in and responded with a level of honesty that surprised me." Nottage also found that when talking with the steel workers, "what they were saying felt very familiar and struck home with me." As she told the *New Yorker*, these laid-off workers felt helpless, ignored, and invisible. "I was sitting with these white men, and I thought, you sound like people of color in America."

The play that resulted from Nottage's research, *Sweat*, debuted off-Broadway in the fall of 2016, just as Donald Trump was elected with strong support from white working-class men like those depicted in Nottage's play. The show then moved to Broadway and was hailed as the "first theatrical landmark of the Trump era." In the spring of 2017, Nottage's play won the Pulitzer Prize. The play doesn't prescribe any easy answers to the social problems it examines—"I feel that my role as an artist isn't to come up with solutions, but to ask the right questions in the right moment," Nottage says. But as one reviewer noted, "Broadway audiences who might not have thought they could empathize with a marginalized steelworker or an opiate addict or even a strikebreaker were finding that they could."

Nottage's research motto—"replace judgment with curiosity"—is a good credo for all of us in these polarized times, a period that journalist Frank Sesno has called "the era of assertion." Just by being willing to sit with someone of a different worldview and listen—while asking the occasional empathetic question—Nottage was able to gain insight and understanding, which she could then pass along to her audiences.

It makes one wonder: What if Nottage's nonjudgmental inquisitive approach were adopted by today's bickering TV pundits? Would it result in greater understanding and empathy all around? And is there a lesson in her play *Sweat* for university students trying to shut down or shout down dissenting voices on campus? And moving still closer to home, might her message bring peace to those family dinners that seem to be blowing up in arguments these days?

During one of my university lectures on questioning, a student sent me the following desperate note afterward: *I have many family members who reside on a different side of the political aisle than I do, and it can be tough to communicate without setting each other off. I wondered if you have any advice to encourage those stuck in their ways (myself AND my family members included) to open their minds to questions about their beliefs?*

For some already in the midst of heated ideological conflict, the act of listening to and asking respectful questions of those on the other side may seem a bridge too far. But for those still interested in promoting civility and understanding, it may be the only bridge we have.

THERE IS MUCH discussion these days about political polarization, but politics isn't the only source of friction or estrangement among neighbors, co-workers, family members, and former friends. An old misunderstanding, a conflict at the office, a family disagreement—whatever the original cause of a rift, over time each side clings to a firm position or "answer" that is in conflict with the other side's "answer." Those opposing answers are likely to keep butting against each other, unless someone is willing to stop defending their position and start asking questions, driven by genuine curiosity.

In using questioning to bridge the gaps, a good place to start is with oneself. Before confronting the hostile uncle or the frosty colleague, ask yourself: *Why might I want to cross this particular divide?* While usually a worthwhile and important thing to do, make sure you're undertaking the debate for the "right" reasons. Those might include: trying to repair or strengthen a personal relationship that's important to you; trying to promote civil discourse and greater understanding among people within your circle at work, among friends, or at home; or, it could be that you want to broaden your own thinking.

As for reasons *not* to proceed: If you're planning to traverse that divide so you can convert someone on the other side to your point of view, be aware that most evidence suggests you're unlikely to succeed—and you may end up doing more harm than good to the relationship.

The questioning approaches discussed here should not be seen as a means to winning the argument. They're better used as tools to defuse the argument and encourage conversation.

In trying to gauge your own motivations, also ask yourself at the outset: *Am I really interested in learning from the other side?* Or, to make this question more open-ended and specific, *What can I learn from those I do not understand?*

As Nottage has observed, curiosity is a critical ingredient. Bring it with you as you cross over to engage with the other side. Not only does curiosity help open up your own thinking to new information, but it also signals to others that you're coming to this exchange to learn, rather than to attack or judge. You can signal your curiosity in simple ways: foremost by listening intently, but also by prefacing your own questions with phrases like, "I'm curious about something," or "I was wondering about this, and maybe you can help me understand . . ."

Researchers of curiosity have stated that it exists in the gap between what we already know and what we want to know more about—so if possible, enter a two-sided discussion about an issue after having given some open-minded thought to both sides of that issue. This is important not only in the context of political differences, but also family disagreements or ongoing difficult relationships with co-workers or estranged friends: *How might I consider both sides of this dispute?*

Is it "wishy-washy" to consider both sides of an issue? Does it put you in danger of accepting all viewpoints as equally valid, even in cases where one view might be uninformed or perhaps malevolent? In a word, no. The willingness to consider other sides is one of the bedrock principles of critical thinking.

Indeed, the best way to determine if you're on the sensible side of an issue is to thoughtfully and fairly evaluate other sides and possibilities (and to do so on an ongoing basis).

If we fail to do that, we can fall prey to "weak-sense critical thinking," in which our critical thinking faculties are used only for purposes of defending what we already believe. There is nothing that says you must accept an opposing view as reasonable or correct—you may end up, after this process, thinking the opposing position is even more wrong than you first thought. But you should be open-minded and fair-minded along the way.

How might I own my own biases?

Start by questioning your own views and beliefs on the issue at hand. In order to be able to go into a conversation with an open mind that's receptive to someone else's point of view, first try to take stock of your own positions, tendencies, and biases. In asking yourself, *Why am I on my side of the divide?*, this harkens back to the earlier discussion of Arno Penzias's "jugular" question: *Why do I believe what I believe?*

Such "self-interrogation" is useful because while you may be well aware of what your positions are, you may not have taken much time lately to consider the rationale behind them. Things may have changed since these views were first formed. *You* may have changed. Then, too, there is the possibility you might not even *know* why you feel strongly on an issue—you just do.

The author Tom Perotta tells a story about a discovery he made soon after he went off to college as a young man. He was from a working-class background and brought certain attitudes and dispositions with him—one being a tendency to make homophobic jokes. "Then one day a friend said to me, 'Why do *you* care? Why does it matter to you what someone else does in their bedroom?'" Perotta recalls. As he thought about this question, Perotta found he had no good answer, other than perhaps his own insecurities. "All it took was a few people asking me, 'Why do you think that way?'—and I changed."

It can be extremely valuable to have a "trusted other" who occasionally asks you to consider your own thinking and biases. But we may not have someone else around to question us, as Perotta did—thus the need to ask ourselves the "jugular" question.

Self-interrogation can sometimes help in detecting, or becoming slightly more aware of, biases (though, of course, biases may also be completely invisible to the person who holds them). Adam Hansen, coauthor of *Outsmart Your Instincts*, observes that to the extent we can gain a glimmer of awareness—through self-reflection, self-questioning, or experience—we should make the most of this self-knowledge. "Be humble about your biases—but also, *own* them," he says. That last point deserves its own beautiful question: *How might I own my own biases?*

If we have a sense that we tend to react to certain subjects in predictable ways, or that we lean a particular way on some issues, we can *own* that bias by acknowledging it and trying to "factor it in" when we take in new information or make new judgments. To sum it up in a question that can be asked situationally: *Knowing that I tend to lean in one direction, how might that be altering my view of this new information or situation?*

That "lean" of yours may be skewing your view of many new things you encounter. It may be attributable to your background, your history, the "media bubble" you inhabit, and the people with whom you associate. That last factor may be the most influential: "The decisions we make, the attitudes we form, the judgments we make, depend very much on what other people are thinking," says Steve Sloman, a professor of cognitive science at Brown University. Whether we care to admit it or not, our thinking is shaped by the people and the culture that surrounds us.

Hence, the psychiatrist and philosopher Iain McGilchrist believes that the question "we should be asking ourselves is, what is it that my culture is preventing me from seeing?" He suggests we must strive to look past what is obvious and clear to us—forget about what every-body around us is "banging on about," says McGilchrist—and try to see that which is obscured, and which perhaps runs counter to what you, and those around you, have been thinking all along.

WHEN YOU ARE face-to-face and asking questions of someone you disagree with, remember this rule: Don't try to persuade. As noted earlier, the problem of giving advice is bad enough. Worse still is trying to foist your opinions on others. The views people hold about various issues often become bound up with identity. When you attack those views, it can be perceived as a personal attack.

Moreover, trying to persuade people they're wrong about some-thing they strongly believe generally doesn't work. *But what if I'm heavily armed with facts to prove my case?* It still won't work, or so the research tells us. In a popular 2017 *New Yorker* article titled "Why Facts Don't Change Our Minds," Elizabeth Kolbert pulled together a number of research studies that came to similar conclu-sions: "Reasonable-seeming people are often totally irrational," particularly once they've made up their minds on a matter. Evidence doesn't sway them. And they're apt to muster all of their weak-sense critical thinking skills to try to dismantle opposing arguments. "Presented with someone else's argument, we're quite adept at spot-ting the weaknesses," Kolbert writes. "Almost invariably, the posi-tions we're blind about are our own."

Rather than trying to attack or disprove someone's strongly held position, an alternative approach is to find nonthreatening ways to ask that person to take another look at their position. Here again, "counterfeit" questions (criticism or judgment in the form of a question) don't work: To ask someone, *How in the world can you believe such a thing?* is a verbal attack—and signals to the person you're talking to that you're not really interested in under-standing their position.

A more effective approach is to start by allowing the other person to explain his position, and to try to show interest as he does. The FBI's Robin Dreeke recommends saying something along the lines of, "That's fascinating—help me understand more about this." And as the person begins to explain their view more, it's a good time to use some of the active listening techniques mentioned previously, such as paraphrasing and mirroring.

There's nothing wrong with using "critical thinking" types of questions to challenge someone to clarify or defend their views. Jay Heinrichs, an expert on rhetoric who wrote the book *Thank You for Arguing*, says it can be effective to show "aggressive interest" by asking questions that seek definition and details from someone stating a case. In asking for definition, you might ask, *When you say "freedom," how are you defining that term?*

The point is to clarify the terms of the discussion, but it serves another purpose, too: When people are "asked to define the meaning of their terms," they "tend to come up with less extreme terms," says Heinrichs. Detail-seeking questions might include, *What are the actual numbers of this epidemic you're talking about?* or *What is the source of that information?* These questions can be seen as a challenge to the speaker, so ask them calmly and politely, not in the tone of an interrogator. (Here again, phrases like "I'm curious," or "I was wondering," inserted at the beginning of the question, can work wonders in softening the tone.)

Having allowed the other person to state their case without judgment, ask for the same for yourself. ("Can I briefly lay out for you what I think?") After you've made your case, try to immediately shift the conversation to a common ground discussion, as opposed to "Let's take turns demolishing each other's arguments." Do this by using "bridge" questions that encourage people to find positive aspects and shared values within opposing arguments.

Here are two good bridge questions, borrowed (and slightly adapted) from the radio host Krista Tippett, who learned them from a guest on her show:

Can you find anything in your position that gives you pause?

Is there anything in my position that you are attracted to or find interesting?

Be sure to answer both questions yourself as well. That way, both of you are encouraged to shift positions to draw closer to each other.

You can use the same approach in talking about political candidates as opposed to issues:

You've done a nice job explaining why you support Candidate A—can you think of a couple of things you dislike about him? And while you don't support Candidate B, can you think of a couple of things about her you find worthwhile or interesting?

These types of questions encourage the other person to be more balanced in their thinking—to look for positives where they might be inclined to see only negatives, and vice versa. In cases where it seems difficult to coax someone to do this, you might try a questioning technique adapted from an area of study known as "motivational interviewing": Ask people to rate something they don't like on a scale of one to ten. For example: *On a scale of one to ten, how much of climate change do you think is true?* (One=None of it is true; ten=All of it is true.)

Researchers have found that even when people are rating something they disagree with or don't like, they rarely pick the lowest number. They're more likely to cite a low-range number like two or three. In which case, you can follow up by asking:

Why did you pick two or three, instead of the lowest number?

At this point, they'll likely offer a couple of reasons why, for example, climate change can't be *totally* written off—which means they are beginning to articulate the other side of their own argument.

Questioning can also be used to encourage people to empathize with, or step into the shoes of, a person they may have strong feelings against. Using a hypothetical "What if?" question such as, *What if you were put in charge of candidate B's campaign tomorrow—how would you encourage her to try to reach out to*

USE THESE "BRIDGE" QUESTIONS TO TRY TO MEET HALFWAY ON A DIVISIVE ISSUE

- What is it in your position that gives you pause?
- What is it in my position that interests or attracts you?
- On a scale of one to ten (one having no value at all, ten being 100 percent right and unassailable), how would you rate my position? And your own?
- If you didn't rate mine a one and yours a ten, why not?
- Can we imagine a position that might at least partly satisfy both of us?

people like you? Understanding that she's not going to come all the way to your side, how do you think she could at least come partway?

Be sure to do likewise on your end: *If I were in a position to advise candidate A on how to reach me, what would I tell him?*

This can begin to move the conversation toward "common ground" questions like these:

Can we imagine a candidate who might make both of us happy? What would a hybrid of Candidates A and B sound like? Or, if you're discussing an issue, *Can we imagine a position on this issue that might at least* partly *satisfy both of us?*

To put it in reverse-engineering terms, you could think of the desired endpoint of the conversation as this: You want to arrive at a "common ground" question along the lines of, *How might we find one small thing we can actually agree on?* Everything else in the conversation should be designed to lead to that shared question. And even if you don't come up with an answer, just getting to that question, and exploring it together, can be enlightening and productive.

"Science Guy" Bill Nye reminds us that we must be patient with those whose views differ from our own. "We tend to say, 'Look at the facts! Change your mind!' But it can take people a couple of years to change their mind." In the meantime, Nye suggests that "the way to overcome that is to say, 'We're all in this together—let's learn about this together.'" Or to quote another "science guy" from an earlier time, Carl Sagan, we must dispense with "the sense that we have a monopoly on the truth . . . that if you're sensible, you'll listen to us; and if not, you're beyond redemption." Instead, Sagan recommended we see our intellectual adversaries as "kindred spirits in a common quest."

How might we form a stronger partnership?

To ask questions of people on the other side of the divide is challenging. But it can also be hard, for very different reasons, to ask questions of and about the people close to us. Whether it's a spouse, a family member, a longtime friend, a business colleague, or maybe even a faithful customer, those near and dear to us are often taken for granted. Because we know them so well, we may feel we don't need to ask about them. But at times we would benefit by doing so.

The blogger Matthew Fray shared an interesting story on his then-obscure website a few years ago and—much to his surprise—his post was soon being passed around by millions of people worldwide. To be sure, the story had an irresistible title: "She Divorced Me Because I Left Dishes by the Sink."

Fray wrote about how his marriage broke up for a number of reasons, not least being that he had a habit of leaving an empty glass by the sink instead of moving it a few extra feet to put it in the dishwasher. To Fray, it was a trivial matter: "I don't care if a glass is sitting by the sink unless guests are coming over . . . I will never care about a glass sitting by the sink." But his wife saw it differently. As Fray eventually came to realize, it was "not about the glass"—it was about a perceived lack of respect. She'd made it clear, again and again, that this simple act mattered to her, and he continually responded by showing that he didn't care. Fray wishes he'd asked himself this question at the time: "The person I love and married is telling me over and over again that this behavior is a problem. Why don't I believe her?"

Another question he wishes he'd asked himself is an example of a "crystal ball" question: *If I knew my marriage would end painfully as a result of something I am doing or not doing, would I continue to make the same choice?*

But Fray didn't ask himself either of the above questions until it was too late. As the problems in his marriage were unfolding, the questions on his mind were rhetorical ones: *Who cares about a glass?* and *Why should it matter?* Those actually wouldn't have been bad questions if he'd asked and considered them honestly. If he had, he might have figured out that the answers were 1) Someone important to him cared; and 2) Therefore it mattered.

Based on his experience, Fray offers this advice to others in a relationship: When you and your partner disagree, try to see if you can articulate each other's feelings and perspective. Start by asking,

Can I try to explain what I think your position is—and then you can do the same for me? "Because until we can accurately present one another's arguments," Fray says, "it's probably safe to conclude that neither of us understands what the other is actually saying."

Fray's questions are all good ones, and each serves a different purpose. They could be summed up in one overarching question that might be asked, regularly, in all close relationships: *What am I missing?*

Close relationships can suffer if we fail to pay attention to what's going on right in front of us. This is one of the central points of research by the psychologist John Gottman on what makes marriages work. Gottman has studied married couples over the past forty years, and one of his key findings is that the health of a relationship is closely linked to whether partners heed each other's "bids" for attention. (A "bid," in Gottman's terms, is an attempt to make a connection, and could be as simple as one partner saying, "Look at that bird outside the window," or "I want to tell you about this interesting story I just read in the paper.")

If the bids are routinely ignored or barely acknowledged by the other partner, Gottman found, the relationship is much more likely to end in divorce. In light of Gottman's research, perhaps the first question everyone in a close relationship should begin asking themselves on a regular basis is: *Am I missing a bid?* (*Was that a bid from a loved one that I just ignored while staring at my iPhone?*)

Another question to ask is, *How should I be responding to the various bids coming from my partner?* Rote answers—*That's nice; That's interesting*—would fall into Gottman's category of "minimal response" (which is almost as bad as ignoring or "turning away"). Much better to engage with and "draw out" the bidder using

---

QUESTIONS TO ASK YOUR BEST BUD

On a long drive with her best friend, the writer Kaitlyn Wylde came up with a lengthy list of questions designed to deepen the relationship. Here are five of them.

- *What do you struggle with on a day-to-day basis?*
- *What have you always wanted to try?*
- *If you could start your own nonprofit, what would it be?*
- *What would be the title of your autobiography?*
- *If you had to live in another country for a year, where would that be?*

questions. (*Yes, that is a beautiful bird—do you know what kind it is? What do you find most interesting about that story in the paper?*)

Some bids are more important than others. When someone tells you about something that is bothering them, it's worth listening closely and inquiring about how you might be able to help. And when a partner or good friend comes bearing good news, that's just as important. Instead of merely saying "Congratulations" or "That's great," a questioner can draw out positive feelings associated with that news. Shelly Gable, a psychologist at UC Santa Barbara, refers to this as "active constructive responding" and in her research, she found it to be a critical ingredient in healthy relationships. (In bad relationships, partners tend to either ignore or downplay good news from each other.)

An "active constructive response" can be expressed through questions such as, *What was going through your mind when you heard the good news?* Using Mark Goulston's approach, you might speculate on those positive feelings as part of your question: *You must have been so proud when you heard about this—what was that like?* Another way to build on good news is to inquire about what led to it, as well as where it might lead: *What new opportunities do you think this might create for you?*

Do I want to be right or do I want peace?

When a close relationship has soured, it's a good time to step back and ask what brought things to this point and how to move forward. But here again, there's a tendency to focus on the wrong question: *Should I get a divorce (or end this friendship/partnership)?* That's a closed, "yes or no" question, and as such, may have value at some point in forcing a decision when it's time to act. But when we ask that question too soon, it closes off options. Better to start with more open-ended, exploratory questions.

Writing in the *New York Times*, Eric Copage collected eleven questions (from talking to therapists and marriage counselors) that should be asked before getting a divorce. Among them: *Have you made clear your concerns about the relationship?* (this relates back to Fray's point about better communication); and *Would you really be happier without your partner?* This is a "crystal ball" question and of course you can't really know whether you'll be happier, but the idea is to weigh potential pros and cons as you try to speculate about a future sans spouse.

And then there's the key one: *If there is a way to save the marriage, what would it be?* This is a question recommended by Reverend Kevin Wright, minister of Riverside Church in New York. I prefer a more open-ended version of the question, such as, *How might we begin to save this marriage?* (because there may be more than "one way" to do so). In trying to answer the "how to save this marriage" question, Wright suggests that each partner make a list—on one side, list what *you* need to do, on the other side, what your spouse needs to do.

There may be countless reasons why a close relationship has gone bad—perhaps too many to ponder. But sometimes it's one big thing: a disagreement, a transgression, something that never was resolved and led to an ongoing feud, or maybe just a gradual distancing. If you think (or know) you might be at least partly at fault, should you apologize? No question about it. But after saying you're sorry, consider adding on a very important "ask"—for forgiveness.

It may seem an apology is enough, but the life coach Michael Hyatt says it is much more effective to say the following three things in ten words, ending with a question mark. Start with the simple apology: *I'm sorry.* Follow with an admission: *I was wrong.* End with the question: *Will you please forgive me?* For maximum effectiveness, say all ten words. As Hyatt acknowledges, it is not easy to do, and the question at the end may be the toughest part—but also the most important. "By phrasing this as a question, we acknowledge that forgiveness is not an entitlement . . . That it is a choice on the part of the other person," Hyatt writes. Given that choice, "in my experience, almost always the other person says, 'I forgive you.'"

Sometimes ending a feud is not so much about forgiving as forgetting—just being willing to let go of the past and the need to be proven "right." That can be hard to do because, as cognitive scientist Steve Sloman points outs, "We have a primitive instinct to prove that we're right."

However, being proven right about an old dispute is not likely to happen. (It's about as probable as the likelihood that you'll persuade somebody to change their political views.) As Oprah Winfrey has written, "Proving I was right used to be a major character flaw." She says it cost her precious time with friends and loved ones by prolonging fights and misunderstandings.

She eventually changed her ways, and notes that "a single question got me started: *Do you want to be right, or do you want peace?*" It's a good question for warring friends—and maybe warring countries, too—to keep in mind.

Can questioning help us connect in the workplace?

If asking the right questions can build trust and rapport with strangers at a party or with family members at home, it can do likewise with coworkers at the office. And yet, our hesitancy to ask questions may be even greater at work than it is in our personal lives. One reason is that business environments have traditionally been hierarchical in structure—and questions, by their nature, can be seen as a challenge to hierarchical authority. This issue seems to come up at almost every company I visit, with managers and employees alike wondering: *How can I ask questions of co-workers without overstepping bounds or putting them on the defensive?*

Before we get into *how* to ask questions at work, consider *why* it's important to do so. First, it enables you to be better at your job, regardless of what it may be. It can also help you collaborate more effectively with colleagues. And if your work involves dealing with clients, customers, or anyone outside the walls of the company, it can help you to better understand those people, satisfy their needs, and persuade them to do business (or keep doing business) with you.

Starting with the first point, you can't do your job well unless you are able to ask, continuously and through various expressions, the following two questions: *What is my job?* and *How might I do it better?*

One might assume that first question is needed only when first starting a job, and then never again. But in fact, the nature of work is changing so rapidly that we must constantly ask the question again and again: *Given all the changes yesterday, what is my job today?* Experienced employees and managers may be reluctant to do this because they think they already know how to do their work. They may see little need to question established methods and work habits, even in times of rapid change.

Experienced people may also consider it risky to ask fundamental questions about their work—fearing that it could be perceived by management as a sign of incompetence. While that's an understandable concern, there are ways to mitigate that risk—and reasons to believe the benefits may outweigh the risks. Having spoken with a number of top executives at various types of companies, I've found most of them are keenly aware of the need for change throughout all levels of their organizations—and one of their primary concerns today is that mid-level managers and front-line employees may not be willing or able to change. Within these organizations, management likely would be relieved and enthused to see employees questioning the established ways of doing things. From what I'm seeing, leaders are more apt to appreciate and reward questioning than to punish it.

When "questioning up"—meaning, asking questions of someone at a higher level—you can increase the likelihood that your questions will be well received by managers if you question with a certain level of respect. Don't use questions to challenge authority or to complain. If a subordinate asks a manager, *Why do we have to do this particular task?* or *Why are we still using this old equipment?*, it can come across as a challenge or a complaint (or both).

To avoid that, start by doing some homework on the issue you're inquiring about. Ask yourself questions before asking a manager:

Why are certain procedures and practices in place? Why is that old equipment still in use? What might be the benefits and costs of making a change (to policies or equipment) and how difficult would it be to do that? Having thought about these issues, and perhaps gathered some relevant facts, the employee can then ask questions that are more informed. The question can be framed as an issue you're interested in and a possibility you're wondering about: As in, *I've been thinking a lot about issue X, and something I was surprised to learn is fact Y. It makes me wonder, do you think should we be looking into possibility Z?*

Even if you don't have a specific idea for a possible change, you can frame a question to indicate that you're open to change—and that you're paying attention to the forces that may be having an impact on your job. For example: *I have noticed that our competitors are using new software that enables them to move much more quickly. I'm wondering how we might adapt to this—and whether there's anything specific that I can do differently in my role?*

When "questioning up," one of the best ways to show respect—and learn important information from managers—is to ask for advice. Previously, we discussed the dangers of *giving* unwanted advice to others; asking for advice is very different. As Wharton's Adam Grant points out, people are usually flattered when you ask them for advice, and managers are no exception. When you ask a manager for advice, you're often making her job a little easier—because you're providing a welcome opening for that manager to give you constructive criticism.

One of the most common ways to solicit advice is to ask, *What would you do in my position?* And that question works in many situations. But there are some interesting variations on it that can be even more effective in helping a manager tell you how to do a better job. Wanda Wallace, a workplace coach and CEO of Leadership Forum, recommends asking your boss, *What does your ideal employee look like?* This question allows the manager to offer constructive criticism in an indirect way, which can be easier on all parties.

Another question shared by Wallace: *What's the one thing if I did it differently would make a difference to you?* Katherine Crowley of K Squared Enterprises puts an interesting tweak on this question: She thinks you should regularly ask your boss, *What is most important on your list to accomplish today—and is there any way I can help?* Both of these questions focus on the manager's key needs and priorities, while making clear that you're interested in more than just doing your own job and you're an available resource. Crowley notes that, "People above you are often juggling multiple tasks and their priorities keep shifting." It's hard to know what they might need most from you at any given time unless you ask.

> **QUESTIONS THAT YOUR BOSS WILL LOVE**
>
> - *What would you do in my position?*
> - *What does your ideal employee look like?*
> - *What's the one thing that, if I did it differently, would make a difference to you?*
> - *What is most important on your list to accomplish today—and is there any way I can help?*

Why is it hard for managers to "question down"?

If employees can benefit by learning to "question up," managers can do likewise by learning to "question down." Many simply are not used to asking interested, authentic questions of people at a lower level. As managers, they may feel their role is to tell, not ask—that can include telling people how to do their jobs, what they're doing wrong, why their performance isn't good enough. When managers do this "it reminds the employee who is in charge," says Cathy Littlefield, chair of the business department at Peirce College. "The power a manager gets from the act of criticizing feeds their ego." But it also can wreak havoc on employee morale.

Certainly, there are times and situations when it is appropriate for a manager to tell someone to do something or to criticize that person's work. But in those situations, questioning can be used to soften the blow and get a better result. And in a general sense, questions can help build a stronger bond with employees—while also helping the manager figure out how to do a better job of managing.

Starting with a situation where an employee might need constructive criticism—something has gone wrong, the job isn't being done as well as it might be—a manager can use questioning to "lead the horse to water." By asking questions such as *Are you satisfied with your own performance?* and *What do you think is working well, and what is not?*, the manager can encourage the employee to identify and articulate problems. Then, following the "guided questions" approach described earlier in this chapter (see the box "Use these questions to help someone figure it out for themselves" on page 121), the manager can lead the employee to begin to think about ways to solve the problem.

Even before work problems surface, managers can use questions to gauge whether people are interested and engaged in their work (a critical issue in the workplace these days: Gallup studies have found that only 30 percent of workers feel "fully engaged" in their jobs). By asking questions such as *What do you* not *have time to work on, that you'd like to be working on?*, a manager can determine what might be getting in the way of someone being fully engaged or doing their best work.

One of the most important questions any manager can ask their employees is: *What questions do you have for me?* If you draw a blank with that question—and you may, because it's unexpected and broad—trying adding some specificity: *Anything you'd like to know about the new policy we're implementing? Or about where we envision this company or this division five years from now?* As a manager, you don't have to have a ready answer for every question—the most important thing is to be receptive to questions, and take them seriously. It's fine to say, *That's an interesting question—I don't have an answer right now, but I'll give it some thought and get back to you.*

Like the people reporting to them, managers should try to ask questions in a non-confrontational way. Standing over a subordinate's desk and barking, *What are you working on?* or *Why are you doing it that way?* can be interpreted as criticism even if it's not intended to be.

How to avoid confrontational questions? The best answer comes down to a word: "curiosity." Questions that are rooted in curiosity tend to be received in a better way. And this can be particularly valuable for managers: If they can convey a sense of curiosity about the people working for them, it lessens the sting sometimes associated with asking questions about someone's work. Again, it can be a simple matter of putting the words "I'm curious" at the beginning of an inquiry: *I'm curious, why did you choose to do it this way?* But this needs to be expressed authentically to generate a useful conversation.

As the FBI's Robin Dreeke observes, questioning works best if you are willing to suspend ego and just "seek someone else's thoughts without judging them."

Curious questions can also show an employee that you're interested in more than just their output. According Dr. Jim Harter, Gallup's chief scientist of workplace management and well-being, today's most effective managers must be able to show they care about and understand the people working for them. One way to do that is by using "open and deep" questions in routine interactions. Instead of asking rote questions (*How's it going?*, *Having a busy day today?*) and quickly moving on to the next cubicle, a deeper connection can be formed by asking questions such as *What's the coolest thing you'll be working on this week? What are you excited about in your job right now?*

"Open and deep" questions also can improve relations between co-workers, enabling you to inquire about what your colleagues care about and where their interests and passions lie. Do you need or even want to know all of that? That's a judgment call based on the person and situation—some co-workers may be best kept on a "How's it going?" basis.

But in work situations where collaboration and teamwork are critical, bonding between workmates may be important. For that, you can use many of the relationship-building questions listed previously in this chapter. Most, with a bit of tweaking, work as

QUESTIONS TO ASK ABOUT A CO-WORKER
YOU REALLY CAN'T STAND

- *Is it possible I'm overreacting?* (Get an "outside view" by describing the situation to a trusted co-worker.)
- *Drill down: Which of this person's specific behaviors most bother me?*
- *Of those, which actually interfere with my ability to do my job?*
- *Of those, which are changeable?*
- *Is there a way to politely ask this person to make one change?*
- *Who could mediate?* (Ideally someone who is known and trusted by both parties.)
- *How might I create distance?* (If possible, move to another desk; if not, consider headphones.)

well in the office as they do at cocktail parties or at home.

One point about questioning and office colleagues: If you're dealing with a truly difficult co-worker, questions might be able to help find common ground; refer to the "bridge" questions cited earlier. But in a situation like that, it's also important to ask yourself a set of questions (in the accompanying box) that can help you determine how to react and adapt to a difficult person from whom there may be no easy escape.

What if we replace the sales pitch with a "question pitch"?

The questions asked within the company's walls are important. But so are the ones taken to the outside world by those representing the company. For businesses, perhaps the most basic way to connect with customers and clients is by being willing to ask, on a regular basis, *What does the world need from us?*

This has always been a "starter" question in business. Many companies are founded and formed as an attempt to answer that question. But in today's business landscape, with customer needs constantly shifting and evolving, a responsive company must keep asking that question again and again. Most often, it is being asked by the people on the frontlines—sales reps, customer service staff, field researchers, and the like. Their critical function is to serve as the company's "chief questioners," though they may not realize that.

Salespeople, for example, are in an ideal position to use questioning to better understand and connect with the lifeblood of the company: its customers. In the past, many salespeople believed their job was to sell, pitch, promise, badger, persuade, and try just about anything *except* asking honest questions. But increasingly, experts on selling are finding that asking questions can be one of the most effective tools in the sales arsenal. Adam Grant of the Wharton School points to research showing that those who listen and ask questions tend to bring in far more revenue than those doing a hard sell.

As to why that's the case, Grant explains, "When people feel you're trying to influence them they put their guard up." But asking questions allows a relationship to build. Grant points to the story of Bill Grumbles, an inexperienced salesman sent to open a regional office for HBO back in the company's early days. Grumbles's approach was to visit customers' offices, look around at the pictures on the walls, and begin asking questions about whatever he saw. He soon became known as a great conversationalist—and a top salesman for HBO. "There was something about this approach of selling by asking questions, as opposed to giving answers, that really worked," Grant says.

Grumbles was creating a rapport with his customers—a great starting point for any salesperson—but a skillful salesperson can use questioning to go well beyond that. The goal is to inspire someone to think of their own reasons why they might want to work with your company or use your products. Daniel Pink, author of *To Sell Is Human*, says: "This is axiomatic in sales and persuasion: When people have their own reasons for doing something—not *your* reasons—they tend to believe those reasons more deeply."

Pink has talked about ditching the sales pitch for a "question pitch"—in which questions are used to encourage the sales prospect to think more deeply about their business problems and explore possibilities. In this capacity, the salesperson steps away from being a "persuader" and takes on a role more like that of a consultant or collaborator. And when that happens, rather than pitching to someone on the other side of a desk, there's a sense of being on the same side as the customer—working together on a collaborative question, along the lines of: *How might we put our heads together to solve this problem your company is having?*

Ideally, the salesperson's offering will be part of the solution, though not necessarily. As Pink has noted, when the seller has transitioned to this more collaborative role, the objective begins to focus more on building a long-term business relationship than making a short-term sale.

If the new rule of selling is "Ask, don't sell," this same rule, adapted slightly, works for all types of business consultants, too— think of it as, "Ask, don't tell." This may seem counterintuitive, because we think of a consultant as someone whose primary function is to give professional advice. But the pioneering business consultant Peter Drucker understood, long ago, that he could best serve clients by asking questions. Drucker said that many company leaders tended to come to him seeking answers to their business problems. However, Drucker's reasoning was that these leaders actually knew far more than he did about their own businesses. They didn't need an outsider with less knowledge of the business to tell them what to do. Instead, they needed someone who could bring an "outside view" to the challenges at hand, ask the questions that weren't being asked (because the company insiders were too close to the problems and too steeped in their own expertise), and in so doing, help these business leaders to come up with their own answers.

Ideally, an organization's questions should flow in all directions: with employees questioning up, managers questioning down, and ambassadors of that company carrying questions to the outside world. It is up to the leader of the organization to ensure that questions freely move up, down, outward, and especially, inward. The leader must be the one to look into the heart and soul of any type of organization or collective and ask, *What is our mission and purpose? Why are we here?*

As we'll see in the next chapter, a new model of leadership is taking hold these days, rooted in the notion that one can, and should, lead by questioning. It is a fundamental change that will impact not just top business executives, but anyone leading—or aspiring to lead—an initiative, a community, a cause, a school, a team, a family. The same powerful questioning tool that enables us to connect with other people can also help us bring those people together and rally them around a larger mission and a shared sense of purpose.

PART IV
Questions for Stronger
LEADERSHIP

"What can we do to right this wrong?"

In 2015, as the eighth-grade student Vidal Chastanet was walking outside his school one day in the Brooklyn neighborhood of Browns-ville, he stopped briefly to answer a question posed to him by a curious stranger. The man asked Chastanet: "Who has influenced you most in your life?"

The boy thought for a moment, then gave a surprising answer. The person who had most influenced him was not a star athlete or storybook hero, not even a parent or teacher. It was the principal of his school, a forty-year-old woman named Nadia Lopez.

"When we get in trouble, she doesn't suspend us," Vidal explained. "She tells us that each time somebody fails out of school, a new jail cell gets built." And one time, Chastanet added, Ms. Lopez "made every student stand up, one at a time, and she told each one of us that we matter."

The curious stranger who had asked the question, Brandon Stanton, took note of Chastanet's reply, snapped his picture, and shared the story on his popular Facebook page, *Humans of New York*. Within days, Vidal and his principal, Ms. Lopez were "Internet famous." And suddenly, many people became aware of what Chastanet and fellow students at his public school already knew: There was a powerful leader walking the halls of Mott Hall Bridges Academy each day.

To see Lopez in action at the school is to see what a "questioning leader" looks like. Mingling with students throughout much of the day, she tries to engage with as many of them as she can, often stopping to look a child in the eyes as she asks questions. Encountering a boy who has been removed from class because of a conflict, Lopez pulls him aside. She doesn't waste time on judgmental "What'd you do and why'd you do it?" questions. She prefers the kinds that prod thinking and problem solving. At one point, Lopez asks him, "What can we do to right this wrong?" The boy ponders that before offering, "Say I'm sorry?" Lopez nods, and says: "It's so simple—you knew the answer."

Lopez, a former nurse who became the founding principal of Mott Hall Bridges Academy in 2010, told me that she learned long ago to use diagnostic questions to try to uncover what might be wrong with a patient. She uses questions similarly with her students: *If they're acting out, what does that really mean? What might be the root cause (could it be a problem at home, or something the child witnessed in the neighborhood)?* Having diagnosed a problem, she uses questions to guide students as they think for themselves about a potential solution.

In classes at Mott Hall Bridges Academy, students are taught to question one another—albeit gently, respectfully. Lopez says that in many underprivileged homes, children don't have as much opportunity to learn how to engage in thoughtful conversation—to express opinions or ask considered questions. "So we show them how to do that here," she says. It's part of the overall mission of the school—posted in signs on the walls—to create "an environment where inquiry is used to develop critical thinkers." To reinforce the message that this school aims to produce lifelong learners, Lopez refers to all of her students as "scholars"—she wants them to think of themselves that way.

It's unusual for a school principal to have such direct and close contact with students. (Lopez even shares her cell phone number with her scholars.) "Teachers at other schools tell me, 'I don't see the principal of my school that much,'" Lopez says. She believes that's almost a dereliction of duty: "If you're the leader, you must lead—you must show your face."

"Just by being present, that holds people accountable," Lopez says. "It says to the teachers, 'You have no excuses, because the principal is just as involved and working just as hard as you are.' And it tells both the teachers and the scholars that this really matters to me."

When Lopez is not roaming the hallways or stopping in at classrooms, she is apt to steal a quiet moment away from the action to think about the larger goals and challenges for her school and its teachers and scholars. She has a vision of the school as a place that doesn't just educate, but actually transforms the way underprivileged young people think about themselves, their circumstances, and the possibilities available to them. During those few quiet moments, Lopez grapples with big, difficult questions. *What is the twenty-first century demanding of these kids, and how can the school provide that? How do you instill a sense of possibility in young people living amid poverty and hopelessness? How do you keep underpaid, overworked teachers from burning out?*

IN SOME WAYS, Nadia Lopez may seem like a throwback—to a cozier time when teachers and even the school principals knew their students by name and inquired about the folks at home. But Lopez also can be seen as a model for a new kind of leadership—not just in schools, but in business, government, and beyond. There are different strains of this new approach and different names attached to it. ("Servant leadership" is among the more popular labels right now.) One way to think about this new type of leader is as a "visionary helper"—a leader who not only charts a course for others to follow but also does whatever it takes (a nudge, a kind word, a supportive gesture) to get them moving in the right direction.

A "visionary helper" tends to exhibit a number of qualities we may not necessarily associate with leadership, including humility, curiosity, and open-mindedness. And such leaders often rely on a skill that was never, until recently, considered critical (or even appropriate) for those in power: the willingness and ability to ask the right questions at the right times.

Doing so enables a new generation of leaders to continually learn, anticipate change, envision new possibilities, empathize, and communicate. Such leaders are comfortable with inward-looking questions—about their own values, judgments, strategies, plans for the future, and even core beliefs. And they're just as adept at asking questions directed outward, toward the people all around them—doing so in a manner that puts people at ease, elicits valuable information, and even provides inspiration to those on the receiving end of those questions.

This new model of leadership can be applied in many contexts and situations, and doesn't necessarily require a plush corner office or a CEO title. A "visionary helper" could be a teacher, parent, community activist, team captain, sales manager, inspirational blogger or thought leader, or anyone who endeavors to rally others around a common goal.

It's a style of leadership that matches up well with the challenges and demands of a "VUCA environment," a term borrowed from military commanders and commonly used these days to describe a world in which all types of leaders must contend with unprecedented "volatility," "uncertainty," "complexity," and "ambiguity." In such circumstances, being "visionary" (which involves trying to anticipate what's coming and designing plans accordingly) is a constant test of imagination and cognitive agility.

The old image of leader as the one who has all the answers (or at very least, an unfailing "gut instinct") simply doesn't hold up in the age of VUCA. What is emerging instead is a profile of a new leader able to continually question those instincts, while seeking out conflicting information and diverse viewpoints. "Today's leader must be a flexible thinker," says the leadership consultant Angie Morgan of the firm Lead Star. Indeed, that new leader must be a *thinker*, period—willing to step away from meetings and cluttered schedules to quietly reflect, consider, and question.

While changing the ways they think, new leaders must also adjust some of the ways they relate to and interact with the people around them. The old "command and control" approach doesn't inspire the kind of company-wide independent thinking and collaboration that is now needed. In the VUCA environment, leadership "is more about influence than control," says David B. Peterson, director of executive coaching and leadership at Google. The leader today can't just order the troops to charge up that hill—they must inspire, coach, and otherwise support them in the effort. To do so, leaders need to build rapport and trust. They must be able to empathize with, and communicate to, a more diverse culture of followers, including people very different from themselves. They must understand—and in order to be able to understand, they must be open-minded questioners.

This is not, however, the reality among many of today's leaders—at least not according to the available evidence. In the real world, we are in the midst of a leadership crisis. That's the view of 86 percent of those surveyed by the World Economic Forum, and it's not hard to understand why so many people feel that way. That crisis manifests itself in scandals among chief executives and politicians, in failing schools, in corporate malfeasance and government shutdowns, and in ongoing failures to prevent (or even adequately respond to) problems ranging from humanitarian crises to rampant sexual harassment in the workplace. In the words of Deborah Ancona, director of the MIT Leadership Center, "The recent past has showcased a leadership stage featuring Greek tragedies filled with leaders who are toxic and corrupt, out of touch and unable to act."

Interestingly, this failure of leadership has come at a time when there is more available information on leadership than ever before—a veritable glut of leadership advice, dispensed in hundreds of thousands of books, articles, and blogs on the subject; an endless cycle of "Eight Things Every Leader Should Do," "Six Leadership Pitfalls to Avoid," "Seven Leadership Lessons to Learn from Steve Jobs," and so forth.

Given that there is so much available knowledge on leadership—so many answers to the questions of "how to be a leader" at our fingertips—why aren't we seeing better results? And moreover, to quote Nadia Lopez, *What can we do to right this wrong?*

DOUGLAS CONANT, A former Campbell Soup chief executive who now heads his own leadership firm, believes that becoming a better leader is an "inside out" process. By this he means one must begin by thinking about and working through some fundamental questions for oneself—without necessarily relying too much on the latest tips and tricks from blog posts or TED Talks. As Conant sees it, the challenge, at least initially, is not to find out what everyone else thinks about leadership, but to clarify what *you* think—about why you want to lead, what matters to you above all else, and how you might start to develop and articulate your own philosophy and strategies. This hard work can help form a solid foundation of values and approaches that will support the leader as she begins to actually do the work.

But most leaders don't do that intellectual groundwork, Conant says. Many ascend without thinking about what awaits them at the top. They rise by way of some combination of productivity, ambition, and deft maneuvering. To quote the author William Deresiewicz, our leaders often become leaders simply because they are able to "climb the greasy pole of whatever hierarchy they decide to attach themselves to."

Having arrived at a position of power—and being unsure what to do next—they begin to practice what Conant calls "seat of the pants leadership." They may take training courses or speed read through some of that vast leadership literature, but the "outside" advice doesn't stick because they haven't done the "inside" work.

"Seat of the pants" leadership has always been a problem, but that's even more the case today, Conant says. The pressures of the VUCA environment cause crises to develop more quickly, and if leaders aren't prepared—because they haven't given enough advance thought to the challenges—they can quickly compound the problems. "They end up cutting corners to make shareholders happy, or spinning half-truths to temporarily placate employees," Conant says, until the whole house of cards comes tumbling down.

So how does a leader, or one who aspires to lead, avoid this trap? Conant and others advise beginning with a few simple yet critical questions.

Why do I choose to lead?

As I've noted previously, it's often wise to begin with the "Why?," and that's certainly true when thinking about leadership. Fundamental "Why?" questions, pertaining to motivation, rationale, and purpose, should be the starting point, but often are not. Conant says it's common for aspiring leaders to be focused on what they hope to *get* from being a leader (status, glory, money) without thinking about what they'll have to *give up* by committing to leading and helping others.

More specifically, aspiring leaders often don't spend enough time considering whether there is a greater purpose driving their leadership aspirations—or clarifying what that purpose might be. The demands of leadership now are so great that unless one is driven by a sense of purpose that transcends personal ambition—and unless one enjoys the actual day-to-day work of engaging with and leading others—the pursuit may not prove satisfying or sustainable in the long run.

If many of those chasing leadership positions are driven by personal ambition alone, we can blame that, at least in part, on our educational system, observes Susan Cain, author of the book *Quiet*. In a *New York Times* essay, Cain noted that universities, and the students entering them, have become extremely focused on leadership. (The schools want to be seen as institutions that produce leaders, while the students all want to become leaders.) But as Cain points out, both sides seem to be defining leadership in shallow terms—based on how many achievements a student can list or the number of clubs that student has become president of. This creates the sense that the overall objective is "to be a leader for the sake of being in charge, rather than in the name of a cause or idea [the student cares] about deeply."

Noting that the world needs leaders who are called to service rather than to status, Cain offered up a beautiful question: *What if we said to our would-be leaders, 'Take this role only if you care desperately about the issue at hand'?*

To reframe Cain's challenge as a "self-question," anyone considering a leadership role in any organization or undertaking might want to first ask, *Why do I want to lead this endeavor or these people—and why would they want me to lead them?*

> **BEFORE TAKING ON A LEADERSHIP CHALLENGE, ASK**
>
> • *Why do I want to lead this endeavor?*
> • *Why would others want me to lead them?*
> • *Does the answer to the first question also work as an answer to the second?* If not, your reasons for wanting to lead may be too self-serving.

If you have a worthwhile answer for the first half of the question, it may apply to the second half as well. For example, Nadia Lopez feels that helping the children of Mott Hall Bridges Academy is a higher calling for her and the teachers. "I tell my teachers that we are chosen to be here because we're supposed to transform a community that doesn't believe in themselves," Lopez says.

That makes clear why she would want to lead this particular school—and why the students and teachers would want her to lead them (who wouldn't want a leader with that kind of conviction?). On the other hand, if Lopez's answer to the first part of the question was more along the lines of *I feel I'm entitled after all these years to be the principal of this school* or *I need the pay raise*, that would be a poor answer to the second part of the question.

Before considering why you'd want to lead a particular organization, the real "starter" question is one that can be applied more generally: *Why do I choose to lead?* The question is designed to force aspiring leaders to really think about what's driving them to pursue a leadership challenge. Conant recommends breaking down the question into a number of others including: *How do you want to leverage your special gifts and interests to make the world a better place?*

The key is to make sure the reasons why you want to lead—perhaps based on your interests, passions, strengths—are aligned with the challenges and everyday realities of being a leader in today's marketplace. Wanting to lead is one thing; being ready or able to do so is quite another.

To this end, four key questions can help determine if you're up to the demands of being a twenty-first-century leader. Starting with the most important one, aspiring leaders should inquire about their own willingness to be helpful. Those with a natural interest in helping others to reach their potential are well-suited to lead in today's environment. Those more focused on their own achievements and goals may be less so.

Indeed, this speaks to what may be the greatest adjustment for high achievers attempting to transition to a leadership role. As Conant puts it, "When you become a leader, it's not about 'you' anymore." Lead Star's Angie Morgan says that many of the executives she coaches were promoted to leadership roles because they excelled at various task-driven, results-oriented jobs within their organizations—which made them rising "stars."

But upon assuming a leadership role, Morgan says, they have had to shift their entire focus and approach. "They were used to being 'doers,' but now they are expected to focus more on building relationships." That often involves more delegation of the work people may love doing, more sharing of responsibility, and a willingness to let others shine as the top performers and producers.

Some overachievers have trouble making that transition. Research by the Hay Group focused on overachievers who become leaders and found they "tend to command and coerce rather than coach and collaborate, thus stifling subordinates," and "may be oblivious to the concerns of others."

With that in mind, aspiring leaders should ask themselves whether they're truly ready to shift from performing to leading. Rather than thinking of leadership as the ultimate starring role in an organization, the question to ask is: *Am I willing to step back from individual achievement—in order to help others move forward?*

The notion that a leader's first and foremost job is to help others succeed is not entirely new. But it has gained much wider acceptance with the growing "servant leadership" movement. Spearheaded by the business guru Robert Greenleaf, the philosophy dictates that a leader should "first make sure that other people's highest priority needs are being served."

In terms of an overall goal, the "servant leader" is advised to try to do several things: help people within the organization to succeed at their jobs; prepare them to become leaders themselves; and simultaneously try to find ways to serve a larger community, beyond the organization.

Morgan, who served as an officer in the Marine Corps before cofounding the Lead Star consultancy, points out that service-based leadership has its roots in the military—where leaders are expected to prepare others to become leaders themselves (on the rationale that the current leader could be lost in battle at any time, and others must be prepared to step forward). Morgan says that military leaders also learn, in the field, that the unit depends—sometimes in life-or-death terms—on each person being capable of succeeding in their role. This incentivizes leaders to do the work necessary to help everyone in the unit improve their skills.

But bringing this kind of service-oriented, relationships-based leadership approach into the business world isn't easy, Morgan and others concede. The notion of a leader as an on the ground "helper" runs counter to the more remote, "command and control" approach favored by many high-powered officials and executives. It requires close contact. It calls for "softer" skills, such as listening, effective communication, and coaching. And it demands another quality that appears to be in short supply in many leadership circles—humility.

Do I have the confidence to be humble?

Research shows that leaderless groups "have a natural tendency to elect self-centered, overconfident and narcissistic individuals as leaders," observes the organizational psychologist Tomas Chamorro-Premuzic, explaining that we "commonly misinterpret displays of confidence as a sign of competence." (And men are usually the beneficiaries of this error, wrote Chamorro-Premuzic in an essay headlined "Why Do So Many Incompetent Men Become Leaders?")

Overconfidence breeds hubris, which can then infect an organization's culture. The consultants Jonathan Mackey and Sharon Toye, who have studied "executive hubris," say the problem often begins with leaders who "exude confidence" (as they are expected and often trained to do), which then manifests in other, more harmful behaviors by the leader—including a tendency to micromanage, to blame others when things go wrong, to treat disagreement as a personal slight, to flout rules, and to engage in self-glorification.

> **TO DETERMINE IF YOU'RE READY TO BE A TWENTY-FIRST-CENTURY LEADER, ASK**
>
> - *Am I willing to step back in order to help others move forward?* Many aspiring leaders are rising stars and high performers, but success as a leader will depend more on helping others achieve success.
> - *Do I have the confidence to be humble?* The balance is to be humble enough to admit you don't have all the answers—while being confident that you can help the organization to figure them out.
> - *Can I learn to keep learning?* Rising uncertainty means today's leaders cannot rely on their own expertise. They must be restless learners.
> - *Do I seek to create an organization in my own image?* Too many leaders surround themselves with similar people, depriving the organization of the diverse thinking needed to be successful today.

Such behaviors by leaders have never been desirable, but today they're an almost surefire recipe for failure—because they tend to work against the increasingly critical needs for innovation, employee engagement and retention, and collaboration. Nevertheless, leaders still must "exude confidence" in order to instill faith in followers. So the balancing act for today's leaders is to be confident yet humble: willing to question one's own judgments, to defer to the needs of others, and share credit, while also projecting a sense of authority, boldness, and a belief in oneself. As Conant puts it: "I must be willing to admit I may not have the answer . . . but at the same time be confident I can help all of us to *find* the answers." Which can be boiled down to a second question that every aspiring leader should ask: *Do I have the confidence to be a humble leader?*

A third question for aspiring leaders involves the U in VUCA: "uncertainty." To be a leader today is to decide you are not just willing to tolerate uncertainty, but to embrace it. In the past, a leader might have been able to develop a strategy and approach to running an organization, then ride on that for years—just keep doing what got you to this point. Because of rapid change, what worked before may not work now, and what works now may not work tomorrow. So today's leaders must constantly shift tactics and change direction—which can be difficult for anyone, even a Silicon Valley entrepreneur like Airbnb cofounder Brian Chesky. "I've had to embrace the fact that I'm constantly going to be in uncharted waters, and I'm constantly going to be doing something I've never done before," Chesky told the *New York Times*, adding that he "had to learn to get comfortable in a role of ambiguity." To succeed in those uncertain circumstances, he said, "the most important thing I've learned how to do is learn." Which gives us the third key question for aspiring leaders: *Can I learn to keep learning?*

To do that, a leader must avoid relying on old ideas and strategies—even the successful ones. Roselinde Torres of the Boston Consulting Group says that today's leaders must ask, *Am I courageous enough to abandon the past?* While moving away from the old, leaders must constantly experiment with the new—by being willing to roll out and test ideas quickly, and change or scrap them just as quickly.

A learning leader also must indulge—and continually feed—one's own curiosity. As with questioning, curiosity was not traditionally thought of as a leadership trait. Today it is being recognized, in a recent PriceWaterhouse study and elsewhere, as a top leadership quality for the twenty-first century. For those wondering, *How might I stimulate my own curiosity?*, John Marshall, chief strategy officer at the creative consultancy Lippincott, suggests looking at everything from your daily schedule to the people you interact with, and asking: *Do I surround myself with inspiring, sometimes even odd, big thinkers? Is my schedule packed with meetings and daily decisions, or freed to explore new frontiers? Do I use every interaction, from the colleague to the driver, to ask new people about how they think and feel?*

Marshall's point about the importance of exposure to diverse influences raises another point about the changing demands of twenty-first-century leadership—and brings us to the last key question for aspiring leaders. Too often, leaders in the past have had a tendency to surround themselves with others who look and think just like them—which can lead to a number of problems. One is that the leader ends up in a homogeneous bubble and doesn't get exposed to a full range of viewpoints and influences when formulating strategies or trying to assess what's happening outside that bubble.

Roselinde Torres notes that being in a bubble can limit the leader's ability to anticipate change. She says that having a diverse network helps in identifying trends and cultural patterns, so every leader must ask, *Am I bringing together diverse people who can share points of view that I might be missing?*

A study by Deloitte found that diverse organizations perform better—but the study also found diversity is seen as one of the *least* urgent issues among most senior leaders. "It's an interesting paradox that diversity correlates to higher performance and yet senior leaders are not taking it very seriously," says Google's David Peterson.

Why the ongoing resistance among leaders to fostering diversity? "We often hear about good ol' boy networks. . . . But to some extent we all have a network of people we're comfortable with," says Torres. And one of the perks of leadership is that leaders get to hire and promote the people they "like," which often consists of people like them—whether it be people of the same gender, race, class, age, or personality type (as in, the extrovert who only wants to work with other extroverts). Leaders who aspire to create a comfortable club of likeminded pals should pause and ask the fourth key question to determine if they're twenty-first-century leadership material: *Am I seeking to create an organization in my own image?* If the answer is yes, start an "ol' boys" club on your own time, but don't put those limits on an organization that needs as much diverse thinking as it can get.

Having considered the four "starter" questions exploring whether you're aspiring to leadership for the right reasons—and assuming the answers come up positive—it's only the beginning of the leadership questioning process. Much of subsequent questioning will happen face-to-face with others, in constant ongoing interactions. But there are still a few more "self-questions" that can guide you as you begin to form a distinct leadership philosophy and strategy. These must be considered alone, and require deep thought and adequate time.

Why must I retreat in order to lead?

When you're the leader, there are endless demands on your time. There's always a decision to be made, a problem that needs solving, an urgent phone call that can't wait.

With all of those pressures, can a leader find time to slow down and think? Just ask Warren Buffett. "I insist on a lot of time being spent, almost every day, just to sit and think," Buffett has said. His business partner, Charlie Munger, says there are days on Buffett's schedule marked simply "haircut day," with nothing else scheduled. On those days, Buffett gets his hair cut—and leaves the rest of the day clear for thinking.

There's a good reason why successful leaders like Buffett set aside time for thinking. According to research by the Boston Consulting Group, "Reflection leads to better insights into innovation, strategy and execution." For leaders who spend much of their time putting out fires, it is critical, BCG maintains, to find time to stop responding and problem solving in order to allow the mind to work in a different way—connecting thoughts, searching for meaning, trying to get at underlying issues, envisioning future possibilities. This type of reflective thinking enables a leader to "clarify the big picture."

It also prepares the leader to respond more effectively to the unexpected challenges that may arise, says Doug Conant. "Reflection is absolutely critical for a leader because it helps you to be well-anchored in your principles. When change comes, you don't want to be responding on your heels." Dedicating set times for reflection is a way of doing your hard thinking in advance, so that you can then "lead on demand."

But how do you find the time? Deep thought and reflection are often squeezed out of the schedule by more pressing demands. The only solution is to schedule time for regular reflection and then protect it from being bumped. It can be scheduled early in the day, late, or anywhere between. "When leaders say they don't have time to think, that's BS," says Conant. "Get up an hour earlier if you must." Conant notes that he developed an early-morning ritual of reflecting on critical questions and ideas while having coffee in his garden. "You can always engineer the time somehow, but you have to have discipline about protecting that time."

Ideally, you want to carve out enough time—an hour, say—to allow for deep uninterrupted thinking and for capturing thoughts and ideas by writing them down. But reflection can also happen in shorter increments—"it is something you can do in one minute a day," says Google's Peterson. Find that minute when you're exercising or on your commute, he adds. Peterson also believes in doing "reflection in action." When you're in the middle of doing something, "think about what's happening, what's really going on here. And then after the action, look at what worked, what didn't work—and ask, *What could I have done differently?*

Reflection is a solo activity, or at least should start out that way, says Conant. "When you're first thinking about some of the leadership questions, you really want to wrestle with them on your own, so that you can land on a point of view that is yours—*Here's what I truly think about this issue.* Then write it down, and think about it some more."

At some point—but not too early—it can be helpful to bring a trusted partner into the reflection process. The partner is there primarily to be a sounding board for your thoughts, Conant says, as you ask questions such as: *Does my thinking sound right to you? Does it sound like me? Am I missing something?"*

What is my code?

For organizational purposes, many of the key questions worth considering during reflective periods can be divided into three main areas: core values, current focus, and future vision. Why these three areas? They're critical to successful leadership; they bring up difficult questions that require deep thought; and they are subject areas that tend to get pushed aside by more immediate concerns.

Core values can be approached in two stages: first, examining individual values (referring to what you, personally, believe in and would like to embody as a leader); and second, organizational values (what the group stands for and aspires to be). The values questions are focused in part on guiding principles but can also encompass purpose, history, identity, and just about anything that might define who you are as a leader and, separately, what the organization represents.

On individual values, Conant suggests beginning with this question: *What is my code?* As he defines it, the code is a set of principles and behaviors that can guide you as a leader. In shaping your own values and principles, you may be guided by others. "Think about those who have had a profound influence on you in your life," Conant says. "It could be a grandparent, a teacher—I find that for many people, the code of values is cultivated during formative years."

On the other hand, Ray Dalio, the founder of the renowned investment firm Bridgewater Associates, warns that simply adapting other people's principles without giving them much thought "can expose you to the risk of acting in ways inconsistent with your goals and your nature."

Both Dalio and Conant say one of the best ways to identify your own leadership principles is to consider your past experiences, focusing in on specific achievements and periods of personal growth. Ask yourself questions such as: *When have I been at my best? What drove or inspired me at those times? What have I learned about working with other people (in doing so, when have I been effective, and what caused that?) When have I taken a principled stand? What have I gone out of my way to defend?*

Conversely, zoom in on failures or setbacks—Dalio found many of his principles were learned from studying his mistakes. So the questions to ask in this case could be, *When have I failed to effectively meet goals or lead others—and what did I seem to be doing wrong? When did I fail to take a stand—and why?*

In thinking about these experiences and lessons, write down the key points—and look for patterns or themes that keep coming up. If, for example, you've found that some of your best experiences came when you were open and transparent—and failures were sometimes associated with a lack of transparency—that could serve as the basis for a guiding principle or value.

USE THESE QUESTIONS TO "CRACK YOUR CODE" AS A LEADER

- **Who are my formative influencers?** Leadership values are instilled early, often from relatives or teachers; revisit those lessons.
- **When have I been at my best?** Study your past successes to assess strengths and productive behaviors.
- **When have I come up short—and why?** Failures usually contain lessons that may be useful in developing guiding principles.
- **What have I taken a stand for (and against)?** This question can help clarify what matters most to you—which should shape your leadership code.
- **What is my logline?** Share your values by way of a story—and boil it down to a line or two that sums up what you're "about" as a leader.

Having a clearer sense of your values can solidify and strengthen your personal "code" as a leader—and it can have a strong influence on your behavior. Lead Star's Angie Morgan talks about the "Galatea Effect" (a phenomenon that derives its name from the Greek myth about an ivory statue that comes to life). Researchers of the Galatea Effect have found that if you think of yourself as honest, you're more apt to behave as an honest person would. As Morgan puts it, "You'll be the person who speaks the truth even when it's uncomfortable to do so."

As a leader, it's important not only to have a code but also to clearly communicate that code to others. Perhaps the best way to communicate what you "stand for" as a leader is through your own behaviors; those values must, like Galatea, come to life on a regular basis.

In conveying your values to others, actions speak loudest, but words do matter. You can share your values and principles in manifesto form, but nothing is more powerful than a narrative. So ask yourself: *What is my story?* To keep it succinct, you might want to boil that story down so that it answers the question *What is my logline?* (A logline is a one- to two-sentence summary of a story, used for Hollywood screenplays).

Every strong leader should have a compact story that tells people where you came from, how you got here, and where you're headed, with values embedded in the subtext. For example: *From humble roots, she started her own company on a shoestring budget in a garage and became a success by doing what no one else had done. Then she nearly lost it all in the recession but battled her way back and now is taking her operation to a whole new level.*

The story should be known by your followers. At her Brooklyn school, Nadia Lopez makes sure her students are very aware of her story: how she came from an immigrant household, worked her way through college, tried different jobs before finding her calling, eventually scraped together the resources to open her own school. The story motivates the followers, but it can also be self-motivating—it pushes us to live up to our own stories, and to keep adding new and better chapters.

How do you know if you're living up to your own values and principles? Ask yourself, on a daily or weekly basis, or immediately after a significant event or action: *Did I live up to my own code?* It can be difficult to meet high standards on an everyday basis, but if you come up short, view it as a learning opportunity: *In what ways did my behavior fail to match my stated values? How would I do it differently?*

IF A LEADER should have a code and a story, so should the organization as a whole. It might not be the same code, though there will likely be overlap. To try to uncover and clarify the company code, substitute "we" for "I" but otherwise ask similar questions about the past, starting with *Why are we here in the first place?* Most organizations begin with a clear sense of purpose (to solve a problem, meet an unmet need) that may become hazy over time. Inquire about highs and lows along the way: *When have we, as an*

organization, been at our best?
What have we stood for throughout
our history? Why do we matter,
and to whom?

   Why do we matter, and to
whom? is worth considerable
thought because it gets at the
essence of why your organization
exists in the first place. In grappling with that question, there
are a number of ways to reframe
it in order to shift the perspective. I like this version, shared by
former Trader Joe's president
Doug Rauch: *If we disappeared*
tomorrow, who would miss us?

> **ASK THESE "MISSION" QUESTIONS TO CLARIFY WHY YOUR COMPANY MATTERS**
>
> • **If we disappeared tomorrow, who would miss us?** This speculative question helps clarify why you matter and to whom.
>
> • **What do we do that others can't or won't?** This shifts the focus to an organization's strengths and uniqueness.
>
> • **What are we against?** It's easy to say what you're for. It's more risky—and therefore carries more weight—for a company to oppose something.
>
> • **How might we be not just a company but a cause?** Increasingly, organizations are expected to contribute something worthwhile—to employees, local communities, and the world.

And here's another way of coming at it, as suggested by the *Fast Company* cofounder William C. Taylor: *What do we do that other organizations can't or won't do?*

   These essential questions inquiring about "why an organization matters" might seem unnecessary—it may feel as if they were answered long ago and don't need to be asked anymore. But one of the key roles of the leader is to keep the company anchored in core ideas, values, and a defining story. The essential questions must be asked periodically to reinforce basic truths about the company and also to see if they still hold up—because an organization's raison d'être can change over time.

   In these politically charged times, the leader of an organiza-tion may need to articulate not only what a company stands for but also what it stands against. "There's a turning point in what's expected from business leaders," says Leanne Meyer, codirector of a new leadership department at Carnegie Mellon University, noting that customers and employees are more interested than ever before in the ethical, moral, and political positions staked out by a company. In the past, business leaders tended to simply avoid any issues deemed controversial or political. To do so today is to risk being seen as not caring about important social justice issues that may matter deeply to a majority of customers and employees.

Leaders must be the ones to ask the questions that look beyond bottom-line concerns, to figure out how the organization should behave as a citizen of the world. The consultant Tim Ogilvie suggests every leader these days should consider: *How might we be not just a company but a cause?* If an organization is seen as being committed to a worthwhile purpose, it can motivate employees and forge a greater bond with customers.

But to *be* a cause demands more than just donating to a cause. It requires a consistent, ongoing commitment (expressed in corporate behaviors and policies, as well as contributions) to a worthwhile idea or endeavor. Ideally, that cause should be one that the organization is in a unique position to lead and support—e.g., the food company that finds ways to feed the hungry, the shoe company that donates a new pair of shoes for every pair purchased. The leader must take stock of the organization's particular strengths and core values, then match that to an appropriate need in the world by asking: *What is our higher calling?*

What is the least I can do?

In a more complex and demanding environment, leaders may feel pressured to do more and more: to chase every opportunity, embrace each new possibility, and capitalize on all the latest trends. And this can quickly lead those leaders into a trap wherein the more they try to do, the less they actually accomplish. The author and business consultant Greg McKeown identifies this as one of the biggest threats leaders face today.

McKeown began his efforts to understand the nature of this threat by pursuing an intriguing question: *Why do otherwise successful people get tripped up by the trivial?* He discovered that many leaders seemed to be operating under the assumption that "more is better." And the problem only seemed to worsen as a leader and an organization became more successful because, as McKeown found, "success diffuses focus."

Hence, a company that began with one simple idea aimed at a specific market finds success and soon begins to expand into various new sectors, pursuing multiple strategies. The products themselves proliferate, with each one becoming more feature laden and complicated. And the leader's schedule collapses under the weight of too many demands, nonstop meetings, and too many "urgent priorities." (The thing about priorities, McKeown points out, is that by definition, you can't have twenty of them.)

Given that leaders are often the ones who determine and set the priorities for others, the ability to focus on what matters most—what McKeown calls "essentialism"—is a critical leadership skill. To get better at doing less, there are a couple of important changes a leader must make. One requires a change of attitude, which McKeown captures in this beautiful question: *What if we stopped celebrating being busy as a measure of importance?*

In addition to that attitudinal change, a fundamental change in behavior is needed. When faced with numerous possibilities, a leader must be willing to choose among and between them. McKeown says that when presented with possibilities A and B, an "essentialist" thoughtfully considers the question *Which problem do I want?*—as opposed to reflexively asking, *How can I do both?*

Questioning is an essential tool for simplifying and for sharpening focus. Perhaps the most effective way to check the "undisciplined pursuit of more" is to train oneself to question every potential addition and expansion to ask, *Is this necessary?* and *If we add this, what do we stand to lose?*

One of the best models for a highly focused approach to leadership is the late Steve Jobs. He was far from a perfect leader, overall. If we apply the "visionary helper" standard to Jobs, he often came up short on the "helper" part, given his well-documented tendencies to berate employees. But on the "visionary" part Jobs excelled, and his laser focus was one reason why. As his biographer Walter

Isaacson observed, Jobs was known for gathering Apple's top thinkers and asking them: "What are the ten things we should be doing next?" The group would jockey to get their ideas on that "top ten" list. Then, Isaacson notes, "Jobs would slash the bottom seven and announce, 'We can only do three.'"

Generally speaking, it's harder to cut than to add, harder to say no than yes. "When a leader says no to something, she is also usually saying no to *someone* and that takes courage," says the executive coach Michael Bungay Stanier. He adds that it also takes discipline and courage to "commit to a few key things that you're going to focus on—as opposed to doing a million other things to cover our backsides."

But by focusing on fewer things, you add momentum and resources to those chosen few. If we have a tendency to think of such tradeoffs in a negative way, says McKeown, then we should reframe the way we think about them: "Instead of asking, *What do I have to give up?*, ask *What do I want to go big on?*"

It's not just new possibilities and options that should be subject to such questioning. In many organizations, existing projects and processes build up over time. Leaders are often interested in adding on the new without subtracting the old. The renowned business consultant Peter Drucker felt that to battle this kind of accretion, a leader needed to regularly ask, *What should we* stop *doing?* Drucker referred to this winnowing practice as "systematic abandonment," and believed it was critical because it kept companies from being stretched too thin.

Almost every bureaucratic process in an organization should be subject to the fundamental "Why?": *Why does this rule (or this process) exist in the first place?* Having considered why it was first implemented, the necessary follow-up question is: *If it made sense once, does it still make sense now?*

When trying to identify and eliminate policies that don't work anymore (and perhaps never did), ask the people who must contend with those policies—employees. The consultant Lisa Bodell recommends giving people in the company the power to decide: *What stupid rule would you most like to kill?* Provide some guardrails, Bodell says. (Some rules may be absolutely necessary and it might even be illegal to get rid of them.) Also, ask why the rule should be eliminated; how they might change it; and whether they think it would be difficult to do so.

In terms of using questions to prioritize a leader's activities and make the best use of limited time, Lead Star's Morgan says that each morning, she asks herself the "HBU" question: *At this moment, what is the highest, best use of my time?*

Of course, to answer that question, you must first ask another question: *What truly matters now?* At any given time, something is deserving of priority status—and the leader's job is to figure out what it is, then devote time and resources to it. Harvard University's James Ryan, who uses *What truly matters?* as one of his own five essential questions, says, "It's a good question to ask whenever you're making a decision, large or small. For example, I think at the start of every meeting, a leader should ask, *What truly matters about this meeting?*" (If nothing comes to mind, then, referring back to Morgan's question, it might not qualify as the "highest, best use" of your time.)

Here's one more question to help leaders focus: It is appropriately called the "focusing" question and was constructed by Gary Keller, cofounder of one of the world's largest real estate companies, Keller Williams. Keller recommends that a leader embarking on a challenge of any kind should begin with the question: *What is the one thing I can do that would make everything else easier or unnecessary?*

TO SHARPEN YOUR LEADERSHIP FOCUS, ASK THESE QUESTIONS

- **What is the one thing I can do that would make everything else easier or unnecessary?** Ask this "focusing" question at the start of any new challenge or project. (Gary Keller)
- **What should we stop doing?** Practice "systematic abandonment." (Peter Drucker)
- **What do I want to go big on?** Ask this instead of "What am I giving up?" (Greg McKeown)
- **Which stupid rule should we kill?** Share this question with employees to see what they choose. (Lisa Bodell)
- **At this moment, what is the highest, best use of my time?** Use the "HBU" question to maximize personal productivity. (Angie Morgan)

Keller's question challenges you to focus on a single priority instead of a lengthy to-do list—so that you can get to work immediately on that one important job. If, for example, a leader wanted to improve employee morale while also spurring innovation, "one thing" that might make all of that easier could be implementing a policy that offers employees more time to work on their own projects.

Depending on the complexity of what you're trying to achieve, figuring out the "one thing" may require some mental reverse engineering, but Keller says he has found when people give some thought to the question, they're usually able to come up with a good answer. He recommends that once you have an answer in mind, you or your group should try to figure out how long it might take to do it—then immediately block off time to get it done.

How can we become the company that would put us out of business?

"The manager has his or her eye always on the bottom line; the leader's eye is on the horizon," declared the leadership guru Warren Bennis. Leaders have always tried to be alert to signs visible in the distance—a new technology or trend just beginning to surface. But today, leaders also have to be futurists, anticipating changes not yet on the horizon because they may still be years away from happening.

To put this in surfer's terms, leaders now must be on the lookout for the "third wave." The first wave "is the wave you're on at the moment, the current core business," according to Dion Weisler, the chief executive at HP Inc. The second wave is just starting to break, and represents new growth opportunities coming your way. But the third wave is in the future—the surfer who wants to ride it goes home "to pull the weather reports and figure out when the next big one is coming."

"Visionary" leaders not only must anticipate that third wave, they must also figure out, in advance, how the organization can best ride it. That requires asking questions that differ from the ones designed to help a leader dig deep for enduring values or hone a sharper focus on present concerns. "Visionary" questions tend to be exploratory and speculative, enabling you to envision a future scenario. I think of them as the kinds of questions that can help you release your inner Elon Musk.

It's not easy for leaders to look into the future, for a number of reasons. Crystal balls are hard to come by and forecasts may be unreliable. Moreover, immediate pressures tend to keep us focused on the latest crisis or impending deadline. We are cognitively biased toward giving more weight to things that are happening now or that happened recently. "If I'm a leader I obsess about the small problems of the moment and don't give enough thought to the major problems a few years down the road," says Don Derosby, a consultant who works with companies on long-term planning. To counter that, Derosby encourages leaders to "shift their temporal references" by encouraging them to try thinking about various current issues from the standpoint of one year in the future—then two years ahead, then five years.

To think about the future, you must first try to envision it—and to do that, begin by asking about it. Derosby, for example, likes to use what he calls "oracle questions," which work as follows: He may ask a client, *If an oracle could tell you what's going to happen three years from now, what would you most want to know?* Obviously, there is no oracle to provide the answer, but the purpose of the question is to encourage one to focus on that future scenario—to begin thinking about current issues with the future in mind, and try imagining what might be most important then. The response to the oracle question may inspire research and scenario planning—in effect, once you've thought of questions for the oracle, you must try to do the oracle's job of answering them.

Speculative inquiry can be used to envision potential future threats. A favorite question along these lines comes from the New York restaurateur Danny Meyer, who likes to ask: *How can we become the company that would put us out of business?* This question invites you to envision that future rival: *What might this predator look like, and why would it have an advantage over us?* Having figured that out, you can think about how to make yourself more like the predator. In Meyer's case, his popular high-quality hamburger-and-milkshakes Shake Shack chain came out of this kind of questioning.

When thinking about future opportunities, leaders can use speculative questions to push the boundaries of what is possible. For example, every leader should ask, *What if we had the capability to do what we now do much faster and more efficiently—what might that enable us to achieve?* We can assume, given the nature of progress, the first part of that question may become a reality—so anticipating it, and planning for the second part, makes sense.

Think about future possibilities from the standpoint of employees: *What if we created the ideal workplace for our employees—what might their workday look like?* And use speculative inquiry on behalf of your customers, too: Professor Michael Schrage of MIT thinks leaders should ask, *Who do we want our customers to become?*

The more accurately you can envision future changes, the better your speculative questions will be. How does one become better at foreseeing those changes? Going back to Dion Weisler's third-wave surfer analogy, you can read "the weather reports." There's no shortage of business futurists and forecasters offering predictive studies and reports. But in addition, Roselinde Torres of Boston Consulting Group urges leaders to be aware of how everyday

---

RELEASE YOUR "INNER STEVE JOBS" BY ASKING "VISIONARY" QUESTIONS

- **How can we become the company that would put us out of business?** Start by envisioning a threat that doesn't exist (yet).
- **How can we brace ourselves for the third wave?** It's not the wave you're on now or the one you can see breaking; it's the big one yet to break.
- **If an oracle could tell us about our business five years from now, what would we ask?** Think of the most critical questions; then go to work on them (because you're the oracle).
- **What would the seventh generation think about what we're doing?** Take a lesson from the Iroquois about long-term planning.
- **How might I make tomorrow visible?** Inspire people by giving them a glimpse of a better future.
- **What is our "vision question"?** Forget the vision statement. Pursue the future with an open-ended query.

activities and interactions can serve to widen your view of what's going on and what may be coming next. *Who are you spending time with? On what topics? Where are you travelling? What are you reading?* These influences will help you identify trends and patterns, she says.

How far ahead should a "visionary leader" look? Derosby recommends thinking about the future in stages: one year ahead, then two years, then five years. The business consultant Suzy Welch suggests a different sliding scale when weighing any major decision: *What are the implications of this decision ten minutes, ten months, and ten years from now?*

On some of the truly important issues—such as how your business operations may be affecting the environment—consider applying a question based on an old Iroquois principle: *What would the seventh generation think about what we're doing?* This principle, codified in the Iroquois Great Law of Peace, held that every decision should take into account its possible effects on descendants seven generations into the future.

"VISIONARY LEADERS" NOT only must develop a guiding vision of where the organization is headed, but they must also be able to share that vision with others. Many do that through some form of published "vision statement," though in giving people a glimpse of the future, it can be more effective to show rather than just tell. How to do this is up to each individual leader, but start by asking: *How might I make tomorrow visible?* One great example of how to do that comes from school principal Lopez. Part of her vision for her scholars is that they'll one day be attending top colleges, but she doesn't just tell them that—she arranges student trips to Harvard University so that the kids can picture themselves there in the future.

Lastly, for those leaders using a vision statement: Consider making a minor change in wording and punctuation to turn that closed statement into a "vision question." When you change a statement into a question, it tends to become more engaging. It is open-ended and forward-looking. It invites people to think about the question and its possibilities.

For example, Nike's vision statement—"To bring inspiration and innovation to every athlete in the world"—could be restated as *"How might we* bring inspiration and innovation to every athlete in the world?" Southwest Airlines' vision statement—"To become the world's most loved, most flown, and most profitable airline"— could be similarly changed by replacing "To" with "How might we . . ."

Having changed the statement to a question, the next step is to take that question and share it with every person you are trying to lead. Request that they take ownership of the vision question and join in the effort of trying to answer it.

Which brings us to the next challenge for the leader as "visionary helper," as we move from inward to outward questioning—going from the "visionary" part to the "helper" part.

What's going on out there—and how can I help?

When asked to describe what the storied Campbell's Soup Company was like when he joined it in 2001, Doug Conant doesn't mince words: He says he waded into a "toxic culture." Conant was brought in as the new chief executive after Campbell's had lost half its market value in one year. The company's prior leadership had made a series of mistakes, started missing their numbers, laying off workers, and even began to compromise product quality. "They literally began to take some of the chicken out of the chicken noodle soup," Conant says.

But perhaps the biggest problem of all was employee morale, as measured by the metric of "engagement" (an assessment of how much people care about their jobs). Conant brought in the research firm Gallup to do a survey of employee engagement and "we had the worst levels of any Fortune 500 company they ever surveyed," he says. For every two employees engaged in the work, one was looking for another job.

So, as Conant set about making many changes—to the advertising, in-store displays, even putting some of that chicken back into the soup—one of his top priorities was to improve morale. To win in the marketplace, you must first win in the workplace, Conant believed, and that philosophy had been borne out in a prior successful stint as the head of Nabisco. The roots of the philosophy actually went back even farther for Conant. Early in his career, he was abruptly fired from a job at General Mills and "ushered out of the building," he recalls. On his way out he was given a phone number for executive outplacement. He called and a counselor picked up the phone and said, "Hello, this is Neil McKenna—*how can I help?*"

McKenna not only helped Conant get his career back on track, but he also inspired him to begin to embrace a managerial approach anchored in that basic question: *How can I help?* "I came to believe that from a leadership standpoint, it is the ultimate question," Conant says. For a leader to ask that question, regularly and effectively, is not as simple as it might seem. To ask it, Conant says, you must have humility; you must be sincere about helping; and you must be willing to act on the responses from the people you ask.

Conant brought his question to Campbell's, along with a pedometer. Believing that the best way to ask his question was through company-wide face-to-face encounters, he set out to walk ten thousand steps each day, covering as much of the company as possible. He wandered the building and at each stop, he inquired about what was going well, what were the biggest challenges that person was facing, and eventually culminating with the clincher: *How can I help?*

Managers are conditioned to be ever on the hunt for problems to fix, and as a result, they often end up asking some version of the question, *What is the problem here?* Conant took a different approach, trying to focus more on positive developments: *What is going well? What are we doing right?* As he identified those small wins throughout the company, he also conspicuously celebrated them. Each day, he handwrote twenty notes, with each note addressed to an individual employee, praising a specific achievement by that employee (over his ten years at Campbell's, Conant figures he wrote thirty thousand notes).

It didn't take long for Conant to reverse Campbell's numbers, as the company's sales, earnings, and stock price began to rise, and did so for much of the next decade leading up to his retirement in 2011. But Conant is particularly proud of the dramatic rise in Campbell's employee engagement levels during his tenure. The company went from being at the bottom of the Fortune 500 to being among the highest-ranked in employee engagement.

Today, in his role as a leadership consultant in his own firm and as the chairman of Northwestern University's Kellogg Executive Leadership Institute, Conant continues to champion an approach to leadership rooted in interacting, questioning, listening, and helping. It can be a tough sell to busy executives, many of whom "brush these interactions aside because they're too busy trying to get the 'real work' done," he says. "But this *is* the real work."

THE PROBLEM CAMPBELL'S Soup faced back in 2001—when a substantial portion of its employees wanted to be somewhere else—can be found at many companies today. Recent studies indicate that employee engagement levels are now alarmingly bad. By some measures, a third of working Americans feel disengaged at their jobs. It represents one of the biggest challenges faced by today's leaders.

There is no panacea—no way to ensure that every person, everywhere, will love going to work. But an on-the-ground, engaged, questioning leader like Conant can do a number of things to raise employee morale and performance levels. The questioning leader can identify employee problems and frustrations before they reach a crisis point; can give support and encouragement when and where it's most needed; and can build trust and rapport between employees and management.

As a leader engages directly with employees, using questioning as a primary mode of communicating, it doesn't just help the employees—it also provides the leader with critical information needed to run the organization.

Edgar Schein, a former MIT Sloan School organizational development expert and author of *Humble Inquiry*, has observed that a problem plaguing most organizations is poor upward communication—it's "a major pathology," he says. "Subordinates know lots of things that would make the place work better or safer that they for various reasons withhold."

When asked why they withhold much-needed information, employees typically answer that bosses and managers don't want to hear about problems, or worse, are likely to "shoot the messenger." The only way to change this, Schein says, is for the manager to go directly to subordinates and say, "I'm really interested and I'm listening." If that doesn't happen, he adds, we will "continue to have accidents and low quality products because the information isn't surfacing."

More than ever before, leaders today must guard against what former General Electric chief Jack Welch refers to as "creeping insularity" that cuts the leader off from people and critical information. Welch notes that "Every day spent behind your closed door is a day you're not out learning about your people, processes, and market realities." He thinks every leader ought to have a sign facing them on their desk that reads, "Why are you still here?"

Assuming we accept the premise that a leader should regularly leave the office and walk the floor asking questions—call it "ambulatory inquiry"—this raises the question: *What should I ask all these people?*

To begin with, a leader should ask questions designed to elicit some kind of meaningful response. In his definition of the term "humble inquiry," Schein describes it as "the skill and the art of *drawing someone out*." To do that, ask open-ended questions, with genuine interest and curiosity behind them.

Schein urges leaders to avoid "leading questions, rhetorical questions, embarrassing questions, or statements in the form of questions." In particular, avoid critical questions—*Whose fault is this?*; *What were you thinking?* Such questions put people on the defensive and can shut down conversation. Leaders who think of themselves as problem solvers and troubleshooters may be used to focusing directly on what went wrong and who's to blame, but interactions usually work better when the focus is on strengths and solutions.

Am I looking for what's broken . . . or what's working?

Case Western Reserve University business professor David Cooperrider, one of the creators of the now-widely-used practice known as "Appreciative Inquiry," believes that business leaders tend to be too problem focused. Cooperrider contends (and has shown in business case studies) that leaders can achieve better results by using questions to highlight what's working and where people's strengths lie, while also inquiring in an optimistic way about possibilities for growth and improvement.

This doesn't mean one should avoid confronting problems employees may be having. Part of the purpose of 'ambulatory inquiry' is to identify problems that are out there and that should be addressed. But it can be done by starting with positive questions. If, for example, an employee delivered work after the deadline, start with any positives (the fact that the project was completed, done well, etc.). That might be followed by a question that broaches the missed deadline, but avoids an accusatory tone: *Help me understand what led to the deadline issues?* Gradually move the questioning toward collaborative solutions: *How might we expedite the work without compromising quality? How can I help?*

Notice in that example of an interaction addressing a problem, the word *Why* did not make an appearance. 'Why' questions can be useful and powerful in many different situations (I'm a strong believer in asking yourself 'Why' as you try to understand a problem or challenge), but be careful about using the word in questions asked directly of employees.

"When someone hears 'why' or 'why not,' they are primed to *justify the current situation*," writes Nathaniel Greene from the consulting firm Stroud International. Greene notes that people often respond to "Why?" questions by "explaining why the problem isn't their fault or why they cannot reasonably change the situation." All of that justification is a waste of time, Greene points out. The real focus should be on solving the problem and moving forward.

If part of the goal is to build rapport and trust with employees, the questioning leader must "remove any judgment or ego from the questions being asked," advises the FBI counterintelligence agent Robin Dreeke. Dreeke often conducts interviews with potential intelligence sources and must try to win their trust quickly. Before any such interactions, he asks himself first: *How can I make sure the conversation is about them—their needs, their interests—and not about me?*

Then, during the conversation, he uses a mental checklist to make sure he isn't going off track. *Am I seeking their thoughts, instead of just offering my own? Am I focused on their priorities, not mine? Am I offering them choices and options, instead of telling them what to do?*

Dreeke has a favorite type of question for building instant rapport with the spies and other intelligence sources he interviews. "I love 'challenge' questions. Everyone has challenges they're dealing with, and if you can get them to talk about that, it does two important things. It tells you what their priorities and concerns are, and it provides an opening for you to offer to help in some way."

WHEN DOING "AMBULATORY INQUIRY," A LEADER SHOULD NOT ASK . . .

- **How's it going?** This is a rote question and elicits rote responses.
- **Why did you ___?** When you ask "why?" questions directly of employees, it shifts them into "justify" mode.
- **Who screwed up here?** Rather than focusing on a scapegoat, inquire about how best to address the issue and move forward.
- **Haven't we tried this already?** Often uttered wearily by "Been there, done that" leaders. Say it enough times, and people will stop offering ideas altogether.

AND SHOULD ASK . . .

- **What's the biggest challenge you're facing?** You can make the "challenge" question more specific ("on this project") or more general ("in your job").
- **Are you making progress?** If employees feel "stuck," frustration sets in.
- **Help me understand what led to . . .** Instead of asking "Why?" about a problem, start the question this way—it's wordier, but less accusatory.
- **Is it clear what we're doing and why?** Ask employees this question with regard to company goals, directives, policy changes, and the vision for the future.
- **How can I help?** Per Doug Conant, the "ultimate leadership question." But only ask it if you mean it.

You can inquire about challenges in a general way (*What are some of the biggest challenges you face in your role within this organization?*) or in a more specific way (*On this project, what is the single toughest challenge?*). Either type of question enables you to identify areas of need and provides a nice setup for the "closing" question, *How can I help?*

One of the most important things for the roaming leader to look for is whether employees are making progress in their work. The Harvard business professor Teresa Amabile says her research has shown that "of all the events that can deeply engage people at work, the single most important is simply making progress on meaningful work." Here's a good way to inquire about progress, shared by the leadership coach Marshall Goldsmith: *Did you do your best to make progress today?* Goldsmith says that by framing the question this way, you allow the responder to take ownership of the effort.

If something is getting in the way of employees' progress, it's the leader's job to identify that obstacle and remove it. It could be too many meetings, lack of resources, inadequate training. Ask people, *What are we doing that's getting in your way?* They'll probably be eager to tell you.

If you observe a chronic problem of an employee being unable to make progress or meet expectations, don't assume the worst. Instead, consultant John Barrett suggests you ask yourself the "Can't, Won't, Don't Question" about this employee's failure to perform: *Is it because they can't do it, they won't do it, or they don't know how to do it?* If it's the last one, that's not the employee's fault—it's your responsibility to make available the needed instruction or training.

In addition to using questions to identify current concerns and needs, you can use them to get a sense of employees' goals, ambitions, strengths, and passions. By asking, for example, *What are you working on right now that you're most excited about?*, you can become more aware of an individual's areas of interest—which could factor into decisions about how to best tap into those passions on future projects. On the other hand, asking *What inspired you to take this approach?* can provide insights on how someone thinks and solves problems. The management coach

William Arruda suggests using questions to try to promote self-discovery in employees by asking, for example, *How would you like to see yourself growing in this role?*

WHILE ASKING EMPLOYEES about their own job challenges, it's an opportune time to check on whether they understand the goals and the larger mission of the organization. Leaders may *think* they've clearly communicated a guiding vision to employees—but that doesn't mean the message has been received. Robert Kaplan of the Harvard Business School thinks leaders should ask themselves: *Would my employees, if asked, be able to articulate the company's vision and priorities?* Rather than wondering, go ahead and ask them, using some version of this question: *Is it clear what we're doing and why?*

The "Why?" part is critical. Anyone can memorize and repeat back a vision statement or a few company buzzwords. What matters is whether people throughout the organization actually understand why the company has chosen to follow a particular path and uphold certain core principles, or why the leaders opted to make that painful decision they announced just last week.

Is there room in these interactions for broader questions about an employee's passions and dreams beyond the job? By asking questions about outside interests—*What do you do in your life outside work that is most inspiring? What do you do to keep learning and growing as a person?*—a leader opens an additional path for building rapport, and might possibly even be able to find a way to connect "outside" interests to the organization's needs. If you can't figure out that connection yourself, ask the employee: *What if we could take that passion you have for X and somehow bring it to life here? How might we do that?*

A few style and tone points to keep in mind when doing ambulatory inquiry: Use a conversational tone, and employ softening phrases, such as "I'm curious," "I was wondering," or "Help me understand." When you've asked a question, give people time to answer and refrain from trying to answer for them. But don't leave them struggling too long if they can't seem to answer your question. Say, "We can come back to that," and then move the conversation forward.

Be careful about performing an interrogation. "No one likes getting questioned by the Spanish Inquisition, although that does appear to be the inspiration for many managers' approaches," observes the coach Michael Bungay Stanier, who offers this helpful reminder: You're seeking "not to reveal incompetence but to help uncover wisdom . . . ratchet down the pressure."

Perhaps most important, follow these guidelines used by the school principal Nadia Lopez: If you're going to ask someone a question, don't do a flyby. Take the time to stop. Look that person in the eye as you're talking to them. Then listen attentively. And ask follow-up questions, based on what you're hearing. If Lopez can find a way to do this with restless junior high students in a jam-packed school hallway, *you* can do it with adults in a work environment.

Do I really want a culture of curiosity?

To this point we've considered ways a leader can begin to ask more questions. But how might a leader encourage others, throughout an organization (or a community or even a family) to inquire more?

As is often the case, it's better to start by first considering "Why?" before "How?" *Why would a leader want to encourage more questioning? Why open the lid and release a potential torrent of employee questions?*

The most obvious answer is that many companies today need new ideas from as many sources as possible, in order to innovate. Questions asked by all sorts of people—a manager reviewing procedures and processes, a worker on the frontlines who detects inefficiencies—can lead to important changes and improvements. Socrates once said, "All of us are smarter than any of us." Companies become smarter and more productive by tapping into the collective intelligence of the group.

A second, related reason to encourage widespread questioning is that companies are having to deal with rapid and constant change, and inquiry is a key, accessible tool for navigating change. People within those changing companies can better adapt and survive if they're able to ask questions and learn on the job.

Moreover, good leaders want their followers to feel content and fulfilled. (If nothing else, it lowers the employee-turnover rate.) One of the ways people feel fulfilled in their work is by learning. In fact, research suggests many people are apt to leave their jobs if and when they stop learning. If you want people within an organization to keep learning, you must give them the freedom to explore, wonder, and inquire.

So that's the "why"—and it's compelling, particularly for organizations that place a premium on innovation, want to encourage learning, and have a tolerance for independent thinking and internal debate.

That tolerance is important. Having a curious, engaged, and inquisitive workforce presents challenges. One question I sometimes ask leaders when discussing this is: *If people start asking more questions at your company, what will you do with those questions?* (Because questions shouldn't be ignored; that just upsets the questioner.) Another point that comes up is, *What if you don't like the questions your employees are asking?*

If leaders are flummoxed by those two points, it indicates they haven't thought through the ramifications of encouraging a questioning culture. Here's another, more common warning sign: Often, top executives say to their employees, "Don't bring me questions; bring me answers." (A similar version of that statement is, "Don't bring me problems; bring me solutions.") If you're a leader and this sounds like something you have said or would say, consider what that statement means.

You're saying, in effect, you'd like someone to bring you solutions and innovations—but you're not interested in the messy process that produces those results. That's not the way innovation works. To encourage innovation, you must embrace questions and experiments as potential opportunities to improve or innovate. As for the person who identifies a problem and raises a question about it—that person has, at that point, already contributed something valuable. In a positive questioning culture, an employee is *not* responsible for answering the question or solving the problem. If that individual happens to know the answer, that's great—but depending on the scope of the problem, it may require a team effort to solve it.

To boil this down to a question, leaders weighing whether they truly desire a culture of inquiry may want to ask themselves: *Am I ready to announce "Bring us the problems you've noticed?"* Because in a questioning culture, people will do just that.

IN TERMS OF how to foster a culture of inquiry, there are different ways to approach the challenge but one thing seems clear: It must start at the top. Research on curiosity shows that it tends to flourish in an environment where questioning and problem solving is modeled and encouraged—whether by a teacher in a classroom, a parent in a home, or a top executive at a company.

"Leaders must be role models for good thinking," says Ed Hess of the University of Virginia's Darden School of Business. They can do that, Hess says, by being very open about what they're curious about, how they're learning and solving problems. "They should be thinking out loud, in front of everyone."

The good news is that many leaders are curious people by nature, as the journalist Adam Bryant observed, based on his hundreds of "Corner Office" profiles appearing over a decade in the *New York Times*. In looking for common characteristics among the many chief executives he interviewed, Bryant found "they share a habit of mind best described as 'applied curiosity.' They tend to question everything. They want to know how things work, and wonder how they can be made to work better. They're curious about people and their back stories."

To begin building a culture of inquiry, a curious, questioning leader should exhibit those tendencies at every opportunity. For example, start meetings "by asking open-ended questions," says Berkeley business professor Morten Hansen. He points out that too many leaders start meetings by stating opinions—which then causes "the rest of the room to fall in behind you."

Rather than expecting people to fall in line, a questioning leader encourages disagreement. Pedro Pizarro, chief executive of the Edison International utility holding company, even goes so far as to ask other senior leaders at his company to disagree with him in open settings "so people see that somebody whom I value can debate with me."

Modeling the behavior of questioning is an important start, but it's only a first step. Doug Conant advises that with any effort to bring about change in an organization's culture, there are three stages: You start by figuring out the culture you want, then you declare it, and then you create practices to support it. The "declaring" part is easy—too many leaders do that without backing up the declaration.

To adjust Conant's formula slightly, leaders might want to start by asking themselves a two-part question: *What is the culture I want, and what actions and conditions are likely to produce such a culture?*

How might we make questioning safe? And rewarding? And productive?

Assuming the culture you desire is one that encourages curiosity, learning, and inquiry, then what conditions will encourage that? In the world of education, this is a question that schools have thought about for some time. With teachers attempting to foster curiosity and questioning, the larger challenge of how to encourage more student inquiry in the classroom could be broken down into four smaller ones: *How can we make questioning safe? How can we make it rewarding? How can we make it productive?* And lastly, *How might we make it a habit?*

These issues all apply as much to business and the workplace as to schools. Consider safety, for instance: In the same way many students are fearful of raising a hand and asking questions in class, many employees—about two-thirds of them, according to one survey—feel "unable to ask a question at work." They worry that the question will be unwelcome for various reasons, or even that it may be seen as insubordination.

So the first job in fostering a culture of inquiry is to create a safe haven for questions. Teachers do this in various ways: by clearly announcing to students that all questions are welcome, and no question shall be judged; by soliciting questions, individually, from students; and sometimes even by organizing student activities and exercises where the whole point of the activity is to ask questions or work on improving questions.

The same approaches that help lessen fear of questioning among kids in the classroom can work with adults in business. For example, classroom questioning exercises can easily be adapted for business, whether small startups or large international companies. Arranging participants in small groups reduces the pressure of having to ask questions in front of many people. And as the participants are instructed to ask as many questions as possible, without fear of being judged, the questions soon begin to flow freely. This sometimes surprises business executives who are used to seeing employees sit quietly, shying away from speaking up and asking questions at large company-wide meetings—but the fact is, almost anyone would feel nervous asking questions in that kind of high-stakes environment.

Business leaders can also adopt the "Ask me anything" policy that the best schoolteachers use. Some companies have, in fact, implemented policies wherein, once a week, the chief executive submits to answering any question from anyone in the company. Google does this and selects the question to be answered by having employees vote up their favorites online. But companies could take the policy further: *Why not have every manager or supervisor throughout the company participate in a weekly or monthly "Ask me anything" session?*

To embolden questioners, make it clear that no one will be judged or punished for asking a question. If that means devising a system that allows people to submit anonymous questions, so be it. But in a healthy questioning culture, questioners shouldn't have to hide their identity. The goal is to have an environment where no one has to fear repercussions for asking, *Why haven't we done something about that problem we've been having with defective parts?*

One subtle way that questioners in business are sometimes punished is by being "rewarded" with more work. The questioner asks, *Why aren't we doing a better job with X?* The manager responds: *So happy you pointed that out. Obviously you care about this issue, so how about we put you in charge of fixing it?* Sounds like an opportunity, but the questioner may already have a full plate or may lack the capability to fix the problem. It's a good way to discourage people from raising their hand to point out a problem.

Once you've stopped punishing questioning, think about how to reward it. That comes down to two words—"recognize" and "incentivize." Here again, consider what inquiry-seeking teachers do: Some of them create "wonderwalls" that showcase the most interesting, creative, sensible, and crazy questions (in other words, all the questions) asked by students. Companies and other organizations could do likewise, using real or online bulletin boards, "question of the week" contests, and other celebrations of questions.

Company leaders could keep notes of the questions they receive and open meetings by saying, *John in accounting asked a great question the other day and I'd like to share it with you all.* Or a leader might borrow the aforementioned approach used by Doug Conant—writing a brief, personalized response to individuals who submitted questions

---

TO ENCOURAGE A CULTURE OF INQUIRY, ASK THESE FOUR QUESTIONS

- *How can we make it safe to question?* Institute a strict "no judging" rule; all questions welcome, the more the merrier.
- *How might we make questioning rewarding?* Celebrate productive questions by verbal recognition. To go further, offer bonuses and other tangible incentives.
- *How might we make questioning productive?* Train people in how to question in ways that produce results.
- *How can we make a culture of inquiry stick?* Make questioning a central part of meetings and other regular activities.

through designated channels. In the end, giving some form of recognition to questions doesn't cost much—but it sends a powerful signal that questions are valued.

Incentives, on the other hand, do cost something, but it may be worth the investment to offer bonuses or other perks to those who ask productive questions. In this case, a "productive" question could be defined as one that leads to a change: a change in corporate policy, a new research effort or employee program, an upgrade to the company's product offering. Companies have traditionally rewarded people for coming up with solutions, but it's time to recognize that the solution might never have come about unless someone first identified and inquired about a problem that needed solving.

Speaking of "productive" questions, this brings up the third of the four culture questions: *How might we make questioning productive?*

The goal is not only for people to ask more questions but also for them to be asking *good* questions—questions that help identify problems or opportunities, questions that posit new ideas and lead to improvements. To that end, organizations should train people in questioning techniques, methods, and practices. This can run the gamut from teaching people how to brainstorm in questions, how to fine-tune and improve a question they may be working on, how to strengthen critical thinking skills, how to use questions to solve problems, and how to question other people in effective ways. (Some brief examples of exercises involving these kinds of questioning skills are included in the next chapter of the book, and most of the exercises are easy to conduct.)

To help people be more productive in their questioning, it's important to teach them that questioning can and should be aimed at achieving a desired outcome. In business, the point is not to debate philosophical questions endlessly, nor to wonder just for the sake of wondering. (Those are fine things to do on one's own time, of course.) The point is to use questioning to drive a process that results in real, tangible results. To that end, employees should understand, for example, the questioning methods that enable an innovator to steadily progress from wondering about a new possibility to eventually figuring out how to make it a reality.

The last question about encouraging a culture of inquiry—*How can we make it stick?*—recognizes that questioning is a habit of mind. The more we do it, the more natural and instinctive it becomes to question things we might have previously ignored or taken for granted. Again, regular questioning exercises can help form the habit. So can rewards. The more questioning can become part of everyday business practice, the sooner the habit will form. So ask yourself, *What if every meeting began with a question? What if the company held regularly scheduled "question days"—during which groups come together to ask, What assumptions can we challenge today? What if you ask employees to come up with one ambitious question a week, to be shared with their colleagues?*

In trying to encourage employees to work on big questions and share those questions with colleagues, businesses could take another lesson from schools—in particular, schools that have adopted a new teaching approach called "Inquiry-Based Learning" (IBL). It's a methodology designed to encourage kids to formulate and take ownership of difficult questions.

Here's how IBL could be adapted for a workplace in four steps: 1) Challenge employees (either individually or in teams) to formulate an ambitious question that addresses an issue relevant to the company. Have them pitch the question to supervisors or management first, for approval. 2) The employee (or team) researches the question (with the company offering a designated amount of "free time" for research). 3) When the research is done, the questioner shares the question and learnings in a presentation to the company or the division. 4) The audience of colleagues then joins together in a collaborative "How might we?" brainstorming session, focused on ways to apply the questioner's learnings to immediate business concerns.

Having programs like IBL projects, question-based meetings, and regularly scheduled questioning exercises can strengthen the questioning habit while sharpening questioning skills.

Two FINAL POINTS on fostering a productive culture of inquiry: First, when people in an organization begin to question more, the potential for conflict increases. It's important, therefore, to teach people about respectful and nonconfrontational questioning. A simple softening of tone and wording can signal that a question is being asked in a spirit of curiosity, not confrontation.

Companies may also need to establish rules of spirited debate based around the principle that it's fine to disagree—up to a point. The idea, says Berkeley's Hansen, is to "fight and unite"—meaning "you want to have real debate among your people, because that supports the best decision-making. But the team also needs to unite behind the final decision." Along those lines, here is a question shared by Amazon's Jeff Bezos, who says that "if you have a conviction on a particular direction even though there's no consensus, it's helpful to say, '*Look, I know we disagree on this, but will you gamble with me on it? [Can we] disagree and commit?*'"

Finally, if you want to have a truly inclusive and widespread culture of inquiry—as opposed to, say, privileged pockets of inquiry—start by recognizing that *everyone* is, or has the potential to be, curious. To quote the curiosity expert Ian Leslie, curiosity "is a state not a trait." It waxes and wanes depending on circumstances, environment, and conditions. If you create an environment that is stimulating, open, and that invites exploration and inquiry, then everyone in that environment is likely to become more curious.

But perhaps some will still be more reticent than others to openly express their curiosity. Questioning can be intertwined with issues involving power and privilege. Some people are more inclined and may even feel entitled to be the person who publicly asks questions. Others—who could be in more of an outsider position, or perhaps are just more polite—might be inclined to hold back their questions.

The leader's job is to encourage quieter folks to share. The consultants Jane Hyun and Audrey Lee urge leaders to ask, *Whose voice might I have missed hearing—and how might I amplify this voice?*

They note that people might be "unheard" based on ethnic group or gender but also other factors—how long they've been with the company or perhaps which department they work in. In a culture of inquiry, none of those boundaries should matter—because great questions can and should come from everyone.

The Inquiring Life

How might I begin to act on my questions?

The preceding chapters have laid out many questions. Reading and considering those questions is one thing; using them is another.

I am of the belief that questioning plus action can lead to change (Q + A = C), whereas questioning minus action equals philosophy (Q − A = P). There's nothing wrong with philosophy, but this book is more geared to using questions to attain practical results—whether in your work, your relationships, or other aspects of your life. For that to happen, you must put the questions to work for you.

Admittedly, this is not always easy to do. The natural human tendency is to behave in instinctive ways, to do things quickly and without much thought or to follow habitual patterns of behavior. Through much of our lives, we're operating on "automatic pilot," and that's not entirely a bad thing. Sometimes it helps us to get more done, or allows for pleasant and even productive daydreaming. But there are times—when we're making a meaningful decision, trying to solve a problem or creative challenge, or having an important conversation, for example—when it can be beneficial to shift to a more deliberate, thoughtful mode, using questioning to prompt or guide our thinking.

Can we simply advise ourselves to "question more" and then expect that shift into questioning mode will happen when needed?

In my interviews with psychologists and behavioral experts, there were differing views on whether people, in general, can train themselves to be more thoughtful or to ask more questions in important situations. One prevailing view is that we have little control over our natural tendencies. This view holds that if you're the kind of person who makes impulsive decisions or who reacts emotionally in conversations, it may be difficult to change that. You can tell yourself to slow down and ask more questions at critical moments, but as those critical moments arise, you will probably do what you've always been inclined to do.

Conversely, a number of experts think it is challenging but possible for people to encourage themselves to question more, though they may need to practice it—and might occasionally need outside help.

That outside help might take the form of "external cues" to serve as reminders. Think of a surgeon or airline pilot, for example, who refers to a printed checklist of important reminders (*Don't forget to do X, Y, and Z before takeoff*); similar checklists could be used to remind us to question. Reminders could also come from a "trusted other" or a wingman—a person who could be relied upon to ask you, at critical moments, *Did you ask the important questions you're supposed to ask?* You could offer to do the same for them.

IN TERMS OF external cues, I suggest using "Q-cards," which can be placed in strategic locations or carried on your person (and can be shared with your co-questioner, of course). The idea is to have some prepared questions readily available for review before encountering various important situations. See

USE "Q-CARDS" TO TAKE YOUR QUESTIONS WITH YOU

All of the "question boxes" in this book—about 200 questions in all, covering about 30 different work or life situations—are in printable PDF format on the book's website, allowing you to print your own set of Q-cards. This is much better than defacing this book by cutting out the boxes or trying to highlight all the questions in an ebook. Simply go to amorebeautifulquestion.com/Q-cards and follow instructions for printing.

There is also a Question Index at the end of this book that includes all the book's questions (the ones in the boxes plus others, totaling more than 500). This full list of questions is also available in a printable format on the website; just click on the "Question Index" tab.

the accompanying box for instructions on how to print your own set of Q-cards.

Think of these questions as a starter kit. Over time, as questioning becomes more habitual and you develop a sense of which types of questions are most effective in different situations, you won't need printed cards or lists. You'll develop your own customized and refined questions on a mental list that will keep growing and evolving.

As you formulate your own "beautiful questions" to be applied as needed, keep in mind the following three main themes from the book—they may help you as you craft your own questions. First, many questions featured in the book (particularly the "Why?" questions) challenge basic assumptions. So as you're compiling your own list of questions in the future, remember that "assumption-busting" is one of the first and most important jobs to be done.

Another theme is the shifting of perspective. A number of questions are designed to encourage you to look at an issue or situation from a different angle—which could be another person's point of view, or a different time perspective (e.g., looking back from the future).

The third major theme is the counterintuitive effect. Many questions in the book encourage you to consider possibilities that might represent the opposite of what's expected. These three themes—challenging assumptions, shifting perspectives, considering opposites—are worth keeping in mind as you think of new questions to add to your list.

IN ORDER TO do more questioning, you must confront "the enemies of questioning": fear, knowledge, bias, hubris, time. While there's really no reason to fear asking the kind of questions that inquisitive four-year-olds do every day, overcoming anything we're reluctant to do inevitably comes down to action.

So here is a suggestion: Try to ask at least one naïve question before noon tomorrow. It can start as a question you ask yourself. (*Why coffee? Why do I drink coffee each morning? How did this whole coffee thing get started? What's the history of coffee? When did they invent these K-cup machines? I wonder, did that invention start with a question? Okay, Google, get ready because I have some questions for you . . .*)

It's good to get into the habit of asking these kinds of fundamental "beginner's mind" questions on your own, but to build questioning courage, take your inquiry public. At the coffee shop, pay attention to what the barista does and politely ask, *I'm curious about that thing you just did when you were making the latte—why do you do it that way?* You'll generally find that true curiosity and interest is welcomed by others.

As for the problems of knowledge, bias, and hubris, here is another challenge: Identify one thing you think you know. Then set out to prove yourself wrong. If you really want to be ambitious, follow the Arno Penzias daily "jugular" question approach. Every day, ask yourself, *Why do I believe what I believe?* Zero in on one particular belief. Then subject it to ruthless questioning.

In trying to develop a questioning habit, that fifth enemy, time, may be the greatest obstacle. Time is the cost of questioning. It takes time to pause and consider before making a rash decision or responding off-the-cuff. It takes even more time to sit alone in a room (or go for a peaceful walk) and reflect on important questions.

The time commitment must be made in two ways: Think of it as "questioning in action" and "questioning in reflection." The first means getting into the habit of slowing down to question while in the midst of making decisions, communicating with people, creating, and doing your job. It may take longer to do those tasks if you add in those important pauses for questioning, so build that in.

In terms of reflection, the challenge is to carve out dedicated time for questioning. You can take the advice of Doug Conant (from the preceding chapter) and get up an hour earlier in the morning, to spend time in the garden for coffee and reflection. Use the time to think about those big questions focused on where you're headed in your career or on a particular large challenge you're trying to solve. Or, as Google's David Peterson suggests, find just a few moments during your daily commute to think about questions—perhaps more immediate ones, involving the challenge of the day. A few minutes may not seem like much, but it adds up. My fellow questionologist Hal Gregersen of the MIT Leadership Center has pointed out that if each of us devotes just four minutes a day to thinking of questions to ask ourselves, it adds up to twenty-four hours—or a full day's worth of questioning—over the course of a year.

If you can't question in the morning, do so at night—it might pay off in the form of a next-day epiphany. The tech entrepreneur Reid Hoffman, a cofounder of LinkedIn, spends a few minutes each night before bed asking himself questions about a particular problem or challenge he's working on. Hoffman finds that when he does this, insights and answers often come to him during the night, making those few minutes spent on questioning a worthwhile investment.

To free up those minutes, try cutting back on social media or cable news. These days, most of us spend hours in "read and respond" mode as we take in the latest tweet, text, or news headline.

Try converting 10 percent of that media consumption time into active thinking time. All it requires you to do is find some version of a cave or tortoise shell or path in the woods—a place where the world cannot get at you for a while. When you go there, leave your phone behind; bring only your questions.

Doing this on a regular basis requires forming a new questioning habit—and research suggests when you're trying to establish a new habit (or break an old one), you should use a system of rewards. So ask yourself, *How might I reward myself for questioning?* Two ideas come to mind: The first is to allow yourself to check email or social media only after a period of quiet reflection. The second is to give yourself one decadent treat for every beautiful question you formulate.

The other thing to do when forming a new habit is to start small, taking baby steps that make it easier to gradually incorporate the new behavior you're trying to adopt. To get you started, what follows are a number of easy-to-do questioning exercises, many of them helping you put into action ideas touched upon in earlier chapters.

How can I warm up my questioning muscles?

It has been said that the way to get better at asking questions is to ask more questions. This is the thinking behind question-formulation or "question-storming" exercises, designed to build the skill of asking questions rapidly and effectively. I use these types of exercises in business workshops, and find they're particularly good for loosening up one's questioning muscles. They also help you look at a problem or challenge in a different way—by attacking it entirely with questions.

Exercise: The Question Formulation Technique
There are a number of question-storming exercises, but among the best is the Question Formulation Technique, developed by the Right Question Institute. This exercise can be done in groups (at a company retreat or in a school classroom) or individually. Here's how it works:

1. **Think of a "Question Focus."** To begin, you need a premise or statement, in two or three words, that can provide a focal point for generating questions. (e.g., "Technological change" or "Encouraging curiosity" or "A balanced life"). Don't use a question as a starting point—it's easier to form questions around a statement or a phrase.

2. **Produce questions.** Within a time limit (try ten minutes), aim to generate and write down as many questions as you can think of, pertaining to that QFocus.

Only questions are welcome—no opinions or answers, and no debating which questions are best. The idea at this point is to just keep inquiring about the subject from different angles.

3. **Improve your questions.** Begin to work on the questions you've written down. Open the closed questions, and close the open ones. For example, a closed question that began as *Is a balanced life desirable?* might be changed to an open one: *Why is a balanced life desirable?* In doing this, you'll see that a question can be narrowed down in some cases, expanded in others—and you begin to see that "the way you ask a question yields different results and can lead you in different directions," says Dan Rothstein of the Right Question Institute.

4. **Prioritize the questions.** Select three favorites. Look for those that stir interest and open up new ways of thinking about the issue.

5. **Decide on next steps.** This includes whether and how you might want to act on the prioritized questions. (*Might you want to share these chosen questions with others? Undertake research in order to answer them?*)

6. **Reflect on what you have learned.** Spend a few moments thinking about what it felt like to "think in questions," and what you learned about the process of formulating questions. (*Did it get easier as you went along? Did you discover any tricks for improving questions or for using one question to develop another?*) This helps solidify the learning and will help you get better at doing it next time.

Can I build a better question?

Having worked on question formulation, let's now try question improvement.

Exercise: Six ways to build a better question
While there are many ways to improve a question, here are six quick methods you can try on favorite questions from a question-storming exercise.

1. **Open it up.** If you want something more than a "yes or no" answer, take a closed question and open it up by starting the question with words like "What?," "Why?," or "How?" So instead of asking, *Have things changed since last year?*, it's better to ask: *How have things changed since last year?*

2. **Close it down.** There are times, however, when closing a question (so that it elicits a simple "yes or no" answer) can help you identify a built-in faulty assumption. Before spending too much time wondering, *Why are we having this problem?*, you may want to ask: *Is it a problem?*

3. **Sharpen it.** Precise questions will tend to yield better answers. Instead of *How will current changes in the market affect us?*, it's better to ask, *How will the rise of e-commerce in the market affect us?*

4. **Add a "Why?" to it.** I'm a big believer in getting to the "question behind the question," and that can often be done by adding "Why?" to the end of a question. So instead of just asking, *What trend are you most concerned about?*, ask *What trend are you most concerned about—and why?*

5. **Soften it.** Questions can be confrontational. It can help to add a softening phrase at the beginning, one that indicates the question is based on genuine interest, not criticism. So instead of, *Why are you doing it that way?*, ask *I'm curious to know: Why are you taking that approach?*

6. **Neutralize it.** Make sure the question is neutral with no agenda, no attempt to lead someone to a desired answer. Leading questions may work for prosecutors and interrogators, but generally should be avoided. Terrible leading

question: *Wasn't that movie awful?* Slightly better: *Do you think that movie lived up to the hype?* Better still: *What did you think of that movie?*

How might I test my built-in baloney detector?

If you want to give your own critical thinking skills a quick tune-up, try this short exercise designed to encourage fair-minded evaluation.

Exercise: Critical thinking workout
Read over an opinion column or essay from a newspaper or blog and then run through these five questions:

1. ***How strong is the evidence?*** Try to list how many points are presented to make the case. Then consider the evidence behind each point: *Does this evidence come from a solid source? Can I identify a possible agenda behind it?*
2. ***What are they not telling me?*** Look for what is missing from the article—insufficient reporting, lack of important details, or of opposing viewpoints.
3. ***Does it logically follow?*** Be on the lookout for flawed reasoning that suggests you should believe A because of B—when in fact there may be a tenuous connection between A and B.
4. ***What is the opposing view?*** If it hasn't been clearly presented, try to think of what someone in opposition would say. If possible think of several opposing points.
5. Finish the exercise by asking yourself the hardest question: ***Which side has more evidence behind it?*** Having thought about opposing viewpoints, are they stronger than the original argument? Or is the author's point (even if imperfect) still valid? An important part of critical thinking is being able to make a reasoned judgment call,

even when there is something to be said for and against both sides of an argument.

Exercises: Combating stinkin' thinkin'

After you've tried applying critical thinking to someone else's claims, see what happens when you use the same kind of thinking on one of your own beliefs—in particular, try to identify something you hold a negative view about. Then use questions to challenge the validity of that negative view, while considering the positive side. Think of this as a way to use critical thinking and inquiry to combat stinkin' thinkin'.

We all are subject to the "negativity bias," a tendency to give too much weight in our thinking to negative events, perceptions, and possibilities. A setback at work can lead to thinking "I'm going to get fired." Listening to the news may convince you that "the world is going to hell in a handbasket."

When you identify a feeling like that, write it down as a definitive statement, then challenge that statement with your critical thinking questions: *What is the evidence behind this claim? How reliable is it? What information is missing from this claim? Does the claim logically make sense? What is the opposing side?*

If, for example, you were to do this exercise with the "hell in a handbasket" assertion, you could easily find that there is lots of evidence against that claim—by various measures of global health and well-being, the world is actually getting better all the time. The problem is that eye-grabbing headlines usually focus on unpleasant surprises and morbid events; the classic "If it bleeds, it leads" news formula still reigns. As critical thinkers, we must factor into our worldview that the source of much of our information about the state of the world is biased toward negativity. That doesn't discredit the news. It just means we have to consider that bias as we make our own judgments.

Critical thinking can help with negative thoughts about the world, but you can also use critical thinking questions as a form of self-therapy to challenge negative thinking about yourself. The psychologist Judith Beck says that a big part of her therapy

approach is teaching patients to question the veracity of their negative thoughts: *Is this bad feeling I have really true? Is there another
way of viewing this situation?*

And here are two more great questions for challenging negative
thoughts about yourself. First, ask, *If my best friend were to say this
same negative thing about himself, what would I say to him?* The
second question to ask yourself is, *What went well today?* Psychologist Martin Seligman says simply asking a positive question like
this each day, and making yourself answer it, can provide a
powerful antidote to negative thinking.

What if I looked at the world around me with a fresh eye?

Questioning can be thought of as a way of looking at the
world—a proclivity to notice and wonder, instead of just accepting.
The challenge is: *How can you get yourself to look at your familiar
everyday world with a fresh eye?* One way, as shown in the 1989
film *Dead Poets Society*, is to stand on top of your desk. As
explained by Robin Williams's character in the film, when you
stand on your desk "the world looks very different from up
here." But there's also the risk that the desk may collapse under
you, so here is a safer exercise designed to help you see things
fresh.

Exercise: Seeing things in a fresh way

1. Take a photo, using your phone camera, of something
    you see every day. It could be a close-up photo of your
    breakfast or your workplace, your coffee shop or your
    health club lobby.
2. Take a close look at what's going on in the photo. Try
    shifting your focus from the object or patterns in the
    foreground to those in the background. Zoom in for
    details; zoom out for context.

3. Try to find three things you notice in the picture that you've never noticed before—small details, juxtapositions, patterns.

4. Turn each of those three things you noticed into a question—then see if you can add another question to the original question. (*Why is one side of my desk so cluttered and the other side so clean? What does that say about the way I work?*)

Once you've mastered the noticing and questioning exercise, try your hand at problem finding. If you can find a good problem to work on, you're well on your way to a great creation.

Exercise: Problem finding

As you go through your everyday routine and travels, document something—but this time, instead of taking a random photo, write down things that "bug" you: You can't find time to read the news; the front door of the building is hard to open; the line waiting for coffee is too long, etc.

Next, subject one of your daily irritations to a "Why?," "What if?," "How?" cycle of questioning. Innovators and inventors often tackle problems by asking "Why?," "What if?," and "How?" questions—in that order. The three types of questions do three different inquiry jobs: "Why?" questions help us to understand a problem; "What if?" questions help us imagine possible alternatives; "How?" questions, which tend to be more practical and action-oriented, lead us toward a solution.

Focusing on one of the problems you've identified, start with as many "Why?" questions as you can think of (*Why does this problem exist in the first place? And why hasn't someone solved it already?*). Then use your imagination to brainstorm multiple 'What If' possibilities (*What if we tried X? What if we tried Y?*). Next, pick the "What if?" question you like best and reframe it as a "How?" question—as in, *How might I take this crazy "what if?" idea and actually own it as a project? How would I take the first step?* Whether or not you keep pursuing this question beyond this exercise, you've probably already identified ways to minimize your daily irritation.

You can also try the Why?," "What if?," "How?" framework on a family issue or a problem at work. *My family never seems to eat dinner together*, or *My department doesn't get included enough in strategic planning*. Watch how the three-question progression leads you to actionable solutions.

Exercise: Connective inquiry

While we're still in "creative questioning" mode, here is an exercise in "connective inquiry" (a term for looking at two separate things and asking, *What if I put this together with that?*). This type of combinatorial thinking is the source of many great creations, from the iPhone to *Hamilton* the musical.

It was also the source of the bestselling 2010 book *Abraham Lincoln: Vampire Hunter*. The author of that book, Seth Grahame-Smith, came up with his mashup idea while in a bookstore, when he noticed one stack of popular books about historical figures near another stack of popular books about vampires. So, for this exercise, go into a bookstore—or any type of store—and try to find two very different themes or items that might be combined to form an interesting hybrid. You can also use items around the house or flip through a magazine looking for possible combinations.

Phrase the combination as a question: *What if Attila the Hun was plopped down in Silicon Valley? What if a potato peeler were combined with gloves?* Once you have your combination idea, subject it to questions: *What's interesting about it, and what doesn't work? Is there a similar but different combination that might be more interesting?* Even if you end up with nothing intriguing, you've given your brain a connections workout. If you think you've got a winning 'What If?' combination, start asking yourself how to begin fleshing out the idea.

How (and with whom) shall I break the ice?

Questioning can establish or deepen a connection with someone. One place to try this is at a cocktail party or any type of gathering where there are people you haven't met before. The challenge is to break the habit of asking rote introductory questions (*How are you? What do you do?*), and try diving in at the deep end of the questioning pool—with questions that seek a more meaningful answer and might possibly draw out a story.

Exercise: "Conversation starting" questions
Before joining a gathering and saying a word to anyone, ask yourself this question: *What if I approached this party as if I were a journalist, looking for stories about the people in attendance?*

Now think about the kinds of questions that can elicit stories. What are some favorite stories you like to share about yourself? Working backwards from that, what kind of questions could someone ask to elicit those stories from you? This will provide a general sense of the kinds of questions you should be asking.

If you want some all-purpose examples, here are a few: *What are you working on that you're really excited about these days? What's the most interesting thing you've done/learned in the past week? If you could pick anyone, who would you like to spend an afternoon with?* Use one of these sample questions if you like, but don't go in heavily scripted. Have a few possible questions in your arsenal and go with one that feels right in the moment.

Once you've initiated a conversation, use tools of active listening, such as paraphrasing or echoing, for clarification and to show you're paying attention (*You actually climbed to the top?*). And use follow-up questions to draw out emotion (*How did it feel when you were up there?*).

People accustomed to being asked only rote questions by strangers at first may give you a look that suggests, *You're overstepping your bounds, stranger.* If that happens, just say, "I like asking these types of questions because when I do, I often hear interesting stories." You've now explained that there's a method to your madness, and the conversational ball is back in the court of the other person, who is probably thinking, *I must have an interesting story! I don't want to be the person with no story.*

Bonus tip: As the conversation naturally shifts from questioning to sharing your own opinions and stories, remember to keep pausing to ask the other person, *What do* you *think?* That is a favorite question of the Harvard University–based questionologist James Ryan, who says "It's a question that's not only useful to ask, but is a good reminder to make sure that you are soliciting the views of other people in a room. If you don't consciously invite people to participate, they might remain silent and the conversation typically suffers because of that."

Exercise: L.I.F.E. questions

Questions can spark lively conversation when the family is together. The L.I.F.E. questions exercise can be done around the dinner table with kids once a week. The idea is to surface the little anecdotes and daily stories that create intimacy and shared memories. Go around the table and ask each person to share their four answers to the four L.I.F.E. questions. (Once your family members know they might be playing the game of L.I.F.E. at dinner next Sunday night, they'll start collecting and remembering moments to be shared at the next gathering.)

L. *What weird LITTLE thing sticks out in your mind from this week?*
The little things that we choose to remember and share with others form the narrative threads of our lives, and focusing on the "weird" helps captures children's attention.

I. *What piece of INFORMATION did you learn this week?*
Sharing something that's news to you or a piece of learning can entertain others and solidify the information in your own brain.

F. *Is there anything you tried and FAILED at this week?*
Sara Blakely, the entrepreneur who founded Spanx apparel, was inspired by this question, asked often by her

father at the dinner table. Acknowledging and discussing trial-and-error in a routine way helps us realize failing happens to all of us, is not something to be afraid of, and indeed helps us become better problem solvers.

E. *What memorable EXCHANGE did you have this week?*
This question reminds us to reach out once in a while beyond *How you doing?*, and show our curiosity about what others think and feel.

Exercise: Using questions instead of giving advice
This conversational questioning exercise is designed to begin training yourself to use guiding questions instead of dispensing advice. Try this exercise one-on-one with a spouse, friend, or colleague at work. The first step is to ask this person: *Do you have a problem or challenge you'd like advice on?* Then, when they share their problem, don't tell them your brilliant idea of what they should do. Instead use questions to help them figure it out for themselves.

Here are some questions to ask:

1. *What's going on?* (Tell me about the challenge you're facing.)
2. *What have you tried already?*
3. *If you could try anything to solve this, what would you try?*
4. *And what else?* (Repeat this question several times, as needed, to surface additional ideas.)
5. *Which of these options interests you most?*
6. *What might stand in the way of this idea, and what could be done about that?*
7. *What is one step you could take to begin acting on this, right away?*

What if I interview myself?

As you use questioning to draw out stories of others, why not do the same to yourself? The self-interview can help you clarify your own personal story. Then you'll be sure you have a good narrative to tell about yourself in a job interview, at a networking function, on an elevator with your boss, or any time you need a strong answer to the question, *So what's your story?*

Exercise: Creating your best story
You want a story that best reflects who you are, what you've accomplished, what matters to you, and where you're headed. These kinds of things are also what people get asked at an in-depth job interview where the interviewer is trying to determine your strengths, ambitions, your awareness of flaws and what you're doing about it. So it makes sense to use job interview questions to help you develop your best story.

The following "killer interview questions" were inspired by those shared by chief executives in a popular post on the site *Quartz*. If you can impress these people, you know you've got a good story. So here are the questions to ask the person in the mirror. Think about each one and write an answer that's at least a few lines long.

1. *Would you rather be respected or feared?*
2. *What is your biggest dream in life?*
3. *When you were a child, who or what did you want to be?*
4. *When you have failed, how did you respond?*
5. *If people were asked how you treat them, what do you think they'd say?*

In addition to these questions from the executives, here are a few more of my own, which you may recognize from earlier sections in the book:

6. *What is your sentence?* (Meaning, if you had to summarize your life in one sentence, what would that sentence be?)
7. *What is your tennis ball?* (What is the thing that you chase as intently as a dog chases a tennis ball?)
8. *What are you trying to get better at?*

Once you have answers to all the questions, think about how to weave those answers together to form a narrative. As in: I am someone who <*fill in "What's your sentence" answer*>. The thing I've always been drawn to is <*"tennis ball" answer*>. When I was a kid I saw myself as <*fill in "child" answer*>. And so forth . . .

Keep working on the story until it fits together well and flows, with a beginning, middle, and end. And have it available in your head to use on short notice, as a whole or in parts.

Can questioning help bring my family closer together?

As discussed in the Leadership section, every leader of a company should make sure the organization has a strong backstory about its history and original purpose, a sense of what the company stands for, and a mission statement—or better yet, a mission question. What if the leaders of families did this? The author Bruce Feiler has explored this theme in his writing, and it was also covered recently in a *New York Times* column by Paul Sullivan. Based on these sources, here's an exercise that uses questioning to develop a family story and an ongoing, inspiring family "mission question."

Exercise: Developing a family story and mission
Begin with a focus on family heritage:

- *Where were our ancestors born? When did they arrive in this country?*
- *What might our ancestors have had to overcome to get here?*
- *What are some traditions that have been passed down through our family? When and how did they get started?*
- *What are some family stories that you know? That I know?*
- *In particular, what difficulties did the family have to bounce back from?*

- *What were some of the greatest accomplishments by family members through the years?*
- *What do the stories mean to us today?*
- *What are some classic family jokes or songs?*

Then, transition to questions about meaning and purpose:

- *What does it mean to be part of this family?*
- *Is how you feel about being part of this family different than how I feel?*
- *Of all the family members you have either known or heard stories about, who do you think lived the most interesting life? Why?*

End with questions exploring a sense of shared mission:

- *What are our family values?*
- *What is this family trying to do beyond daily living? What's the greater purpose of our family?*
- *How might we create a "How might we . . ." mission question for the family?*
- *How might I contribute to the mission?*

What if I trade my resolutions for "questolutions"?

Research indicates that creating a resolution in question form may be more effective than a typical resolution in the form of a statement. A study at the University of Illinois found that when people were trying to motivate themselves to do something, they had better results asking (*Will I do X? How can I do X?*) as opposed to declaring (*I will do X!*)

Why do questions motivate us more than resolutions? First of all, questions are more engaging than statements. They invite you (or even challenge you) to think about potential solutions. They get your brain working right away on a problem. For example, suppose instead of resolving that *I will meet more interesting people this year!* you were to ask yourself, *How might I meet more interesting people this year?*

That question is likely to trigger speculative thought: *Well, what if I were to do X?* or *What if I tried to do Y?* Already, you are thinking of potential new ways to meet people.

Questions are also less intimidating than resolutions. They put less pressure on you. Some people might feel they need pressure to get themselves to act, but the self-imposed pressure of resolutions rarely produces immediate results—and this, in turn, can cause us to quickly abandon those resolutions. A question, on the other hand, is more forgiving and offers more leeway. It doesn't necessarily have to be answered right away, or definitively—we can be working on the question, taking steps, making progress toward an answer.

Plus, questions tend to be more "shareable" than statements. No one really wants to hear your declarations of the wonderful things you're promising to do. But when you share a question with others (*I wonder how I could do a better job of X*, or *How might I improve Y?*), it invites people to think about that question themselves—and they may end up helping you to arrive at an answer.

Here's an exercise in which you can use questioning to try to change your own behavior by composing a resolution, with a twist. Call it a "questolution."

Exercise: Create your own "questolution"

1. In thinking of a questolution for yourself, phrase it as "How might I?" question (e.g., *How might I get myself to drink more water?*).

2. Write or print the question in bold type at the top of a sheet of paper and tape the sheet to the wall.

3. Each time you think of an idea that might help you achieve the goal, phrase that idea as a "What if?" question (*What if I begin carrying a reusable water bottle to*

work each day?) and jot it down under the overarching "How might I?" questolution.

4. This very visible list of "What if?" questions you're creating will cry out for action, and you're likely to find yourself making step-by-step progress on your questolution.

How can I encourage others to question more?

Fostering a "culture of inquiry" at a company or a school isn't only the purview of chief executives or school principals. If you believe that questioning is a positive thing then it's your responsibility to encourage others around you—at work, in your home, your school, your neighborhood—to question more.

Exercises: Making questioning fun and appealing to others

- At home, make one night a week "question night," during which family members can only communicate with one another by questions. Try to think of songs with a question for the title. (I've got a running list going at www .amorebeautifulquestion.com/50-question-songs). Do a question-storming or another question-related activity; some examples can be found here www.questionweek.com /exercises-to-build-your-questioning-muscles.
- If you're trying to encourage kids to question more, it helps if you can convince them that questioning is cool. This is difficult because many young people over a certain age think questioning is decidedly "uncool." But you might try pointing out that many things they probably love—the iPhone, Instagram, and many popular apps— started as questions. (If they demand specifics on that, you can find stories about cool stuff that started as a question on this book's website.) And while you're pointing this out

to them, also point out that questioners are rebels and mavericks and rule breakers (from Elon Musk to Beyoncé). And if that's still not enough, you can point out that a lot of questioners, particularly in Silicon Valley, have become some of the most successful people in the world because of their questions.

- Celebrate good questions that your kids or your friends ask. Write the question down and tape it on the refrigerator or share it on social media.

- When your kids come home from school, ask them if they asked a good question that day. This tip is inspired by a quote from the Nobel Laureate scientist Isidor Isaac Rabi, who said that when he was growing up in Brooklyn, all the other mothers asked their kids, "So did you learn anything today?" But Rabi's mother would ask him, "Izzy, did you ask a good question today?" Rabi believes his mother's question about questions had a profound influence that contributed to him becoming a scientist.

- If you are a manager or boss, ask for questions as if you really value them and want to hear them. Consider giving rewards to people for asking a question. When I do a talk, I often give a free book to the first person in the audience to ask a question. "First question" askers are courageous, and they make it safe for everyone else to ask questions.

- When someone asks a good question, don't say simply, "That's a good question." Tell them why you think it's a fascinating or important question—and ask them what they might like to do with that question, now that it has been given life.

What is my one "big beautiful question"?

There are a myriad of beautiful questions out there—questions that can be used again and again to help you decide, create, connect, and lead. In addition to the ones in this book, there are many more you can devise yourself. But I also believe that you should try to identify *one particular question* to pursue over time—call it your "big beautiful question" (BBQ). It should be bold and ambitious and actionable.

My own BBQ started a decade ago as *How might I encourage more questioning?* Writing this book is just one of the ways I am still trying to explore that question. I do other things in pursuit of my question—such as visiting various types of organizations to proselytize and share questioning tips and techniques. But I am particularly focused these days on going to schools, spending time with teachers, and exploring ways to bring more questioning into classrooms, because I believe the future depends on our ability, right now, to develop the questioners, critical thinkers, innovators, and lifelong learners that the world will very much need in the days to come.

Where and how might you find *your* big beautiful question? Start by looking to where your interests and passions lie. Ask yourself some questions about what moves you, what you care deeply about, what you feel you were meant to do (refer back to part I's "tennis ball" section for some questions to help with this). And keep your eyes open for the right "problem"—one that stirs you, and that you might be able to "own" in your own way. It might turn out to be a problem right in front of you—but you may need to step back to see it fresh.

You may have a goal in mind and are already actively pursuing it. But if you haven't put it into question form, give it a try. The evidence suggests this will help get your mind thinking about the challenge in a new way, as well as make it more shareable with others.

As you construct your BBQ, think about phrasing it in the "How might I" format—or if you're collaborating with others on a shared mission, "How might we." This form of questioning is powerful. It is used increasingly by tech innovators, inquiry-based educators, and other forward thinkers because it enables one to construct a question that is open and expansive, yet still action oriented. As explained by Tim Brown, chief executive at the innovation firm IDEO, "How might" questions free you to do your best creative thinking. "The 'how' part assumes there are solutions out there—it provides creative confidence," Brown says. "The word 'might' says we can put ideas out there that might work or might not—either way, it's okay."

Don't be afraid of constructing a multi-part, compound BBQ. You might need to build onto the original question, in order to address different aspects of a complex challenge. For instance, my own question has expanded to the point that in its full form it now reads, *How might I encourage more questioning, through writing and in-person contact, at businesses as well as nonprofit organizations, but with a primary focus on education?* The reason to expand your question in this way is to remind yourself of key things you should be focused on within the overall challenge.

Make your question ambitious—but not overly so. If your BBQ is along the lines of *How might I end all wars, starting today?*, you will find that it's not actionable, and thus it won't stick. The physicist Edward Witten describes the sweet spot of questioning as "a question that is hard (and interesting) enough that it is worth answering—and easy enough to actually answer it."

If you're a leader, try to find the big beautiful question for your organization or group—the forward-looking vision question that everyone can rally around. Take this opportunity to work on a "How might we" question that encapsulates your organization's goals, dreams, and vision for the future.

Once you've devised your question, write it down, tell your friends, put it out there on social media—share it any way you can. You'll be amazed at how people tend to support and help someone pursuing a beautiful question. If you want to share it with the readers of this book, there is a designated area on the website where I am posting an array of beautiful questions sent in by readers. (Go to amorebeautifulquestion.com/whats-your-beautiful-question). If you haven't thought of your question yet, go to the site and check out some of the questions others are pursuing—it may spark an idea.

Most important, stay with your question. In the age of Google, we have come to expect instant answers to our questions. But the best questions, the beautiful ones, cannot be answered by Google. They require a different kind of "search." Be willing to go on that journey of inquiry—and try to enjoy working on your question, grappling with it, sleeping with it, and just being in its engaging company.

Acknowledgments

I want to start by thanking three people who made this book happen: the editors George Gibson and Ben Hyman, and literary agent Jim Levine. George encouraged me to write a follow-up to *A More Beautiful Question* (a book he'd edited and championed), while Jim closed the deal with Bloomsbury. Then, something unexpected happened: Before I finished writing the new book, George left his longtime editorial perch at Bloomsbury—which meant my book had no editor and was an "orphan," in publishing parlance. Fortunately, Bloomsbury handled all of this just the right way. They allowed George, after leaving the company, to continue to edit the book, so there would be no disruption. At the same time, they named Ben as the in-house editor of the book. Ben and George collaborated beautifully, and were supported by an excellent team of marketers, publicists and production people at Bloomsbury.

This was a challenging book to write, because I was attempting to cover so much ground with it. Fortunately, many people helped along the way. I am particularly indebted to David Cleary, Lauren Dial, Marshall Saenz, and Emeka Patrick, who conducted extensive research for the book.

Thank you to all those who granted interviews. When people agree to give an interview to a book author, it is an act of generosity. It's not the same as talking to a news media outlet, which provides a faster and often bigger reward in terms of publicity. A book interviewee doesn't know for sure when the book will come out or how many people will read it. They do the interviews because they are genuinely interested in the subject of a book—and they simply want to be helpful.

With that in mind, here's to those who took time to talk to me about questioning, including (but not limited to): Adam Grant, Nadia Lopez, Douglas Conant, Arthur Aron, Angie Morgan, Daniel J. Levitan, Katherine Milkman, Neil Browne, Ed Hess, David Burkus, Adam Hansen, Robin Dreeke, Don Derosby, Michael Bungay Stanier, Khe Hy, Tom Kelley, Kwame Dawes, Keith Yamashita, Lisa Kay Solomon, James Ryan, Steve Sloman, Katherine Crowley, Matthew Fray, Jay Heinrichs, Scott Barry Kaufman, Rachel Sussman, Christopher Schroeder, David Cooperrider, and Ron Friedman. Bruce Mau, Jonathan Fields, John Seely Brown, and Eric Maisel talked to me for previous books, and were quoted again in this one. George Kohlrieser, Nancy Kessler, and Mark Strauss also shared great insights and material.

The whole time I was working on *The Book of Beautiful Questions*, I was also "going to school"—visiting classrooms and university research centers, talking to students and teachers, conducting questioning exercises, and constantly learning. I'd like to thank Bowling Green State College, New York's School of Visual Arts, the University of Colorado at Boulder, the California College of Art, the University of South Carolina, the University of Oklahoma, Maryland Institute College of Art, Johns Hopkins University, and New York University (special thanks to Luke Williams).

I think I've learned the most in my visits to high schools and elementary schools. I don't have room to name them all here, but I want to give special thanks to the Los Angeles County Office of Education, the public schools in Westchester County (I've run questioning clinics with several of them), the CASA Middle School in the Bronx (thank you for the invite, Jamaal Bowman), the Carroll County schools in rural Georgia, the Dalton School, the Loyola School, the Avenues World School, the Berkshire School, the Charles River School, and the Nueva School. All of these schools, teachers, and students contributed to this book, mostly by showing me questioning in action.

Thank you also to business and government organizations that have invited me to share questioning techniques and refine my learning. There are too many to name them all, but a few that stand out are Pepsico, Novo Nordisk, Boeing, Chanel, and Oracle. And my thanks to NASA for bringing me in to discuss questioning with some of the world's top scientific minds.

I want to salute my fellow "questionologists," starting with the Right Question Institute's Dan Rothstein and Luz Santana. They have championed my work (and I've tried to do likewise for them) and been a great source of information and contacts, while also helping to co-sponsor "Question Week" each year. Thanks also to Frank Sesno, the former CNN anchor and author of *Ask More*, who is advancing the study of questioning at George Washington University. Hal Gregersen of MIT has been a pioneer in this area, as has the author Marilee Adams. Bob Tiede's blog, *Leading with Questions*, has been an invaluable resource. Edgar Schein and his book *Humble Inquiry* have been highly influential. And I keep meeting new people—such as Aileen Gibb, Gerard Senehi, and Kurt Madden—who are specializing in this area. Our ranks are growing; now we need to make questionology an officially-recognized "thing."

In lieu of a full bibliography, I want to acknowledge a handful of books that had a very big influence on this book, starting with Daniel Kahneman's *Thinking, Fast and Slow*, and continuing with Chip and Dan Heath's *Decisive*, Tom and David Kelley's *Creative Confidence*, Ed Hess and Katherine Ludwig's *Humility is the New Smart*, Greg McKeown's *Essentialism*, Ian Leslie's *Curious*, Neil Browne's *Asking the Right Questions*, Carl Sagan's *The Demon-Haunted World*, and Mark Goulston's *Just Listen*.

I also relied on the research and writings of Richard Larrick, Jack Soll, Katherine Milkman and John Payne, Charan Ranganath, KH Kim, Ethan Koss, Emily Esfahani Smith, Martin Seligman, Dan Ariely, John S. Hammond, Ralph L. Keeney and Howard Raiffa, Mihaly Csikszentmahalyi, Paul Sloane, Daniel Pink, Elizabeth Gilbert, Cal Newport, Dan Rockwell, Scott Belsky, the late Dr. Richard Paul of the Foundation for Critical Thinking, and Julia Galef of the Center for Applied Rationality.

For the Creativity section of this book, I was inspired by the work and wise words of a number of artists, including John Cleese, Lin-Manuel Miranda, Lynn Nottage, Ann Patchett, Mike Birbiglia, and the late George Carlin (thank you to his daughter, Kelly Carlin, for sharing inside information about Carlin's questioning ways).

Thanks to *Fast Company* and *Harvard Business Review* for running my articles and posts about questioning; to *Quartz* for publishing my work on critical thinking; and to *Psychology Today* for providing a platform for my "Questionologist" blog.

And I want to express appreciation for all the publications and blogs that produce so many great posts and articles about questioning, curiosity, and creative thinking—in particular, the *New York Times*, *Wired*, *O, The Oprah Magazine* (which designated 2018 as a year of "Big Questions"), *Big Think*, Maria Popova's *Brain Pickings*, Shane Parrish's *Farnam Street*, and Eric Barker's *Barking Up the Wrong Tree*.

Special thanks to my local Monday martini club and its leader, Ben Cheever, for helping me get through the writing process by providing encouragement, moral support, and Hendricks gin.

As always, deepest thanks and love to Barbara, Walter, and Kathy Berger and to the Kelly family, with a special nod to the late Lawrence Kelly, who learned from his formidable father to "always ask why."

I close by honoring the most important person in my work and my life, Laura E. Kelly—my wife, creative partner, business partner, constant companion, and fellow questioner. She was deeply involved in the creation of this book from start to finish, as she has been with all of my previous works. Many years ago, I asked a beautiful question aimed at her: *Will you accompany me on this journey?* Thankfully, she answered yes.

Notes

Introduction: Why Question?

PAGE 1: ***What if I just declared myself a questionologist?*** ... Warren Berger, "The Power of Why and What If?," *New York Times*, July 3, 2016.

PAGE 5: **we become more likable to others by asking questions** ... Karen Huang, Michael Yeomans, Alison Wood Brooks, Julia Minson, and Francesca Gino, "It Doesn't Hurt to Ask: Question Asking Increases Liking," *Journal of Personality and Social Psychology* Vol. 113, mentioned in the *Boston Globe* Ideas column by Kevin Lewis, May 12, 2017, www.bostonglobe.com/ideas/2017/05/12/nYdE1qm6gpihhxChjdrpXP/story.html.

PAGE 6: **when we're working on questions in our minds we're engaged in "slow thinking"** ... Daniel Kahneman, *Thinking, Fast and Slow* (New York: Farrar Strauss and Giroux, 2011).

PAGE 7: **children at that age may ask anywhere from one hundred to three hundred questions a day** ... Paul Harris, *Trusting What You're Told: How Children Learn from Others* (Boston: Harvard Press, 2012). Studies also cited in the article "Mothers Asked Nearly 300 Questions a Day, Study Finds," *Telegraph*, March 28, 2013.

PAGE 7–8: **young children discover early on that the information they seek can be easily extracted from other human beings** ... Ibid.

PAGE 8: **Neurological research shows that merely wondering about an interesting question** ... "The Power of the Question," Liesl Gloecker, The Swaddle (blog), March 3, 2017, www.theswaddle.com/how-to-stimulate-curiosity-questions.

PAGE 8: **Think of curiosity as a condition—"like an itch," says the neuroscientist Charan Ranganath** ... Ibid.

PAGE 8: **The asking of questions (at least the ones that are verbalized by young students in school) tends to subside steadily** . . . Right Question Institute study based on question-asking data gathered by the National Center for Education Statistics for the 2009 Nation's Report Card. For more on the study, see www.rightquestion.org.

PAGE 10: **we can easily fall into the "trap of expertise"** . . . This is a widely used term. A recent article on the subject: www.scientificamerican .com/article/you-don-t-know-as-much-as-you-think-false-expertise.

PAGE 11: **"Some people see things that are and ask, 'Why?' "** . . . from *Brain Droppings*, by George Carlin (New York: Hyperion, 1997).

PAGE 11: **"I always asked why we're doing things the way we're doing them,"** Jobs said . . . From *Steve Jobs: The Lost Interview*, a documentary released to theaters in 2012 consisting of an original seventy-minute interview that Steve Jobs gave to Robert X. Cringely in 1995 for the Oregon Public Broadcasting documentary, *Triumph of the Nerds*.

PAGE 15: **"People are united by questions. It is the answers that divide them"** . . . From Elie Wiesel's essay "The Loneliness of Moses" in *Loneliness* by Leroy S. Rouner (Boston: University of Notre Dame Press, 1998); quoted by Maria Popova in "Loneliness of Leadership, How Our Questions Unite Us, and How Our Answers Divide Us," *Brain Pickings*, May 29, 2017, www.brainpickings.org/2017/05/29/elie -wiesel-the-loneliness-of-moses.

PAGE 15: **A growing body of research shows that human connection is central to leading a happier, more meaningful life** . . . Scott Stossel, "What Makes Us Happy, Revisited," *Atlantic*, May 2013.

PAGE 16: **"It's hard to transcend a combative question"** . . . Krista Tippett, *Becoming Wise: An Inquiry into the Mystery and Art of Living* (New York: Penguin Press, 2016).

PAGE 17: **"If we are not able to ask skeptical questions"** . . . Carl Sagan's last interview in 1996 on *Charlie Rose*. Available on YouTube: www .youtube.com/watch?v=U8HEwO-2L4w.

PAGE 17–18: **"We've become less critical in the face of information overload"** . . . From my interview with Daniel J. Levitin in Apr. 2017, and from his August 2014 Talks at Google, "The Organized Mind: Thinking Straight in the Age of Information Overload," www.youtube.com/ watch?v=aRiTNEHRY-U, uploaded Oct. 28, 2014. These themes are also covered in Levitin's book *Weaponized Lies: How to Think Critically in the Post-Truth Era* (New York: Dutton, 2016).

PAGE 18: **we can do what Carl Sagan called "baloney detection"** . . . Sagan's Baloney Detection Kit was featured on *Brain Pickings* on Jan. 3, 2014, in Maria Popova's "The Baloney Detection Kit: Carl Sagan's Rules for Bullshit-Busting and Critical Thinking," www

.brainpickings.org/2014/01/03/baloney-detection-kit-carl-sagan, which excerpted it from Sagan's *The Demon-Haunted World: Science as a Candle in the Dark* (New York: Ballantine, 1996).

Part I: Questions for Better
DECISION-MAKING

PAGE 22: **"The science simply doesn't support the value of following your gut"** . . . From my interview with Katherine Milkman of the University of Pennsylvania, Sept. 2017.

PAGE 22: **"your gut is going to be wrong more than it is right"** . . . From my email exchanges and interview with Daniel Levitin, Apr. 2017. Levitin also covers this theme in his book *Weaponized Lies*.

PAGE 23: **rather than spending time analyzing small decisions, "have fun with them"** . . . Mike Whitaker's advice in Stephanie Vozza's "How Successful People Make Decisions Differently," *Fast Company*, Aug. 7, 2017.

PAGE 23: **Questions enable us to "organize our thinking around what we don't know"** . . . From my interviews with Steve Quatrano of the Right Question Institute, at various points in 2014 and 2015. This quote also appeared in *A More Beautiful Question*.

PAGE 24: **"It's going against evolution"** . . . From my interview with Levitin, Apr. 2017.

PAGE 24: **humans resort to snap judgments because "we're cognitive misers"** . . . Jack B. Soll, Katherine Milkman, and John Payne, "Outsmart Your Own Biases," *Harvard Business Review*, May 2015.

PAGE 24: **we are prone to falling into "a raft of traps"** . . . John S. Hammond, Ralph L. Keeney, and Howard Raiffa, "The Hidden Traps of Decision Making," *Harvard Business Review*, Jan. 2006.

PAGE 25: **We form a story in our heads based on what little we know, without allowing for all we do *not* know** . . . Daniel Kahneman, "Don't Blink! The Hazards of Confidence," *New York Times Magazine*, Oct. 19, 2011.

PAGE 26: **"Overconfidence arises because people are often blind to their own blindness"** . . . Ibid.

PAGE 27: **Facebook's newsfeed algorithm steadily feeds confirmation bias** . . . Nelson Granados, "How Facebook Biases Your News Feed," *Forbes*, Jun. 30, 2016.

PAGE 27: **he made a daily habit of asking what he called the "jugular question"** . . . Arno Penzias said this at a Fast Company conference, and it was reported in *The Art of Powerful Questions* by Eric E. Vogt, Juanita Brown, and David Isaacs of the World Café (Whole Systems Associates: Mill Valley, CA, 2003).

PAGE 27: ***What did I once believe that is no longer true?*** ... Daniel Pink shared this question during an online interview with Adam Grant, conducted Aug. 2015 on Parlio.com, www.parlio.com/qa/daniel-pink.

PAGE 27: **don't overlook the "desirability bias"** ... Ben Tappin, Leslie Van Der Leer, and Ryan McKay, "Your Opinion is Set in Stone," Gray Matter, *New York Times*, May 28, 2017.

PAGE 28: **"What are some reasons that my initial judgment might be wrong?"** ... Richard Larrick, "Debiasing," a chapter in the *Blackwell Handbook of Judgment and Decision Making* (New York: Wiley-Blackwell, 2004).

PAGE 28: **there is at least some scientific basis for the "Opposite George" strategy** ... "The Opposite" aired May 19, 1994, the twenty-first episode of the fifth season of *Seinfeld*. The idea originates when Jerry suggests to George, "If every instinct you have is wrong, then the opposite would be right."

PAGE 29: **You must be "humble enough to admit that you don't know something"** ... From my interview with Daniel J. Levitin, Apr. 2017. Unless otherwise indicated, all quotes from Levitin in this chapter are from that interview.

PAGE 29: ***Am I a soldier or a scout?*** ... From Julia Galef's TED Talk, "Why You Think You're Right Even When You're Wrong," Mar. 9, 2017, www.ted.com/talks/julia_galef_why_you_think_you_re_right_even_if_you_re_wrong.

PAGE 30: **one quality the company looks for when hiring is intellectual humility** ... Thomas Friedman, "How to Get a Job at Google," *New York Times*, Feb. 22, 2014.

PAGE 30: **Defined as "a state of openness to new ideas, a willingness to be receptive to new sources of evidence"** ... Cindy Lamothe, "How 'Intellectual Humility' Can Make You a Better Person," The Cut, Feb. 3, 2017, www.thecut.com/2017/02/how-intellectual-humility-can-make-you-a-better-person.html.

PAGE 30: **We can't compete with artificial intelligence unless we humans keep learning, experimenting, creating, and adapting** ... From my interview conducted with Edward Hess, Nov. 2017. Hess is also quoted from a podcast interview with Knowledge@Wharton, Jan. 24, 2017. www.knowledge.wharton.upenn.edu/article/why-smart-machines-will-boost-emotional-intelligence.

PAGE 31: ***Would I rather be right or would I rather understand?*** ... Christopher Schroeder shared this question during my interview with him in Oct. 2017.

PAGE 31:   **"If we really want to improve our judgment as individuals and as societies"** . . . From Julia Galef's TED Talk "Why You Think You're Right . . . ," Mar. 9, 2017.

PAGE 32:   **"It's a terrible name"** . . . From my interview conducted with Neil Browne at Bowling Green State College in Feb. 2017.

PAGE 32:   **It's really just a matter of asking a few fundamental questions** . . . The five critical thinking questions featured are based on my interviews with Neil Browne and also drawn from his book *Asking the Right Questions: A Guide to Critical Thinking*, coauthored with Stuart Keeley (London: Pearson, 2007), as well as from my interviews with Daniel Levitin, and from the chapter on critical thinking/baloney detection in Carl Sagan's 1996 book, *The Demon-Haunted World: Science as a Candle in the Dark*.

PAGE 34:   **An excellent resource for identifying common logical fallacies is Carl Sagan's "baloney detection kit"** . . . Featured on Maria Popova's *Brain Pickings* blog, Jan. 3, 2014, www.brainpickings.org /2014/01/03/baloney-detection-kit-carl-sagan/, which excerpted it from Sagan's book *The Demon-Haunted World*.

PAGE 35:   **a common behavior that he labeled "weak-sense critical thinking"** . . . Dr. Richard Paul's thoughts on critical thinking are featured at the website for his Foundation for Critical Thinking (www .criticalthinking.org), and in Dr. Paul's talks available on YouTube, including "Critical Thinking: Standards of Thought," www.youtube .com/watch?v=gNCOOUK-bMQ. "Weak-sense critical thinking" is also discussed in Neil Browne's *Asking the Right Questions*.

PAGE 36:   **Kahneman found that "people who face a difficult question often answer an easier one instead, without realizing it"** . . . Daniel Kahneman, "Don't Blink! The Hazards of Confidence," *New York Times Magazine*, Oct. 19, 2011.

PAGE 36:   **A decision can be no better than the best option under consideration** . . . Jack B. Soll, Katherine Milkman, and John Payne, "Outsmart Your Own Biases," *Harvard Business Review*, May 2015.

PAGE 36:   **"the first villain of decision making—'narrow framing'** . . . Chip and Dan Heath, *Decisive: How to Make Better Decisions in Life and Work* (New York: Currency, 2013).

PAGE 37:   **Milkman, Soll, and Payne suggest generating at least three options for any decision** . . . from "Outsmart Your Own Biases," *Harvard Business Review*, May 2015.

PAGE 37:   **Paul Sloane suggests that the third option you generate should be an unusual one** . . . From Paul Sloane's blog, *Destination Innovation*, "Got a Big Decision to Make? Try the Three by Three Method," May 2017, www.destination-innovation.com/got-big -decision-make-try-three-three-method.

PAGE 38:   **Whenever you're trying to decide between existing choices, try asking yourself the "vanishing options" question** . . . Chip and Dan Heath, *Decisive: How to Make Better Decisions in Life and Work.*

PAGE 38:   **we give more sensible advice to others than we give ourselves** . . . Dan Ariely, "A Simple Mind Trick Will Help You Think More Rationally," Big Think, www.bigthink.com/videos/dan-ariely-on-how-to-be-more-rational.

PAGE 38:   **"When we think of our friends we see the forest. When we think of ourselves, we get stuck in the trees"** . . . Chip and Dan Heath, *Decisive: How to Make Better Decisions in Life and Work.*

PAGE 38:   **try asking yourself about a decision by using the third person** . . . Ethan Kross's research on using the third person to make decisions is covered in a number of articles, including Pamela Weintraub's "The Voice of Reason," *Psychology Today*, May 4, 2015, www.psychologytoday.com/articles/201505/the-voice-reason.

PAGE 39:   **"If we got kicked out and the board brought in a new CEO, what do you think he would do?"** . . . This anecdote involving Intel cofounders Andrew Grove and Gordon Moore has been widely reported. When Grove died last year, it appeared in a number of obituaries, including one by Phil Rosenthal, "What the Late Intel Boss Andrew Grove Can Teach about Managing," *Chicago Tribune*, Mar. 22, 2016.

PAGE 40:   **They needed to "step back from the process and see it objectively as I did"** . . . Dave LaHote, "Improvement for the Sake of Improvement Means Nothing," *The Lean Post* (blog of the Lean Enterprise Institute), Apr. 4, 2014, www.lean.org/LeanPost/Posting.cfm?LeanPostId=179.

PAGE 40:   **"Most decisions should probably be made with somewhere around 70% of the information you wish you had"** . . . From Amazon CEO Jeff Bezos's "2016 Letter to Shareholders," Apr. 12, 2017, www.amazon.com/p/feature/z609g6sysxur57t.

PAGE 40:   **there are times when we should avoid making decisions—when we're tired, stressed** . . . Various sources, including Marcia Reynolds, "When You Should Never Make a Decision," *Psychology Today*, Apr. 17, 2014. Also covered in Daniel Kahneman's book *Thinking, Fast and Slow* (New York: Farrar Strauss and Giroux, 2011).

PAGE 40:   *Is it possible to shoot holes in this decision?* . . . A variation of this question is found in T. A. Frank, "The Fine Art of Making the Right Decision," *Monday* (an online magazine from The Drucker Institute), Jan.–Feb. 2017.

PAGE 41:   *Where in my life right now am I living under the fog of indecisiveness?* . . . Todd Henry shared this question and other quotes on

Srini Rao's *Unmistakable Creative* podcast episode titled "Todd Henry: Becoming the Leader Creative People Need," www .unmistakablecreative.com/podcast/todd-henry-becoming-leader -creative-people-need.

PAGE 41:   **"we'll end up dead and broke on the side of the road"** . . . From my interview conducted with Khemaridh Hy, May 2017. Unless otherwise indicated, other quotes from Hy in this chapter are from this interview.

PAGE 42:   **CNN dubbed him "an Oprah for millennials"** . . . Heather Long, "Meet Khe Hy, the Oprah for Millennials," CNN Money, Dec. 31, 2016. money.cnn.com/2016/12/30/news/economy/khemaridh -hy-rad-reads-oprah-for-millennials/index.html.

PAGE 42:   **the "negativity bias"** . . . Hara Estroff Marano, "Our Brain's Negative Bias," *Psychology Today*, June 20, 2003.

PAGE 42:   **people continuing to choose to drive instead of fly long after the 9/11 tragedy** . . . James Ball, "Sept. 11's Indirect Toll: Road Deaths Linked to Fearful Fliers," *Guardian*, Sept. 5, 2011.

PAGE 42:   **those "jungle instincts"—the same ones that can cause us to feel we must react** . . . From my fall 2017 series of interviews with Adam Hansen, coauthor of *Outsmart Your Instincts: How the Behavioral Innovation™ Approach Drives Your Company Forward* by Adam Hansen, Edward Harrington, and Beth Storz (Minneapolis: Forness Press, 2017). Unless otherwise indicated, subsequent quotes from Hansen in this chapter are from this interview.

PAGE 43:   **Phil Keoghan, a lifelong adventurer and fear conqueror who hosts the television series *The Amazing Race*** . . . These tips are extracted from my interview with Keoghan for the book *No Opportunity Wasted* (New York: Rodale, 2004).

PAGE 43:   **The life coach Curt Rosengren points out that it's critical to emphasize the *Why?*** . . . Curt Rosengren, "8 Fear-Busting Questions," *Passion Catalyst* (blog), www.passioncatalyst.com/newsletter /archive/fear.htm.

PAGE 44:   ***What is the worst that could happen?*** . . . The benefits of asking this question are discussed by Eric Barker in "Stoicism Reveals 4 Rituals That Will Make You Mentally Strong," *Barking Up the Wrong Tree* blog, Dec. 2016 www.bakadesuyo.com/2016/12/mentally-strong/.

PAGE 44:   **when we think about failure, "we do so in a vague, exaggerated way"** . . . From my interview with Jonathan Fields in 2013 for *A More Beautiful Question*. A couple of Fields's comments here originally appeared in that book, as well as in my Mar. 10, 2014 post for *Fast Company*, "Scared of Failing? Ask Yourself These 6 Fear-Killing Questions," www.fastcodesign.com/3027404/scared-of-failing-ask -yourself-these-6-fear-killing-questions.

PAGE 45:   **decision-making expert Gary Klein is a proponent of using "premortems"** . . . Gary Klein, "Performing a Project Premortem," *Harvard Business Review*, Sept. 2007, www.hbr.org/2007/09 /performing-a-project-premortem.

PAGE 45:   **"What if I succeed—what would that look like?"** . . . Also from my 2013 interview with Jonathan Fields.

PAGE 46:   *What would I try if I knew I could not fail?* . . . This question, also featured in *A More Beautiful Question*, was used in a slightly different version by Pastor Robert H. Schuller in *Possibility Thinking: What Great Thing Would You Attempt . . . If You Knew You Could Not Fail?* (Chicago: Nightingale-Conant Corp., 1971). The question, worded as "What would you attempt to do if you knew you could not fail?," was also featured in Regina Dugan's March 2012 TED Talk, "From Mach 20 Glider to Hummingbird Drone" www.ted.com/talks/ regina_dugan_from_mach_20_glider_to_humming_bird_drone.

PAGE 46:   **"In order for imagination to flourish, there must be an opportunity to see things as other than they currently are"** . . . From my interview conducted in 2013 with John Seely Brown, also taken from an article by Brown and Douglas Thomas, "Cultivating the Imagination: Building Learning Environments for Innovation," *Teachers College Record*, Feb. 17, 2011, www.newcultureoflearning .com/TCR.pdf.

PAGE 47:   **An interesting variation of the "What if I could not fail?" question was explored** . . . Ron Lieber, "'What Would You Do If You Weren't Afraid?' and 4 Money Questions from Readers," Your Money, *New York Times*, Sept. 2, 2016, www.nytimes.com/2016/09 /03/your-money/what-if-you-werent-afraid-and-4-more-money -questions-from-readers.html.

PAGE 47:   **that question "caused me to re-examine my situation to make sure I wasn't doing what was easy"** . . . Ibid.

PAGE 47:   **The economist Steven Levitt wanted to find out, and conducted a study** . . . Levitt's study is described in a column by Arthur C. Brooks, "Nobody Here but Us Chickens," *New York Times*, Jul. 22, 2017.

PAGE 48:   **people under age thirty today are much less likely than their counterparts in the past to relocate** . . . Ibid.

PAGE 48:   **A friend of Galef's was offered a job that would amount to a $70,000 pay increase** . . . This is story is told by Julia Galef in a video titled "Decision Making: Reframing," featured on the Center for Applied Rationality website. (www.rationality.org/resources/videos.)

PAGE 49:   **"Good decision-making is tied to our ability to anticipate future emotional states"** . . . Ed Batista, "Stop Worrying about Making the Right Decision," *Harvard Business Review*, Nov. 8, 2013.

PAGE 49: *If I look back years from now, will I wish that I'd made a change*
          when the opportunity was ripe? . . . Rob Walker, "Finding a New
          Direction When a Plum Job Turns Sour," from Walker's Workolo-
          gist column, *New York Times*, Apr. 17, 2016.

PAGE 49: **"Human beings are works in progress that mistakenly think
          they're finished"** . . . From Dan Gilbert's March 2014 TED Talk,
          "The Psychology of Your Future Self," www.ted.com/talks/dan_
          gilbert_you_are_always_changing.

PAGE 49: **Adam Grant offered several more targeted questions** . . . Adam
          Grant, "Which Company is Right for You?," *New York Times*, Dec. 20,
          2015. (Additional quotes by Grant in this section are from this article.)

PAGE 50: **the social component of work—it is a large and often under-
          rated factor** . . . Ron Friedman is quoted in Ron Carucci's "Before
          You Accept That Job Offer, Make Sure the Company Does These 3
          Things Well," *Forbes*, Jul. 27, 2016, www.forbes.com/sites/roncarucci
          /2016/07/27/before-you-accept-that-job-offer-make-sure-the
          -company-does-these-3-things-well.

PAGE 51: **"Why are people fully aware that benefits are important in their
          current job"** . . . Ayelet Fishbach, "In Choosing a Job, Focus on the
          Fun," *New York Times*, Jan. 13, 2017. (Other quotes from Fishbach
          are from the same article.)

PAGE 51: **think of each important decision as a chapter within a larger
          story** . . . All quotes from Joseph Badaracco in this section are from
          a post by Jared Lindzon, "Ask Yourself These 5 Questions before
          Making Any Major Decisions," *Fast Company*, Aug. 15, 2016. www
          .fastcompany.com/3062721/ask-yourself-these-five-questions-before
          -making-any-major-decisions.

PAGE 52: *If I'm saying yes to this, what am I saying no to?* . . . This ques-
          tion was shared by Michael Bungay Stanier during my interview
          conducted with him Sept. 2017.

PAGE 52: **He calls it the "cancel-elation" question** . . . Dan Ariely shared
          this question during an interview with Ron Friedman during the
          Peak Work Performance Summit (www.thepeakworkperformance
          summit.com). It is also discussed on Dan Ariely's website: www
          .danariely.com/2014/08/30/ask-ariely-on-mandatory-meetings-the
          -meaning-of-free-will-and-macroeconomist-musings.

PAGE 53: **"What if putting experience first makes us happier, more
          fulfilled, more creative and more memorable people?"** . . . Carl
          Richards, "A Life Full of Experiences May Not Mean Less Finan-
          cial Security," Your Money, *New York Times*, May 24, 2016.

PAGE 53: *When I look back in five years, which of these options will make
          the better story?* . . . This question from John Hagel also appeared
          in *A More Beautiful Question*, and originated in Hagel's post "The

Labor Day Manifesto of the Passionate Creative Worker," *Edge Perspectives with John Hagel* (blog), Sept. 2012, www.edgeperspectives .typepad.com/edge_perspectives/2012/09/the-labor-day-manifesto -of-the-passionate-creative-worker.html.

PAGE 54:   **Young people get paralyzed by the idea that 'I'm going to find this thing I'm meant to do'"** . . . Cal Newport said this to Dr. Scott Barry Kaufman on Kaufman's *The Psychology Podcast*, Episode 47: "Deep Work," www.acast.com/thepsychologypodcast/dr-cal-newport -on-deep-work.

PAGE 54:   **Elizabeth Gilbert says she has stopped advising people to "follow your passion"** . . . OWN's Super Soul Sessions, "The Advice Elizabeth Gilbert Won't Give Anymore," Oct. 13, 2015, www .oprah.com/own-supersoulsessions/the-advice-elizabeth-gilbert -wont-give-anymore_1.

PAGE 54:   **"They remind me of a dog chasing a tennis ball"** . . . Drew Houston's comments excerpted from his commencement speech at Massachusetts Institute of Technology, Jun. 7, 2013.

PAGE 55:   *What personal strengths did I display when I was at my best?* . . . Martin Seligman discusses this in Julie Scelfo, "The Happy Factor: Practicing the Art of Well-Being," *New York Times*, April 9, 2017.

PAGE 55:   *What are my superpowers?* . . . This question was shared by Keith Yamashita during my 2013 interview with him for *A More Beautiful Question*.

PAGE 55:   **Tom Rath's popular "StrengthsFinder 2.0" program, with its menu of thirty-four traits** . . . Tom Rath, *StrengthsFinder 2.0* (New York: Gallup Press, 2007).

PAGE 55:   **The idea is to become "an anthropologist of your own life"** . . . Greg McKeown, "How to Design Your Life's Mission into Your Career," posted Nov. 27, 2014 on McKeown's blog, www .gregmckeown.com/blog/design-lifes-mission-career/.

PAGE 55:   *What did I enjoy doing at age ten?* . . . From my 2012 interview with Dr. Eric Maisel for *A More Beautiful Question*.

PAGE 56:   *What makes me forget to eat?* . . . Mark Manson, "7 Strange Questions That Help You Find Your Life Purpose," posted Sept. 18, 2014 on Manson's blog, www.markmanson.net/life-purpose.net.

PAGE 56:   **the work of psychologist Mihaly Csikszentmahalyi on "flow"** . . . Mihaly Csikszentmahalyi, *Flow: The Psychology of Optimal Experience* (New York: Harper & Row, 1990).

PAGE 56:   **people who pursue the "Well-Planned Life"** . . . David Brooks, "The Summoned Self," *New York Times*, Aug. 2, 2010, www.nytimes .com/2010/08/03/opinion/03brooks.html.

PAGE 57:   *In what way do I wish the world were different?* . . . Angela Duckworth, "No Passion? Don't Panic," Preoccupations, *New York Times*, Jun. 5, 2016.

PAGE 57:   **"You can think of Purpose with a capital P"** . . . Daniel Pink shared this during his interview with Ron Friedman during the 2017 Peak Performance Summit.

PAGE 57:   **But even if you do find an opportunity that seems to answer that question, Cal Newport has a warning** . . . From Newport's discussion with Scott Barry Kaufman on *The Psychology Podcast*, episode 47.

PAGE 58:   **Considering how hard it is to do anything worthwhile, perhaps a good question to keep in mind is this off-color one** . . . From Manson's post "7 Strange Questions That Help You Find Your Life Purpose."

PAGE 58:   *What is my sentence?* . . . Pink's quotes, plus the original quote by Clare Booth Luce, drawn from Daniel Pink's *Drive: The Surprising Truth about What Motivates Us* (New York: Riverhead Books, 2009). This question and the description of its origin also was featured in *A More Beautiful Question*.

Part II: Questions for Sparking
CREATIVITY

PAGE 61:   **Some years ago, David Kelley, founder of one of the most successful consulting firms** . . . Kelley's story comes from my Sept. 2017 interview with Tom Kelley, earlier interviews (between 2008 and 2012) with Tom Kelley and David Kelley, plus their book *Creative Confidence: Unleashing the Creative Potential Within Us All* (New York: Crown Business, 2013). See also David Kelley's 2012 TED Talk "How to Build Your Creative Confidence," www.ted.com/talks/david_kelley_how_to_build_your_creative_confidence.

PAGE 62:   **"an angel of the Lord appears"** . . . Linda Tischler, "IDEO's David Kelley on Design Thinking," *Fast Company*, Feb. 1, 2009, www.fastcodesign.com/1139331/ideos-david-kelley-design-thinking.

PAGE 63:   **The psychologist Robert Sternberg studied successful creative people** . . . Tom Kelley and David Kelley, *Creative Confidence*.

PAGE 64:   **Research has shown that just doing one creative task, no matter how small** . . . Girija Kaimal, Kendra Ray, and Juan Muniz, "Reduction of Cortisol Levels and Participants' Responses Following Art Making," *Art Therapy: Journal of the American Art Therapy Association*, Vol. 33, Apr. 2016.

PAGE 64: **"Creativity is yoga for the brain"** . . . Phyllis Korkki, *The Big Thing: How to Complete Your Creative Project Even if You're a Lazy, Self-Doubting Procrastinator Like Me* (New York: Harper, 2016).

PAGE 64: **"The excitement of the artist at the easel or scientist in the lab"** . . . Mihaly Csikszentmihalyi, *Creativity: The Work and Lives of 91 Eminent People* (New York: HarperCollins, 1996).

PAGE 64: **"I write in what is probably a vain effort to somehow control the world in which I live"** . . . Quote from poet and author Kwame Dawes, drawn from Jeremy Adam Smith, Jason Marsh, "Why We Make Art," *Greater Good Magazine*, Dec. 1, 2008, www.greatergood .berkeley.edu/article/item/why_we_make_art.

PAGE 64: **The "sense of control" associated with creation is also cited by Gina Gibney** . . . Ibid.

PAGE 65: **"In the twenty-first century, what the market values is the ability to produce something rare and valuable"** . . . Cal Newport said this to Dr. Scott Barry Kaufman on Kaufman's *The Psychology Podcast*, Episode 47: "Deep Work," www.acast.com/thepsychology-podcast/dr-cal-newport-on-deep-work.

PAGE 66: **one of the primary myths is what he calls the "breed myth"** . . . from my Sept. 2017 interview with David Burkus, also discussed in his book *The Myths of Creativity: The Truth About How Innovative Companies and People Generate Great Ideas* (New York: Jossey-Boss, 2015). Unless otherwise indicated, all quotes in this chapter from Burkus are from this interview.

PAGE 66: **a third of those she interviewed could recall a "creativity scar"** . . . From *Creative Confidence*. Brené Brown has talked about creative scars on Elizabeth Gilbert's *Magic Lessons* podcast.

PAGE 68: **even experienced creative people had trouble predicting whether their individual projects would be successful** . . . Thomas Oppong, "To Get More Creative, Become Less Judgmental," *The Mission* (blog), Nov. 19, 2017. www.medium.com/the-mission/to-get-more-creative-become-less-judgemental-14413a575fa9.

PAGE 68: **Fadell didn't have to search for his idea—it was staring him in the face** . . . Unless otherwise indicated, all of Fadell's quotes in this chapter are from his May 2012 talk at the 99U conference titled "Tony Fadell on Setting Constraints, Ignoring Experts, and Embracing Self-Doubt," www.99u.adobe.com/videos/7185/tony-fadell -on-setting-constraints-ignoring-experts-embracing-self-doubt.

PAGE 69: **As for playwright Miranda, his idea was waiting for him in a bookstore** . . . Blake Ross, "Lin-Manuel Miranda Goes Crazy for *House* and Hamilton," Playbill, Sept. 21, 2009, and many other sources.

PAGE 69: **as he began reading it, something clicked for him** . . . Rebecca Mead, "All about the Hamiltons," *New Yorker*, Feb. 9, 2015.

PAGE 69: creativity arises "from looking at one thing and seeing
another" . . . Quote from the designer Saul Bass is from his 1968
short film, "Why Man Creates." www.fastcodesign.com/3049941
/watch-legendary-designer-saul-bass-explains-why-we-create.

PAGE 69: Miranda looked at the story of the immigrant Hamilton . . .
Rebecca Mead, "All About the Hamiltons."

PAGE 69: "smart recombinations" . . . This term was used and defined in
John Thackara's book *In the Bubble: Designing in a Complex World*
(Cambridge: MIT Press, 2005).

PAGE 70: "What is at issue is not the fact of 'borrowing' or 'imitating' " . . .
Oliver Sacks, from the essay "The Creative Self," in the posthumous
book *The River of Consciousness* (New York: Knopf, 2017).

PAGE 71: "It is the discovery and creation of problems" . . . Csikszentmihalyi and Getzel's study is described in Maria Popova's interview of
Daniel Pink in "Ambiverts, Problem-Finders and the Surprising
Psychology of Making Your Ideas Happen," *BrainPickings*, Feb. 1,
2013. www.brainpickings.org/2013/02/01/dan-pink-to-sell-is-human/.

PAGE 72: "Something about it just grabbed me" . . . Blake Ross, "Lin-
Manuel Miranda Goes Crazy for *House* and Hamilton," Playbill,
Sept. 21, 2009.

PAGE 73: When asked about the source of his creativity, Fadell focuses on
the word "frustration" . . . "Tony Fadell on Setting Constraints,"
2012 99U Conference.

PAGE 73: Grant collects ideas in a notebook . . . From my interview with
Adam Grant, Sept. 2017. Unless otherwise indicated, all quotes from
Grant in this chapter are from this interview.

PAGE 73: "didn't recognize it until about my seventh book" . . . Anthony
Breznican, "Dennis Lehane's Place in the Sun," *Entertainment
Weekly*, May 12, 2017.

PAGE 74: we must "shift our focus from objects" . . . Robert I. Sutton,
*Weird Ideas That Work: 11 and ½ Practices for Promoting, Managing
and Sustaining Innovation* (New York: The Free Press, 2000).

PAGE 75: "customers are *always* beautifully, wonderfully dissatisfied" . . .
From Bezos's "2016 Letter to Shareholders," Apr. 12, 2017, www
.amazon.com/p/feature/z608g6sysxur57t.

PAGE 75: One study found 85 percent of companies surveyed admitted
they had trouble diagnosing their own problems . . . Thomas
Wedell-Wedellsborg, "Are You Solving the Right Problems," *Harvard
Business Review*, Jan.–Feb. 2017.

PAGE 75: "Look at your work and ask, *When am I most resonant? What
are people responding to in my work?*" . . . From Todd Henry's
interview on Srini Rao's *Unmistakable Creative* podcast episode
titled: "Harnessing the Power of Your Authentic Voice with Todd

Henry," https://unmistakablecreative.com/podcast/harnessing-the
-power-of-your-authentic-voice-with-todd-henry/.

PAGE 78: **when she can frame the idea she's working on as a question,
          it provides "a focus"** . . . Amy Tan, "Where Does Creativity
          Hide?" TED Talk, Feb. 2008, www.ted.com/talks/amy_tan_on_
          creativity.

PAGE 78: **Miranda began to immerse himself in research on the man and
          his life** . . . Edward Delman, "How Lin-Manuel Miranda Shapes
          History," *Atlantic*, Sept. 29, 2015, www.theatlantic.com/entertain
          ment/archive/2015/09/lin-manuel-miranda-hamilton/408019.

PAGE 78: **Research feeds creativity** . . . KH Kim, *The Creativity Challenge:
          How We Can Recapture American Innovation* (Amherst, NY:
          Prometheus Books, 2016).

PAGE 78: **"they don't come into existence from nothing"** . . . John Kounios,
          "Eureka? Yes, Eureka!" Gray Matter, *New York Times*, Jun. 11, 2017.

PAGE 79: **"I read the script and ask, 'Why?' until there's no more 'Why?'
          to ask"** . . . Camille Sweeney and Josh Gosfield quoting Laura
          Linney in *The Art of Doing: How Superachievers Do What They Do
          and How They Do It So Well* (New York: Plume, 2013).

PAGE 79: **A few years ago, while watching one of Cleese's creativity
          talks** . . . Cleese has discussed this in speeches on creativity, as noted
          in Chris Higgins, "John Cleese: Create a Tortoise Enclosure for Your
          Mind," Mental Floss, Nov. 11, 2009.

PAGE 80: **does his best work in close proximity to the buzz of a crowd** . . .
          Scott Adams, "Creativity Hack," Aug. 18, 2014, www.blog.dilbert
          .com/2014/08/18/creativity-hack.

PAGE 80: **"Focus is the new IQ"** . . . Cal Newport said this to Dr. Scott
          Barry Kaufman on Kaufman's *The Psychology Podcast*, Episode 47:
          "Deep Work," www.acast.com/thepsychologypodcast/dr-cal-newport
          -on-deep-work.

PAGE 81: **"the tiny cracks of inactivity in our lives"** . . . Andrew Sullivan,
          "I Used to Be a Human Being," *New York* magazine, Sept. 19, 2016
          issue.

PAGE 81: **"It is easier to react than to create"** . . . Stefan Sagmeister said
          this to me in my 2008 interview with him for my book *Glimmer*
          (New York: Penguin Press, 2009).

PAGE 81: ***What if we saw attention in the same way that we saw air or
          water, as a valuable resource that we hold in common?*** . . .
          Matthew B. Crawford, "The Cost of Paying Attention," *New York
          Times*, Mar. 7, 2015, www.nytimes.com/2015/03/08/opinion/sunday/
          the-cost-of-paying-attention.html.

PAGE 81: **"Instead of taking breaks *from* digital media"** . . . Cal Newport
          said this to Dr. Scott Barry Kaufman on Kaufman's *The Psychology*

Podcast, Episode 47: "Deep Work," www.acast.com/thepsychology-podcast/dr-cal-newport-on-deep-work.

PAGE 81:   **For those who can't bring themselves to disconnect completely ...** Khe Hy shared these tips with me during my May 2017 interview with him.

PAGE 82:   **Recent studies have shown that bored people tend to come up with more ideas ...** Clive Thompson, "How Being Bored Out of Your Mind Makes You More Creative," *Wired*, Jan. 25, 2017, www .wired.com/2017/01/clive-thompson-7.

PAGE 82:   **psychologist Sandi Mann says, because "we try to extinguish every moment of boredom in our lives with mobile devices" ...** Ibid.

PAGE 83:   **"the maker's schedule" and "the manager's schedule" ...** Paul Graham in a July 2009 post on his blog: "Maker's Schedule, Manager's Schedule," www.paulgraham.com/makersschedule.html, Jul. 2009.

PAGE 83:   **"You open your calendar and you see a blank space" ...** Dan Ariely, "Forget Work-Life Balance. The Question is Rest Versus Effort," Big Think, www.bigthink.com/in-their-own-words/forget -work-life-balance-the-question-is-rest-versus-effort.

PAGE 83:   **You must make a conscious effort to "prune the vine" ...** From Todd Henry's interview with Ron Friedman during the 2017 Peak Work Performance Summit. www.thepeakworkperformancesummit .com/.

PAGE 84:   **suggests giving yourself a "flow test" ...** from Pink's 2009 book *Drive*; also discussed in his new book, *When: Scientific Secrets of Perfect Timing* (New York: Riverhead Books, 2018).

PAGE 84:   **72 percent of them did their best work in the morning ...** Paul Thagard, "Daily Routines of Creative People," *Psychology Today*, Apr. 27, 2017, www.psychologytoday.com/blog/hot-thought/201704 /daily-routines-creative-people; analysis of Mason Currey's book *Daily Rituals: How Artists Work* (New York: Knopf, 2013).

PAGE 84:   **"To have the full benefit of the richness of the unconscious" ...** Dorothea Brande, *Becoming a Writer*. This book was originally published in 1934, and has been subsequently republished by Tarcher-Perigee in 1981, and by other publishers.

PAGE 85:   **"No matter what happens at the end of this 45 [minutes], you are free" ...** Jessie Van Amburg, "Elizabeth Gilbert Never Imag-ined Being a Childless Adult," *Time*, Nov. 25, 2016.

PAGE 86:   **"if you let your mind wander" ...** From my interview with Kaufman in July 2017.

PAGE 86:   **Tending the garden is a favorite of many artists ...** KH Kim, *The Creativity Challenge: How We Can Recapture American Innovation.*

PAGE 86:   **Michael Stipe of REM composed songs in his head** . . . Marc
            Myers, *Anatomy of a Song: The Oral History of 45 Iconic Hits That
            Changed Rock, R&B and Pop* (New York: Grove Press, 2016).

PAGE 86:   **What one needs, according to Scott Adams, are "distractions
            that don't distract"** . . . Scott Adams, "Creativity Hack," Aug. 18,
            2014, www.blog.dilbert.com/2014/08/18/creativity-hack.

PAGE 86:   **"Museums are custodians of epiphanies"** . . . Hugh Hart, "7
            Pieces of 'Damn Good' Creative Advice From '6os Ad Man George
            Lois," *Fast Company*, Mar. 22, 2012, www.fastcompany.com/1680316
            /7-pieces-of-damn-good-creative-advice-from-60s-ad-man-george-lois.

PAGE 87:   **"the cacophony in which it is impossible to hear your own
            voice"** . . . William Deresiewicz, "Solitude and Leadership" lecture
            at West Point, NY, Mar. 1, 2010.

PAGE 87:   **"I reach up and pluck the butterfly from the air"** . . . Ann Patch-
            ett's quotes about "killing the butterfly" are from her essay "The
            Getaway Car: A Practical Memoir About Writing and Life," which
            appears in the book *This is the Story of a Happy Marriage* (New York:
            Harper, 2013).

PAGE 88:   **"A surplus of ideas is as dangerous as a drought"** . . . Scott
            Belsky, *Making Ideas Happen: Overcoming the Obstacles between
            Vision and Reality* (New York: Portfolio, 2010).

PAGE 89:   **"Projects that you do quietly by yourself are much easier to
            abandon"** . . . From Phyllis Korkki's interview with Chris Baty in
            her book *The Big Thing: How to Complete Your Creative Project Even
            if You're a Lazy, Self-Doubting Procrastinator Like Me* (New York:
            HarperCollins, 2016).

PAGE 89:   **Bruce Mau shares a story about a writer friend of his who was
            about to embark on an ambitious new book** . . . From my 2008
            series of interviews with Bruce Mau for the book *Glimmer*.

PAGE 90:   **"What can I do with what I have?"** . . . Scott Sonenshein, "How
            to Create More from What You Already Have," *Time*, Feb. 27–Mar. 6,
            2017.

PAGE 90:   **a favorite quote from the maverick composer John Cage: "Begin
            anywhere"** . . . From my 2008 series of interviews with Bruce Mau
            for the book *Glimmer*.

PAGE 90:   **"I saw it with such clarity and intensity that I couldn't get it out
            of my head"** . . . William Grimes, *New York Times* obituary of
            novelist and critic William McPherson, Mar. 29, 2017.

PAGE 91:   **If you shift to the "editor off" mode of your mind** . . . Stephen
            Watt, "Questions for Robert Burton," *Rotman Magazine*, Winter 2010.

PAGE 92:   **"You start out making something wrong and then see if you can
            turn that bad thing into something good"** . . . From my 2012
            interview with Tom Monahan for *A More Beautiful Question*.

PAGE 92: **Grant describes five stages that tend to trigger different emotional responses in the creator** . . . From my interview with Grant in Sept. 2017.

PAGE 93–94: **Lee Clow, felt that a good idea should be able to withstand scrutiny** . . . I interviewed Clow many times during the late 1990s and early 2000s in my reporting for *Advertising Age*, *Wired*, and other publications.

PAGE 94: **Seth Godin has a word he uses often and persuasively, and that word is "ship"** . . . Seth Godin, "Fear of Shipping," *Seth's Blog*, June 11, 2010, sethgodin.typepad.com/seths_blog/2010/06/fear-of -shipping.html.

PAGE 94: **"Creativity is a consequence of sheer productivity"** . . . Dean Keith Simonton quoted by Robert I. Sutton, "Forgive and Remember: How a Good Boss Responds to Mistakes," *Harvard Business Review*, Aug. 19, 2010, www.hbr.org/2010/08/forgive-and-remember-how-a-goo.

PAGE 95: **"We have the words 'Done is better than perfect' painted on our walls"** . . . From Mark Zuckerberg's 2012 letter to investors, "The Hacker Way," published in *Wired*, Feb. 1, 2012, www.wired .com/2012/02/zuck-letter.

PAGE 95: **"if you wait for ideal circumstances . . . the market will pass you by"** . . . Guy Kawasaki, *The Art of the Start: The Time-Tested, Battle-Hardened Guide for Anyone* (New York: Portfolio, 2004).

PAGE 95: **we have a strong need "to feel accepted, respected and safe"** . . . Douglas Stone and Sheila Heen, *Thanks for the Feedback: The Science and Art of Receiving Feedback Well* (New York: Viking, 2014).

PAGE 96: **"If you know that feedback will meet resistance or dismissal from you"** . . . From my interview with Kwame Dawes, Oct. 2017.

PAGE 97: **"ask them hard questions like: 'What do you like *least* about the script?'"** . . . Mike Birbiglia, "6 Tips for Making It Small in Hollywood," *New York Times*, Sept. 4, 2016.

PAGE 97: ***How do you figure out when to listen to other people—and when to listen to yourself?*** . . . Laurel Snyder, "When to Listen to Other Readers . . . and When to Ignore Them," *The NaNoWriMo Blog*, Jan. 13, 2014, http://blog.nanowrimo.org/post/73214585258/when-to -listen-to-your-readers-and-when-to.

PAGE 97: **"he doesn't do it to be told what the movie's vision should be"** . . . Mike Birbiglia, "6 Tips for Making It Small in Hollywood."

PAGE 97: **"A good note says what's wrong, what's missing, what makes no sense"** . . . Ed Catmull, *Creativity, Inc.: Overcoming the Unseen Forces That Stand in the Way of True Inspiration* (New York: Random House, 2014).

PAGE 98: **a then-young comedian Jon Stewart interviewed a then-aging comedian George Carlin** . . . From a YouTube video, "George

Carlin Dropping Words of Wisdom," posted Aug. 20, 2013, www
.youtube.com/watch?v=oWmTtoynTdQ.

PAGE 98:   **her father's willingness to continually "begin again"** . . . Kelly
Carlin said this in my Nov. 2016 interview with her.

PAGE 99:   **"As expertise goes up, creative output tends to go down"** . . .
from my Sept. 2017 interview with David Burkus.

PAGE 99:   **Elizabeth Gilbert, in a talk extolling the benefits of "the
curiosity-driven life"** . . . From Gilbert's talk on Oprah Winfrey's
SuperSoul Conversations, Oct. 17, 2015. www.oprah.com/ownsu
persoulsessions/elizabeth-gilbert-the-curiosity-driven-life-video.

PAGE 99:   **If curiosity is unfocused (or, to use the term applied by
researchers, "diverse")** . . . Ian Leslie, *Curious: The Desire to
Know and Why Your Future Depends on It* (New York: Basic Books,
2014).

PAGE 100: **"You have to reject one expression of the band first before you
get to the next expression"** . . . Quote from Bono, the lead singer
of the band U2, in the documentary *From the Sky Down*, directed
by Davis Guggenheim and broadcast on Showtime Oct. 2011.

PAGE 100: **"To reach a new generation of music fans, he reinvented his
approach to performing"** . . . Jon Friedman, "Bob Dylan's Relentless Reinvention," *Boston Globe*, May 23, 2016.

PAGE 101: **"The minute you try to grab hold of Dylan, he's no longer where
he was"** . . . Todd Haynes, director of the 2007 film *I'm Not There*,
which was about Dylan, said this, and it has been widely quoted,
including here: www.moma.org/calendar/events/1485.

PAGE 101: **The late novelist Ursula K. Le Guin did just that when, at age
eighty-one, she started her own blog** . . . Robert Minto, "What
Happens When a Science Fiction Genius Starts Blogging?," *New
Republic*, Sept. 7, 2017.

PAGE 101: ***Where is my petri dish?*** This question was shared by Tim Ogilvie
during my 2013 interview with him for *A More Beautiful Question*.

Part III: Questions to Help
CONNECT WITH OTHERS

PAGE 103: **Arthur Aron and Elaine Spaulding, a pair of psychology
students** . . . Interview with Arthur Aron, Oct. 2017. Additional
information from: Yasmin Anwar, "Creating Love in the Lab: The
36 Questions That Spark Intimacy," *Berkeley News*, Feb. 12, 2015,
www.news.berkeley.edu/2015/02/12/love-in-the-lab; Elaine N. Aron,

"36 Questions for Intimacy, Back Story," *Psychology Today*, Jan. 14, 2015, www.psychologytoday.com/blog/attending-the-undervalued -self/201501/36-questions-intimacy-back-story.

PAGE 104: **"To Fall in Love with Anyone, Do This"** . . . Mandy Len Catron, Modern Love, "To Fall in Love with Anyone, Do This," *New York Times*, Jan. 11, 2015, www.nytimes.com/2015/01/11/fashion/modern -love-to-fall-in-love-with-anyone-do-this.html.

PAGE 105: **at the FBI, Robin Dreeke's job** . . . From my interview with Robin Dreeke, Dec. 2017. Unless otherwise indicated, all quotes from Dreeke in this chapter are from this interview.

PAGE 106: **Children come to realize, at an early age, that a question is a means to engage** . . . Paul L. Harris, *Trusting What You're Told: How Children Learn from Others* (Boston: Belknap Press, 2012). Studies also cited in the article "Mothers Asked Nearly 300 Questions a Day, Study Finds," *Telegraph*, March 28, 2013.

PAGE 107: **But research suggests that if we truly want to be happy** . . . Tara Parker-Pope, "What Are Friends For? A Longer Life," *New York Times*, Apr. 21, 2009.

PAGE 107: **Various studies, including the landmark Grant Study** . . . Scott Stossel, "What Makes Us Happy, Revisited," *Atlantic*, May 2013.

PAGE 107: **"Only connect!"** . . . E. M. Forster, *Howards End*, originally published in 1910 by Edward Arnold (London).

PAGE 107: **People who have companionship are not only happier and healthier, but they also are likely to have a greater sense of "meaning"** . . . Emily Esfahani Smith, "Psychology Shows It's a Big Mistake to Base Our Self-Worth on Our Professional Achievements," Quartz, May 24, 2017, www.qz.com/990163/Psychology-shows-its-a -big-mistake-to-base-our-self-worth-on-our-professional-achieve ments. These themes are also covered in Emily Esfanani Smith's *The Power of Meaning: Finding Fulfillment in a World Obsessed with Happiness* (New York: Crown, 2017).

PAGE 107: **having friends at work is critical** . . . Sarah Landrum, "Millennials Are Happiest When They Feel Connected to Their Co-Workers," *Forbes*, Jan. 19, 2018, www.forbes.com/sites/sarahlandrum/2018/01/19 /millennials-are-happiest-when-they-feel-connected-to-their-co -workers.

PAGE 108: *Why do we go around asking each other such pointless questions?* . . . Tony DuShane, "Chris Colin, Rob Baedeker Are the Kings of Conversation," *SFGate*, Mar. 16, 2014, www.sfgate.com/books/ article/Chris-Colin-Rob-Baedeker-are-the-kings-of-5351986.php. All quotes from Colin and Baedeker are from this article and the article "27 Questions to Ask Instead of What Do You Do?" by

Courtney Seiter, Buffer Open, Nov. 30, 2015, www.open.buffer.com /27-question-to-ask-instead-of-what-do-you-do.

PAGE 108:   **coauthors of the 2014 book *What to Talk About* . . .** Chris Colin and Rob Baedeker, *What to Talk About: On a Plane, at a Cocktail Party, in a Tiny Elevator with Your Boss's Boss* (San Francisco: Chronicle Books, 2014).

PAGE 109:   **writer Tim Boomer, who believes we should be should be asking just such questions . . .** Tim Boomer, "Dating in the Deep End," Modern Love, *New York Times*, Jan. 17, 2016.

PAGE 111:   ***Did your family throw plates?* . . .** Eleanor Stanford, "13 Questions to Ask Before Getting Married," *New York Times*, Mar. 24, 2016.

PAGE 111:   ***What would marriage offer us that we don't already have?* . . .** Mandy Len Catron, "To Stay in Love, Sign on the Dotted Line," Modern Love, *New York Times*, Jun. 25, 2017.

PAGE 111:   **Questions to ask your spouse instead of *How was your day?* [box] . . .** The six questions in the box were selected from a longer list compiled by Sara Goldstein, "21 Questions to Ask Your Spouse Instead of "How Was Your Day?," Mother.ly, Mar. 16, 2016, www .mother.ly/parenting/21-questions-to-ask-your-spouse-instead-of -how-was-your-day-after-work.

PAGE 111:   **her father would ask his children, *What was the most difficult problem you had today?* . . .** Adam Bryant, "Deborah Harmon, on Playing to Your Team's Strengths," Corner Office, *New York Times*, Nov. 1, 2014.

PAGE 112:   **her father often asked at the dinner table: *What have you failed at this week?* . . .** From an Oct. 2017 Quiet Revolution interview, " 'The Power of Moments': An Interview with Chip and Dan Heath," www.quietrev.com/power-moments-interview-chip-dan-heath.

PAGE 112:   **consider using a question jar, a strategy recommended by Glennon Doyle . . .** "Save Your Relationships: Ask the Right Questions," Momastery, Jan. 16, 2014, www.momastery.com/blog/2014 /01/16/save-relationships-ask-right-questions. Unless otherwise indicated, all quotes in this chapter from Doyle are from this article.

PAGE 113:   **"The simple act of asking, and of listening without comment or judgment" is powerful . . .** From my 2017 interviews with Frank Sesno, and this is covered in his book, *Ask More: The Power of Questions to Open Doors, Uncover Solutions, and Spark Change* (New York: AMACOM, Jan. 10, 2017).

PAGE 113:   **"Increasingly, listening is a forgotten skill" . . .** Nick Morgan, "How to Use Improv to Make Your Work Day Better: Interview with Cathy Salit," Public Words, Jul. 28, 2016, www.publicwords.com /2016/07/28/use-improv-make-work-day-better.

PAGE 114: **"Your office space is a breeding ground for distractions"** . . . Alison Davis, "Dramatically Improve Your Listening Skills in 5 Simple Steps," *Inc.*, Jul. 27, 2016, www.inc.com/alison-davis/dramat ically-improve-your-listening-skills-in-5-simple-steps.html.

PAGE 114: **"Good listeners have a *physical*, *mental*, and *emotional* presence"** . . . Judith Humphrey, "There Are Actually 3 Kinds of Listening–Here's How to Master Them," *Fast Company*, Aug. 16, 2016, www.fastcompany.com/3062860/there-are-actually-3-kinds-of -listening-heres-how-to-master-them.

PAGE 114: **"picture what the speaker is saying"** . . . Dianne Schilling, "10 Steps to Effective Listening," *Forbes*, Nov. 8, 2012, www.forbes.com /sites/womensmedia/2012/11/09/10-steps-to-effective-listening /#1731bd7a3891.

PAGE 115: **"The second that I think about my response, I'm half listening to what you're saying"** . . . Eric Barker, "How to Get People to Like You: 7 Ways from an FBI Behavior Expert," Barking Up the Wrong Tree interview with Robin Dreeke, Oct. 26, 2014, www.bakadesuyo .com/2014/10/how-to-get-people-to-like-you.

PAGE 115: **As a reminder to talk less and listen more, try asking yourself the "WAIT question"** . . . Ronald Siegel, "Wisdom in Psycho-therapy," *Psychotherapy Networker*, Mar.–Apr. 2013.

PAGE 115: **if social media users got into the habit of asking the WAIT question** . . . Michael J. Socolow, "How to Prevent Smart People from Spreading Dumb Ideas," *New York Times*, Mar. 22, 2018.

PAGE 115: **people are prone to "conversational narcissism"** . . . Heleo editors in conversation with Celeste Headlee and Panio Gianopou-lous, "Conversation Is a Skill. Here's How to Be Better at It," Heleo, Oct. 2, 2017, www.heleo.com/conversation-conversation-is-a-skill -heres-how-to-be-better-at-it/16595.

PAGE 116: **the analogy of a tennis match** . . . Mark Goulston, *Just Listen: Discover the Secret to Getting Through to Absolutely Anyone* (New York: AMACOM, 2010). Unless otherwise indicated, all quotes in this chapter from Goulston are from this book.

PAGE 117: **a shortened form of paraphrasing known as "mirroring"** . . . "Influence Anyone with Secret Lessons Learned from the World's Top Hostage Negotiators with Former FBI Negotiator Chris Voss," *The Science of Success* podcast, Oct. 20, 2016, www.podcast .scienceofsuccess.co/e/influence-anyone-with-secret-lessons-learned -from-the-world%E2%80%99s-top-hostage-negotiators-with -former-fbi-negotiator-chris-voss.

PAGE 117: **the "AWE" question** . . . From my interview with Michael Bungay Stanier, Oct. 2017, and also appearing in his book *The Coaching*

Habit: Say Less, Ask More & Change the Way You Lead Forever
(Toronto: Box of Crayons Press, 2016).

PAGE 118: **Salit recommends using what she calls "empathetic listening"** . . . Nick Morgan, "How to Use Improv to Make Your Work Day Better: Interview with Cathy Salit."

PAGE 119: **"powerless communicators" who listen and ask questions . . .** Susan Cain, "7 Ways to Use the Power of Powerless Communication," Quiet Revolution, Apr. 2015, www.quietrev.com/7-ways-to-use-powerless-communication.

PAGE 119: **Why are we inclined to advise others on what they should do?** . . . From my interview with Michael Bungay Stanier, Oct. 2017.

PAGE 121: **see through what Hal Mayer calls the "fog"** . . . Hal Mayer, "Can You Actually Help People by Just Asking Them Questions?" Leading with Questions, Apr. 27, 2017, www.leadingwithquestions.com/leadership/can-you-actually-help-people-by-just-asking-them-questions-2.

PAGE 122–123: **if you're thinking of criticizing friends and family, "the professional consensus boils down to one word: don't"** . . . Martha Beck, "The 3 Questions You Need to Ask Yourself Before Criticizing Someone," Oprah.com, Oct. 5, 2017, www.oprah.com/inspiration/martha-beck-how-to-stop-criticizing-everyone.

PAGE 124: **This type of question "is, unfortunately, the starting point of 80 percent of meetings in management"** . . . From my interview with David Cooperrider for my *Harvard Business Review* article "The 5 Questions Leaders Should Never Ask," Jul. 2, 2014, www.hbr.org/2014/07/5-common-questions-leaders-should-never-ask.

PAGE 124: **When she first went to Reading in 2011, she said, "I did not know anything about the city"** . . . "Another Round with SWEAT: In Conversation with Lynn Nottage and Kate Whoriskey, posted on YouTube by Sweat Broadway, Mar. 22, 2017, www.youtube.com/watch?v=nfGaZuCE6TY.

PAGE 125: **But as Nottage told the *New York Times*, "I like to replace judgment with curiosity"** . . . Liz Spayd, "New Voices, but Will They Be Heard?," Public Editor, *New York Times*, Apr. 23, 2017.

PAGE 125: **As she told the *New Yorker*, these laid-off workers felt helpless, ignored, and invisible** . . . Michael Schulman, "The First Theatrical Landmark of the Trump Era," *New Yorker*, Mar. 27, 2017.

PAGE 125: **hailed as the "first theatrical landmark of the Trump era"** . . . Ibid.

PAGE 125: **"I feel that my role as an artist"** . . . Liz Spayd, "New Voices, but Will They Be Heard?"

PAGE 125: **"Broadway audiences who might not have thought they could empathize with a marginalized steelworker"** . . . Alexis Soloski,

"Breaking 'Sweat': How a Blue-Collar Drama Crossed Over to the Great White Way," *Village Voice*, Apr. 5, 2017.

PAGE 127: **most evidence suggests you're unlikely to succeed** . . . Elizabeth Kolbert, "Why Facts Don't Change Our Minds," *New Yorker*, Feb. 27, 2017.

PAGE 127: **Researchers of curiosity have stated that it exists in the gap between** . . . Ian Leslie, *Curious: The Desire to Know and Why Your Future Depends On It* (New York: Basic Books, 2014).

PAGE 128: **The author Tom Perotta tells a story about a discovery he made** . . . From Terry Gross's interview with Tom Perotta on NPR's *Fresh Air* radio program, Jul. 31, 2017.

PAGE 129: **It can be extremely valuable to have a "trusted other"** . . . From my 2017 interview conducted with Edward D. Hess, author of multiple books on innovation and a professor of business administration at University of Virginia's Darden School of Business.

PAGE 129: **Adam Hansen, coauthor of *Outsmart Your Instincts*, observes that to the extent we can gain a glimmer of awareness** . . . From my 2017 interview with Hansen.

PAGE 129: **"The decisions we make, the attitudes we form, the judgments we make"** . . . Sean Illing, "Why We Pretend to Know Things, Explained by a Cognitive Scientist," Nov. 3, 2017, Vox, www.vox.com /conversations/2017/3/2/14750464/truth-facts-psychology-donald -trump-knowledge-science.

PAGE 129: **"what is it that my culture is preventing me from seeing?"** . . . Kenneth Primrose interview of Iain McGilchrist on *The Examined Life* (blog), Dec. 2016, www.examined-life.com/interviews/iain -mcgilchrist.

PAGE 130: **In a popular 2017 *New Yorker* article** . . . Elizabeth Kolbert, "Why Facts Don't Change Our Minds."

PAGE 131: **it can be effective to show "aggressive interest" by asking questions** . . . Jay Heinrichs, "How to Talk to Someone You Hate," Vice's *Tonic* blog, Nov. 8, 2017, www.tonic.vice.com/en_us/article /gqymzx/how-to-talk-to-someone-you-hate.

PAGE 131: **two good bridge questions, borrowed (and slightly adapted) from the radio host Krista Tippett** . . . Krista Tippett, *Becoming Wise: An Inquiry into the Mystery and Art of Living* (New York: Penguin Press, 2016). The questions were shared with Tippett by Frances Kissling, retired head of Catholics for Choice.

PAGE 132: **Ask people to rate something they don't like on a scale of one to ten** . . . This "motivational interviewing" technique is described by Yale professor Michael V. Pantalon in his book *Instant Influence* (New York: Little, Brown and Company, 2011). Hat tip to Adam Grant for calling this to my attention.

PAGE 133:   **"Science Guy" Bill Nye reminds us that we must be patient . . .**
From "Hey Bill Nye! How Do You Reason with a Science Skeptic?,"
Big Think, April 4, 2017, www.bigthink.com/videos/hey-bill-nye
-how-do-you-reason-with-a-science-skeptic.

PAGE 133:   **we must dispense with "the sense that we have a monopoly on
the truth" . . .** Carl Sagan in his 1996 book *The Demon-Haunted
World: Science as a Candle in the Dark*, and as quoted by Maria Popova
in "Carl Sagan on Moving Beyond Us vs. Them, Bridging Conviction
with Compassion, and Meeting Ignorance with Kindness," on her
Brain Pickings blog, Nov. 9, 2016, www.brainpickings.org/2016/11/09
/carl-sagan-demon-haunted-world-ignorance-compassion.

PAGE 134:   **"She Divorced Me Because I Left Dishes by the Sink" . . .**
Matthew Fray, from a Jan. 14, 2016 post on his blog, *Must Be This
Tall to Ride*, www.mustbethistalltoride.com/2016/01/14/she-divorced
-me-because-i-left-dishes-by-the-sink. The background info is from
an Aug. 2017 interview I conducted with Fray.

PAGE 134 : **"The person I love and married is telling me" . . .** These and
other Matthew Fray quotes are from an Aug. 2017 interview I
conducted with Fray.

PAGE 135:   **Close relationships can suffer if we fail to pay attention to
what's going on right in front of us . . .** Emily Esfahani Smith
citing psychologist John Gottman in "The Secret to Love Is Just
Kindness," *Atlantic*, June 2014.

PAGE 135:   **"Questions to ask your best bud" [box] . . .** The five questions in
the box were selected from a longer list compiled by Kaitlyn Wylde,
"20 Things to Ask Your Best Friend to Make Your Relationship Even
Stronger," Bustle, Oct. 26, 2015, www.bustle.com/articles/119084-20
-things-to-ask-your-best-friend-to-make-your-relationship-even
-stronger.

PAGE 136:   **Shelly Gable, a psychologist at UC Santa Barbara, refers to this
as "active constructive responding" . . .** Jeremy McCarthy, "The
3 Magic Words That Create Great Conversations," HuffPost, Dec. 12,
2013, www.huffingtonpost.com/jeremy-mccarthy/conscious-relation
ships_b_4414955.html.

PAGE   *Have you made clear your concerns about the relationship? . . .*
136–137:   Eric V. Copage, "Questions to Ask Before Getting a Divorce," Vows,
New York Times, May 28, 2017.

PAGE 137:   *If there is a way to save the marriage, what would it be? . . .* Ibid,
quoting Rev. Kevin Wright, minister of Riverside Church in New York.

PAGE 137:   **It may seem an apology is enough, but the life coach Michael
Hyatt says . . .** Michael Hyatt, "Ten Difficult, But Really Important
Words," an Aug. 4, 2017 post of Hyatt's blog, www.michaelhyatt
.com/Ten-Difficult-But-Really-Important-Words.

PAGE 138: **"We have a primitive instinct to prove that we're right"** . . . From my 2017 interview with Brown University cognitive scientist Steven Sloman, coauthor with Philip Fernbach of *The Knowledge Illusion: Why We Never Think Alone* (New York: Riverhead Books, 2017).

PAGE 138: **"Proving I was right used to be a major character flaw"** . . . Oprah Winfrey, "What Oprah Knows for Sure about Letting Go," Oprah.com, Jul. 11, 2017, www.oprah.com/inspiration/what-oprah-knows-for-sure-about-letting-go.

PAGE 140: *What does your ideal employee look like?* . . . Wanda Wallace, "Questions Employees Should Ask Their Managers," Jan. 5, 2017, in a guest post on *Leading with Questions*, www.leadingwithquestions.com/personal-growth/questions-great-employees-should-ask-their-leaders.

PAGE 141: *What is most important on your list to accomplish today* . . . From my Aug. 2017 interview with Katherine Crowley of K Squared Enterprises in New York.

PAGE 141: **"it reminds the employee who is in charge," says Cathy Little-field** . . . Lydia Dishman, "This Is Why We Default to Criticism (and How to Change)," *Fast Company*, Nov. 3, 2017, www.fastcompany.com/40487947/this-is-why-we-default-to-criticism-and-how-to-change.

PAGE 142: **only 30 percent of workers feel "fully engaged" in their jobs** . . . Mark C. Crowley, "Gallup's Workplace Jedi on How to Fix Our Employee Engagement Problem," *Fast Company*, Jun. 4, 2013, www.fastcompany.com/3011032/gallups-workplace-jedi-on-how-to-fix-our-employee-engagement-problem.

PAGE 143: **today's most effective managers must be able to show they care** . . . Ibid.

PAGE 145: **those who listen and ask questions tend to bring in far more revenue** . . . Adam Grant in "The Power of Powerless Communication," a May 2013 TedxEast talk, www.youtube.com/watch?v=n_ffqEA8X5g.

PAGE 145: **the story of Bill Grumbles, an inexperienced salesman** . . . Ibid.

PAGE 145: **"This is axiomatic in sales and persuasion"** . . . Daniel Pink, "How to Persuade Others with the Right Questions," Big Think, May 21, 2014, www.youtube.com/watch?v=WAL7Pz1i1jU. Ideas derived from Pink's book *To Sell is Human: The Surprising Truth about Moving Others* (New York: Riverhead Books, 2012).

page 146: **"Peter Drucker understood, long ago, that he could best serve clients by asking questions"** . . . Drucker's belief in the power of questions was described to me by Drucker Institute executive director Rick Wartzman in our 2013 conversations, as well as in Wartzman's article "How to Consult Like Peter Drucker," *Forbes*, Sept. 11, 2012.

Part IV: Questions for Stronger
LEADERSHIP

PAGE 149: **"Who has influenced you most in your life?"** . . . Posted on Brandon Stanton's *Humans of New York* Facebook page, Jan. 19, 2015, www.facebook.com/humansofnewyork/photos/a.102107073196735 .4429.102099916530784/865948056812629.

PAGE 150: **"What can we do to right this wrong?"** . . . Footage of Nadia Lopez in action at the school from "Why Principals Matter," *Atlantic*, Feb. 26, www.theatlantic.com/video/index/385925/why-principals -matter.

PAGE 150: **use diagnostic questions to try to uncover what might be wrong with a patient** . . . From my Jan. 2018 interview with Nadia Lopez.

PAGE 152: **"VUCA environment," a term borrowed from military commanders** . . . Lisa Kay Solomon, "How the Most Successful Leaders Will Thrive in an Exponential World," SingularityHub, Jan. 11, 2017, www.singularityhub.com/2017/01/11/how-the-most -successful-leaders-will-thrive-in-an-exponential-world.

PAGE 152: **"Today's leader must be a flexible thinker"** . . . From my interview with Angie Morgan of Lead Star, Oct. 2017. Morgan also discusses this concept in her book *Spark: How to Lead Yourself and Others to Greater Success* by Angie Morgan, Courtney Lynch, and Sean Lynch (New York: Houghton Mifflin Harcourt, 2017).

PAGE 153: **leadership "is more about influence than control"** . . . David B. Peterson, "The Paradox of Leadership: Navigating the New Realities," speech from World Business Executive Coach Summit 2017, June 15, 2017, www.wbecs.com/wbecs2017/presenter/david-peterson.

PAGE 153: **we are in the midst of a leadership crisis. That's the view of 86 percent of those surveyed** . . . Shiza Shahid, World Economic Forum, "Crisis in Leadership Underscores Global Challenges," Nov. 10, 2014, https://www.weforum.org/press/2014/11/crisis-in -leadership-underscores-global-challenges/.

PAGE 153: **"The recent past has showcased a leadership stage featuring Greek tragedies filled with leaders who are toxic and corrupt"** . . . Deborah Ancona and Elaine Backman, "Distributed Leadership: From Pyramids to Networks: The Changing Leadership Landscape," MIT whitepaper, Oct. 2017, https://mitsloan-php.s3.amazonaws .com/leadership_wp/wp-content/uploads/2015/06/Distributed-Lead ership-Going-from-Pyramids-to-Networks.pdf.

PAGE 154: **becoming a better leader is an "inside out" process** . . . From my interview with Douglas Conant in Jan. 2018. The concept of "inside out" leadership is also featured in Conant's essay "Leaders,

You Can (And Must) Do Better. Here's How" on LinkedIn, (www
.linkedin.com/pulse/leaders-you-can-must-do-better-heres-how
-douglas-conant), and in Conant's book *TouchPoints: Creating
Powerful Leadership Connections in the Smallest of Moments*, coauthored with Mette Norgaard (New York: Jossey-Bass, 2011). Unless
otherwise indicated, quotes from Conant in this chapter are from
the interview cited above.

PAGE 154: **"climb the greasy pole of whatever hierarchy they decide to
attach themselves to"** . . . William Deresiewicz, "Solitude and
Leadership," *The American Scholar*, Mar. 1, 2010.

PAGE 154: **"They end up cutting corners to make shareholders happy"** . . .
Douglas Conant, "Leaders, You Can (And Must) Do Better. Here's
How," on LinkedIn.

PAGE 155: **"to be a leader for the sake of being in charge, rather than in
the name of a cause or idea [the student cares] about deeply"** . . .
Susan Cain, "Followers Wanted," *New York Times*, Mar. 26, 2017.

PAGE 157: **Research by the Hay Group focused on overachievers who
become leaders** . . . Scott Spreier, Mary H. Fontaine, and Ruth
Malloy, "Leadership Run Amok: The Destructive Potential of Overachievers," *Harvard Business Review*, June 2006.

PAGE 158: **"first make sure that other people's highest priority needs are
being served"** . . . Robert K. Greenleaf, "The Servant as Leader,"
an essay first published in 1970, now available on from the Robert K.
Greenleaf Center for Servant Leadership (www.greenleaf.org/prod
ucts-page/the-servant-as-leader).

PAGE
158–159: **leaderless groups "have a natural tendency to elect self-centered,
overconfident and narcissistic individuals as leaders"** . . . Tomas
Chamorro-Premuzic, "Why Do So Many Incompetent Men Become
Leaders?," *Harvard Business Review*, Aug. 22, 2013, www.hbr.org/2013
/08/why-do-so-many-incompetent-men.

PAGE 159: **Overconfidence breeds hubris, which can then infect an orga-
nization's culture** . . . Jonathan Mackey and Sharon Toye, "How
Leaders Can Stop Executive Hubris," *Strategy+Business*, Spring 2018 /
Issue 90.

PAGE 160: **"I've had to embrace the fact that I'm constantly going to be in
uncharted waters"** . . . Adam Bryant, "Brian Chesky: Scratching
the Itch to Create," Corner Office, *New York Times*, Oct. 12, 2014.

PAGE 160: **today's leaders must ask, *Am I courageous enough to abandon
the past?*** . . . Roselinde Torres's TED Talk, "What It Takes to Be a
Great Leader," Feb. 2014, www.ted.com/talks/roselinde_torres_
what_it_takes_to_be_a_great_leader.

PAGE 160: **a recent PriceWaterhouse study and elsewhere, as a top leadership
quality for the twenty-first century** . . . Taken from the 2015 CEO

survey by PwC, "Responding to Disruption." Published Jan. 2016, www.pwc.com/gx/en/ceo-survey/2015/assets/pwc-18th-annual -global-ceo-survey-jan-2015.pdf. Also discussed in Will Yakowicz, "This Is the Most Valuable Leadership Trait You Can Have," *Inc.*, Sept. 15, 2015, www.inc.com/will-yakowicz/why-leaders-need-to-be -curious.html.

PAGE 160–161: ***Do I surround myself with inspiring, sometimes even odd, big thinkers?*** . . . John Marshall, "Why Relentless Curiosity Is a Must for CEOs," *TNW*, Jul. 29, 2017, www.thenextweb.com/contributors /2017/07/29/relentless-curiosity-must-ceos.

PAGE 161: ***Am I bringing together diverse people who can share points of view that I might be missing?*** . . . Roselinde Torres's TED Talk, "What It Takes to Be a Great Leader," Feb. 2014, www.ted.com/talks /roselinde_torres_what_it_takes_to_be_a_great_leader.

PAGE 161: **"It's an interesting paradox that diversity correlates to higher performance"** . . . David B. Peterson, "The Paradox of Leadership: Navigating the New Realities," speech from World Business Executive Coach Summit 2017, June 15, 2017, www.wbecs.com/wbecs2017/ presenter/david-peterson. Peterson refers to the following Deloitte study on diversity: Juliet Bourke, Stacia Garr, Ardie van Berkel and Jungle Wong, "Diversity and Inclusion: The Reality Gap," Deloitte Insights, Feb. 28, 2017, www2.deloitte.com/insights/us/en/focus/ human-capital-trends/2017/diversity-and-inclusion-at-the-workplace .html.

PAGE 162: **"I insist on a lot of time being spent, almost every day, just to sit and think"** . . . Erica Anderson, "23 Quotes from Warren Buffett on Life and Generosity," *Forbes*, Dec. 2, 2013, www.forbes.com/sites /erikaandersen/2013/12/02/23-quotes-from-warren-buffett-on-life -and-generosity. Charlie Munger's comments about Buffett's "haircut day" are from Munger's speech at the 2016 Daily Journal annual meeting, captured by Shane Parrish, "Charlie Munger Holds Court at the 2016 Daily Journal Meeting," posted on *Medium*, Feb. 14, 2016, www.medium.com/@farnamstreet/charlie-munger-holds-court -at-the-2016-daily-journal-meeting-542e04784c5e.

PAGE 162: **"Reflection leads to better insights into innovation, strategy and execution"** . . . Roselinde Torres, Marin Reeves, Peter Tollman, and Christian Veith, "The Rewards of CEO Reflection," BCG blog, June 29, 2017, www.bcg.com/en-us/publications/2017/leadership -talent-people-organization-rewards-ceo-reflection.aspx.

PAGE 164: **"can expose you to the risk of acting in ways inconsistent with your goals and your nature"** . . . Ray Dalio, *Principles: Life and Work* (New York: Simon & Schuster, 2017).

PAGE 165: **"You'll be the person who speaks the truth even when it's uncomfortable to do so"** . . . Angie Morgan, Courtney Lynch, and Sean Lynch, *Spark: How to Lead Yourself and Others to Greater Success* (New York: Houghton Mifflin Harcourt, 2017). The "Galatea effect," as described by Morgan, is defined here: www.psychologyconcepts .com/galatea-effect/.

PAGE 167: *If we disappeared tomorrow, who would miss us?* . . . Shared with me during a 2013 interview I conducted with Doug Rauch for *A More Beautiful Question.*

PAGE 167: *What do we do that other organizations can't or won't do?* . . . William C. Taylor, "Simply Brilliant: 8 Questions to Help You Do Ordinary Things in Extraordinary Ways," *ChangeThis*, Issue 145, www.changethis.com/manifesto/show/145.01.SimplyBrilliant. Taylor also explores these themes in his book *Simply Brilliant: How Great Organizations Do Ordinary Things in Extraordinary Ways* (New York: Portfolio, 2016).

PAGE 167: **"There's a turning point in what's expected from business leaders"** . . . David Gelles and Claire Cain Miller, "Business Schools Now Teaching #MeToo, N.F.L. Protests, and Trump," *New York Times*, Dec. 25, 2017.

PAGE 168: *How might we be not just a company but a cause?* . . . From my 2013 interview with business consultant Tim Ogilvie for *A More Beautiful Question.*

PAGE 168: *Why do otherwise successful people get tripped up by the trivial?* . . . Greg McKeown's question from "Essentialism," Talks at Google, Apr. 29, 2014, www.youtube.com/watch?v=sQKrt1-IDaE. He also covers this theme in his book *Essentialism: The Disciplined Pursuit of Less* (New York: Crown Business, 2014).

PAGE 169: an **"essentialist"** thoughtfully considers the question *Which problem do I want?*—as opposed to reflexively asking, *How can I do both?* . . . From Greg McKeown's book *Essentialism.*

PAGE 170: **"Jobs would slash the bottom seven and announce, 'We can only do three'"** . . . Walter Isaacson, "The Real Leadership Lessons of Steve Jobs," *Harvard Business Review*, April 2012.

PAGE 170: **"When a leader says no to something, she is also usually saying no to *someone* and that takes courage"** . . . From the interview I conducted with executive coach Michael Bungay Stanier Sept. 2017.

PAGE 170: **"systematic abandonment"** . . . The concept, sometimes referred to as "purposeful abandonment," is described in Leigh Buchanan, "The Wisdom of Peter Drucker from A to Z," *Inc.*, Nov. 19, 2009. www.inc.com/articles/2009/11/drucker.html.

PAGE 171: *What stupid rule would you most like to kill?* . . . Lisa Bodell for
futurethink, "Killer QuickWin: Kill a Stupid Rule," Mar. 9, 2012,
www.youtube.com/watch?v=eqN3AYjkxRQ.

PAGE 171: **Harvard University's James Ryan, who uses** *What truly matters?*
as one of his own five essential questions . . . From my interview
with James E. Ryan Oct. 2017. Ryan's five questions are featured in
his book *Wait, What? And Life's Other Essential Questions* (New
York: HarperOne, 2017).

PAGE 171: *What is the one thing I can do that would make everything else*
easier or unnecessary? . . . Dan Schawbel, "Gary Keller: How to
Find Your One Thing," *Forbes*, May 23, 2013. Also see Gary Keller's
book, coauthored with Jay Papasan, *The ONE Thing: The Surprisingly*
Simple Truth Behind Extraordinary Results (Austin: Bard Press, 2013).

PAGE 172: **"The manager has his or her eye always on the bottom line; the**
leader's eye is on the horizon" . . . Warren Bennis, *On Becoming*
a Leader (New York: Basic Books, 2009; originally published in 1989).

PAGE 172: **The first wave "is the wave you're on at the moment, the current**
core business" . . . Adam Bryant, "Surfing the Three Waves of
Innovation," Corner Office, *New York Times*, Oct. 8, 2017.

PAGE 173: **"If I'm a leader I obsess about the small problems of the moment**
and don't give enough thought to the major problems a few years
down the road" . . . From multiple interviews I conducted with
business consultant Don Derosby in the fall of 2017.

PAGE 173: **New York restaurateur Danny Meyer, who likes to ask:** *How can*
we become the company that would put us out of business? . . .
Leigh Buchanan, "100 Great Questions Every Entrepreneur Should
Ask," *Inc.*, April 2014.

PAGE 174: **Professor Michael Schrage of MIT thinks leaders should ask,**
Who do we want our customers to become? . . . Ibid.

PAGE 175: **The business consultant Suzy Welch suggests a different sliding**
scale when weighing any major decision: *What are the implica-*
tions of this decision ten minutes, ten months, and ten years from
now? . . . Ibid.

PAGE 175: *What would the seventh generation think about what we're*
doing? . . . Molly Larkin, "What Is the 7th Generation Principle
and Why Do You Need to Know About It?," from her blog, May 15,
2013, www.mollylarkin.com/what-is-the-7th-generation-principle
-and-why-do-you-need-to-know-about-it-3.

PAGE 176: **he waded into a "toxic culture"** . . . Rodger Dean Duncan, "How
Campbell's Soup's Former CEO Turned the Company Around,"
Fast Company, Sept. 18, 2014, www.fastcompany.com/3035830/how
-campbells-soups-former-ceo-turned-the-company-around.

PAGE 176: **"They literally began to take some of the chicken out of the chicken noodle soup"** . . . Art Kleiner, "The Thought Leader Interview: Douglas Conant," *Strategy+Business*, Autumn 2012 / Issue 68.

PAGE 178: **"brush these interactions aside because they're too busy trying to get the 'real work' done"** . . . Ibid.

PAGE 178: **By some measures, a third of working Americans feel disengaged at their jobs** . . . Mark C. Crowley, "Gallup's Workplace Jedi on How to Fix Our Employee Engagement Problem," *Fast Company*, June 4, 2013, www.fastcompany.com/3011032/gallups-workplace-jedi-on-how-to-fix-our-employee-engagement-problem.

PAGE 179: **poor upward communication—it's "a major pathology"** . . . Tim Kuppler, "Leadership, Humble Inquiry & the State of Culture Work—Edgar Schein," Mar. 10, 2014, CultureUniversity.com, www.cultureuniversity.com/leadership-humble-inquire-the-state-of-culture-work-edgar-schein.

PAGE 179: **"Every day spent behind your closed door is a day you're not out learning about your people"** . . . Jack and Suzy Welch, "The One Question Every Boss Should Ask," LinkedIn, Dec. 2, 2014, www.linkedin.com/pulse/20141202054906-86541065-the-one-question-every-boss-should-ask.

PAGE 180: **David Cooperrider, one of the creators of the now-widely-used practice known as "Appreciative Inquiry"** . . . David L. Cooperrider and Diana Whitney, *Appreciative Inquiry: A Positive Revolution in Change* (Oakland: Berrett-Kohler, 2005).

PAGE 180: **"When someone hears 'why' or 'why not,' they are primed to justify the current situation"** . . . Nathaniel Greene, "Misguided Questions Kill Businesses," *Leadership Freak* (blog), Apr. 5, 2017, www.leadershipfreak.blog/2017/04/05/misguided-questions-kill-businesses.

PAGE 182: **"of all the events that can deeply engage people at work, the single most important is simply making progress on meaningful work"** . . . Teresa Amabile, "The Progress Principle," TEDxAtlanta Talk, Oct. 12, 2011, www.youtube.com/watch?v=XD6N8bsjOEE.

PAGE 182: **"Is it because they can't do it, they won't do it, or they don't know how to do it?"** . . . John Barrett, "The Can't, Won't, Don't Question . . . ," *John Barrett Leadership* (blog), Nov. 21, 2017, www.johnbarrettleadership.com/the-cant-wont-dont-question.

PAGE 183: *How would you like to see yourself growing in this role?* . . . William Arruda, "Coaching Skills Every Leader Needs to Master," *Forbes*, Oct. 17 2015, www.forbes.com/sites/williamarruda/2015/10/27/coaching-skills-every-leader-needs-to-master.

PAGE 183:   *Would my employees, if asked, be able to articulate the compa-*
            ny's vision and priorities? . . . Robert S. Kaplan, "What to Ask
            the Person in the Mirror," *Harvard Business Review,* Jan. 2007.

PAGE 184:   **"No one likes getting questioned by the Spanish Inquisition,**
            although that does appear to be the inspiration for many
            managers' approaches" . . . Michael Bungay Stanier, "The Right
            Way to Ask a Question," *Toronto Globe and Mail,* Apr. 6, 2016.

PAGE 184:   **"All of us are smarter than any of us"** . . . Socrates says this to the
            playwright Agathon at a dinner party at the start of Plato's
            dialogue, the "Symposium." Ronald Gross, *Socrates' Way: Seven Keys
            to Using Your Mind to the Utmost* (TarcherPerigee, Oct. 2002).

PAGE 185:   **research suggests many people are apt to leave their jobs if and**
            when they stop learning . . . Annie Murphy Paul, "This Is the
            Biggest Reason Talented Young Employees Quit Their Jobs," *Busi-
            ness Insider,* Sept. 18, 2012, www.businessinsider.com/why-young
            -employees-quit-their-jobs-2012-9.

page 186:   **"Research on curiosity shows that it tends to flourish in an**
            environment" . . . This has been the focus of work by educator
            Susan Engel and is covered in her article "The Case for Curiosity,"
            Educational Leadership, Feb. 2013. Environmental effects on curi-
            osity are also discussed Ian Leslie's *book Curious: The Desire to Know
            and Why Your Future Depends on It* (New York: Basic Books, 2014).

PAGE 186:   **"Leaders must be role models for good thinking"** . . . From my
            Dec. 2017 interview with Ed Hess of the University of Virginia.

PAGE 186:   **"they share a habit of mind best described as 'applied curi-**
            osity'" . . . Adam Bryant, "How to Be a CEO, from a Decade's
            Worth of Them," Corner Office, *New York Times,* Oct. 27, 2017.

PAGE 187:   **start meetings "by asking open-ended questions"** . . . Chuck
            Leddy, "The Seven Principles of Productivity: Author Morten
            Hansen Explains How to Be Great at Work," National Center for
            the Middle Market, Jan. 22, 2018, www.middlemarketcenter.org
            /expert-perspectives/the-7-principles-of-productivity. See also Morten
            Hansen's book *Great at Work: How Top Performers Do Less, Work
            Better, and Achieve More* (New York: Simon & Schuster, 2018).

PAGE 187:   **"so people see that somebody whom I value can debate with**
            me" . . . Adam Bryant, "Pedro J. Pizarro: A Leader Who Encour-
            ages Dissent," Corner Office, *New York Times,* Oct. 27, 2017.

PAGE 187:   *How can we make questioning safe? How can we make it
            rewarding? How can we make it productive?* . . . Warren Berger,
            "5 Ways to Help Your Students Become Better Questioners,"
            Edutopia, Aug. 18, 2014, www.edutopia.org/blog/help-students
            -become-better-questioners-warren-berger.

PAGE 188: **many employees—about two-thirds of them, according to one survey—feel "unable to ask a question at work"** . . . Todd Kashdan, "Companies Value Curiosity, But Stifle It Anyway," *Harvard Business Review*, Oct. 21, 2015, www.hbr.org/2015/10/compa nies-value-curiosity-but-stifle-it-anyway.

PAGE 191: **a new teaching approach called "Inquiry-Based Learning" (IBL)** . . . Heather Wolpert-Gawron, "What the Heck is Inquiry-Based Learning?" Edutopia, Aug. 11, 2016, www.edutopia.org/blog /what-heck-inquiry-based-learning-heather-wolpert-gawron.

PAGE 192: **"you want to have real debate among your people, because that supports the best decision-making"** . . . Chuck Leddy, "The Seven Principles of Productivity: Author Morten Hansen Explains How to Be Great at Work," National Center for the Middle Market, Jan. 22, 2018, www.middlemarketcenter.org/expert-perspectives/the-7-princi ples-of-productivity.

PAGE 192: *I know we disagree on this, but will you gamble with me on it? [Can we] disagree and commit?* . . . From Bezos's "2016 Letter to Shareholders," Apr. 12, 2017, www.amazon.com/p/feature/z608g6sys xur57t.

PAGE 192: **curiosity "is a state not a trait." It waxes and wanes depending on circumstances** . . . Ian Leslie, *Curious: The Desire to Know and Why Your Future Depends on It* (New York: Basic Books, 2014).

PAGE 192: **The consultants Jane Hyun and Audrey Lee urge leaders to ask,** *Whose voice might I have missed hearing* . . . Leigh Buchanan, "100 Great Questions Every Entrepreneur Should Ask," *Inc.*, April 2014.

Conclusion: The Inquiring Life

PAGE 196: **Think of a surgeon or airline pilot, for example, who refers to a printed checklist of important reminders** . . . The effectiveness of checklists is explored at length in Atul Gawande's *The Checklist Manifesto: How to Get Things Right* (New York: Henry Holt & Co., 2009).

PAGE 199: **if each of us devotes just four minutes a day to thinking of questions to ask ourselves, it adds up to twenty-four hours** . . . Hal Gregersen of the MIT Leadership Center created an initiative, the 4-24 Project, encouraging 4 minutes a day of questioning. The project's website: www.4-24project.org.

PAGE 199: **Reid Hoffman, a cofounder of LinkedIn, spends a few minutes each night before bed asking himself questions** . . . Michael Simmons, "Why Successful People Spend 10 Hours a Week on

Compound Time," *The Mission* (blog), August 10, 2017, www
.medium.com/the-mission/why-successful-people-spend-10-hours
-a-week-on-compound-time-79d64d8132a8.

PAGE 199: **when you're trying to establish a new habit (or break an old
one), you should use a system of rewards** . . . For more on how to
use rewards to encourage habit changes, see Charles Duhigg, *The
Power of Habit: Why We Do What We Do In Life and Business* (New
York: Random House, 2012).

PAGE 200: **among the best is the Question Formulation Technique** . . . For
more on this technique, visit the Right Question Institute website
(www.rightquestion.org) or refer to the book by Dan Rothstein and
Luz Santana, *Make Just One Change: Teach Students to Ask Their Own
Questions* (Cambridge, MA: Harvard Education Press, 2012).

PAGE 204: **Combating stinkin' thinkin'** . . . to borrow a phrase from the
Saturday Night Live character Stuart Smalley, played by Al Franken.

PAGE 204: **by various measures of global health and well-being, the
world is actually getting better all the time** . . . Here's just one of
a number of articles that makes this point: Nicholas Kristof, "Good
News, Despite What You've Heard," *New York Times*, July 1, 2017.

PAGE 205: *Is this bad feeling you have really true?* . . . the negative-thinking
questions were shared by psychologist Judith Beck in my interview
with her in 2013 for *A More Beautiful Question*.

PAGE 205: *What went well today?* . . . Psychologist Martin Seligman discusses
the importance of reflecting on positive events in an article by Julie
Scelfo, "The Happy Factor: Practicing the Art of Well-Being," *New
York Times*, April 9, 2017.

PAGE 206: **Innovators and inventors often tackle problems by asking
"Why?," "What If?," and "How?" questions** . . . This is covered at
length in *A More Beautiful Question*, but for a shorter explanation of
the "Why?," "What If?," and "How?" questioning cycle, see my
post "Tackle Any Problem with These 3 Questions," *Fast Company*'s
Co.Design site, May 19, 2014, www.fastcodesign.com/3030708/tackle
-any-problem-with-these-3-questions.

PAGE 207: **Seth Grahame-Smith, came up with his mashup idea while in a
bookstore** . . . In this video interview, posted March 22, 2012 on
the site ComicBookMovie.com, Grahame-Smith discusses the inspiration for his mashup idea. www.comicbookmovie.com/horror
/abraham-lincoln-vampire-hunter-seth-grahame-smith-on-his
-inspiration-a56768.

PAGE 209: **keep pausing to ask the other person, *What do* you *think?*** . . .
James Ryan's quote comes from an article by Christina Nunez,
"These 5 Questions Might Boost Your Curiosity—and Make You
Happier," *National Geographic*, May 26, 2017, news.national

geographic.com/2017/05/wait-what-book-talk-chasing-genius-jim
-ryan-commencement-speech.

PAGE 209: **L.I.F.E. questions . . .** This is an original exercise created for this
book by Laura E. Kelly, based on her research of family conversation techniques.

PAGE 209: **Sara Blakely, the entrepreneur who founded Spanx apparel,
was inspired by this question . . .** From an Oct. 2017 Quiet Revolution interview, "'The Power of Moments': An Interview with
Chip and Dan Heath," www.quietrev.com/power-moments-interview
-chip-dan-heath.

PAGE 210: **Using questions instead of giving advice . . .** The list of questions
is inspired by Hal Mayer, "Can You Actually Help People by Just
Asking Them Questions?" Leading with Questions, Apr. 27, 2017,
www.leadingwithquestions.com/leadership/can-you-actually-help
-people-by-just-asking-them-questions-2.

PAGE 211: **The following "killer interview questions" were inspired by
those shared by chief executives . . .** Jason Karaian, "We Got 10
CEOs to Tell Us Their One Killer Interview Question for New
Hires," Quartz, Feb. 4, 2016, www.qz.com/608398/be-prepared-we
-gotasked-10-ceos-to-tellgive-us-their-killer-interview-questions.

PAGE 212: **a mission question. What if the leaders of families did this? . . .**
Author Bruce Feiler has explored the idea of having a family mission/
purpose in his book, *The Secrets of Happy Families: Improve Your
Mornings, Rethink Family Dinner, Fight Smarter, Go Out and Play,
and Much More* (New York: William Morrow, 2013). In addition,
ideas for this passage on family questioning, and several of the questions listed, were drawn from Paul Sullivan, "Keeping the Family
Tree Alive," *New York Times*, Dec. 29, 2017.

PAGE 213: **Research indicates that creating a resolution in question form
may be more effective . . .** Based on more than 100 studies spanning
forty years of research, as reported in, among other sources, Chey-
enne MacDonald, "Will You Stick to Your New Year's Resolutions?
Psychologists Say Asking Questions Rather than Making Statements Helps People Follow Goals," *The Daily Mail*, Dec. 28, 2015.

PAGE 218: **"How might" questions free you to do your best creative
thinking . . .** Quote is from my interview with Tim Brown for my
post "The Secret Phrase Top Innovators Use," *Harvard Business
Review*, Sept. 17, 2012.

PAGE 218: **"a question that is hard (and interesting) enough that it is worth
answering—and easy enough to actually answer" . . .** From
my email interview with physicist Edward Witten in Feb. 2013 for *A
More Beautiful Question*. Witten originally said this in an interview
for "Physics' Sharpest Mind Since Einstein," CNN, Jul. 5, 2005.

Index of Questions

261

Part III: Questions to Help *CONNECT WITH OTHERS*

Conclusion: The Inquiring Life

A Note on the Author

Warren Berger has studied hundreds of the world's foremost innovators, entrepreneurs, and creative thinkers to learn how they ask questions, generate original ideas, and solve problems. His writing and research appears regularly in *Fast Company* and *Harvard Business Review*. He is the author of the internationally acclaimed *Glimmer*—named one of *Businessweek*'s Best Innovation and Design Books of the Year—and the bestseller *A More Beautiful Question*. He lives in New York.

650.1   Berger, Warren.
BER
         The book of beautiful
         questions.

$28.00

DATE			